HIERARCHIES
of CARE

GIRLS, MOTHERHOOD, AND INEQUALITY IN PERU

KRISTA E. VAN VLEET

UNIVERSITY OF
ILLINOIS PRESS
Urbana, Chicago, and Springfield

© 2019 by the Board of Trustees
of the University of Illinois
All rights reserved
1 2 3 4 5 C P 5 4 3 2 1

Library of Congress Control Number: 2019950172

For My Parents

Contents

Acknowledgments

THIS BOOK HAS EMERGED from the generosity and support of many people. Although I alone am responsible for what is written here, I also want to express my deep gratitude to the individuals and organizations that have contributed to my research. Most important, I offer my admiration, respect, and thanks to the young women who were residents of Palomitáy and to the staff, interns, volunteers, and directors of the home during my fieldwork period and since. Although your names do not appear here, this book would not have been possible without you.

Bowdoin College has supported this project in various stages, including field research in Peru during a sabbatical in 2009–2010 and the summer of 2013, data analysis and writing during a sabbatical in 2015–2016, and preparation of the manuscript for publication. Thanks to the College for generous funding from the Fletcher Family Fund and the Faculty Research and Travel Fund, including a subvention to support the inclusion of several images. I am also thankful for the intellectual community of the Department of Sociology and Anthropology and the Program in Latin American Studies. Especially Susan Bell, Sara Dickey, Susan Kaplan, Scott MacEachern, Nancy Riley, and Allen Wells have offered moral support, intellectual challenge, and advice at crucial moments.

During fieldwork in Cusco, Jean-Jacques Decoster, his wonderful golden retriever Q'uri, and the staff at Centro Tinku always made my husband, two young daughters, and me feel warmly welcomed. Thanks also to Juan Rubén Aguierre Gómez, Hugo Alvarez Espinoza and Heather Lewis, Vanessa Cunéo, Steve and Sheri Dyer, Ana Escalante Gutiérrez, Raquel Garcia Matias, Rosalia Sutta Ccapa, Sergio Velásquez Calvo, Maureen Van Norden, and Andrew

Wallach, all of whom enriched our lives in Cusco. The Ausangate Bilingual School and Colegio Pukllasunchis graciously incorporated our daughters into their learning communities. I am also grateful to Centro Bartolomé de las Casas for providing me with access to their library.

Through conversations, conference presentations and discussions, and commentary on earlier versions of chapters, many deserve my gratitude. I thank Bruce Mannheim for his intellectual insight and love of the Andes, which has challenged and inspired me over the course of many years. Cristina Alcalde, Jeanine Anderson, Florence Babb, Greg Beckett, Andrew Canessa, Paja Faudree, Margarita Huayhua, Michelle Lambert, Jessaca Leinaweaver, Charlene Makely, Linda Seligmann, and Maria Tapias have all shaped the intellectual contours of this project in large and small ways. Special thanks to Nancy Riley for reading the very first drafts, of what I thought would be an article but turned into this book. Thanks to Jen Edwards for editing images and Michelle Becket for copyediting the initial manuscript. Several undergraduate students have contributed to research assistance for this book. Special thanks to Bill de la Rosa, Daniel Edgerton-Dickey, Abigail Gonneville, Isabel Kovacs, Ariana Reichert, and Natasha Soto.

Thanks to Norm Whitten for his enthusiasm for this project and sage advice. Marika Cristofides has been a wonderful editor. The two anonymous reviewers of the manuscript offered excellent commentaries, and I hope I have done justice to their suggestions. I appreciate the hard work of several people at University of Illinois Press who have supported the production of this book, including Jennifer Comeau, Walt Evans, Jennifer Fisher, and Roberta Sparenburg.

Laura Henry and Hadley Horch have been intrepid and inspiring writing partners. This book might not have seen the light of day without their willingness simply to be present. Dana Bateman deserves special recognition for imposing a deadline (and celebrating its completion). I especially am grateful to my parents-in-law, Dr. Ernest Kovacs and Rhonda Buam, and my parents, Lyle and Marian Van Vleet, who made it possible for me to take a research leave in the fall of 2016 and devote full attention to completing the manuscript.

A heartfelt thank you to the many friends and family members who have kept me going as I have worked on this project over many years. In addition to those already named, I acknowledge Jack Bateman, Alex and Katherine Dauge-Roth, Lelia DeAndrade and Derek Burrow, Kate Dempsey and Tim Blair, Nancy Donsbach, Anne Henshaw and Bruno Marino, Jerry Herrera, Helen Hudson and Matt Wierzba, Lisa and Mark Klein, Diane Kovacs, David Kovacs and Megan Son, Laura Lee, Peter and Gail Schneider, Karen Topp and Thomas Baumgarte, Jim and Carmella Van Vleet, Matt Van Vleet, and Dave Van Vleet.

I cannot fully express the extent of my gratitude for my husband, Lawrence Kovacs, and our daughters, Isabel and Sophia (who were eleven- and four-years-old, respectively, when we arrived in Cusco). Their curiosity, courage, and laughter made that trip to Peru (and others since) much more than an intellectual endeavor. Lawrence, without your love, patience, and care, I could not have written this book, truly. Isabel and Sophia—you bring me joy, always.

This book is dedicated to my mom and dad, who first taught me that actions as well as words reveal what matters. My dad, Lyle Van Vleet, died in January 2019. I miss him more than words can convey. In his memory, the royalties from the sale of this book will be donated to support domestic violence prevention and youth advocacy in Kansas City, Kansas, and Cusco, Peru.

HIERARCHIES
of CARE

CHAPTER 1

Young Mothers, Moral Experience, and the Politics of Care

"Just Me and My Child Are Enough"

"I don't ever want another child. Just me and my child are enough."[1]

Walking down the street, it's clear to me that Jeni is in her old neighborhood. The length of her stride in slightly faded but freshly ironed blue jeans, her level gaze, and her decisive turn into the beauty shop—Ángela's hand in hers—indicated her comfort with this neighborhood. "I would rather live just on my own (*sapalla*)."

We had been making our way back from one of Cusco's sprawling markets to Palomitáy, the home for young mothers and their children, where Jeni and her daughter, Ángela, lived. When Jeni asked if she might stop and say hello to a friend, we jumped off the bus but continued the conversation that we had begun during our long ride. I suggested that perhaps her circumstances would change; she was just sixteen, I pointed out, and her daughter was only two. She then reiterated that she was not at all interested in acquiring a boyfriend or getting married. In a refrain that had become familiar since I had begun conducting research at Palomitáy several months before, Jeni said that she planned to work hard and take care of Ángela so that her daughter might "move ahead" and have a "better life." Just the two of them were "enough."

An exclamation of surprise greeted Jeni as she stepped through the doorway into the beauty shop. After introducing me to Margarita, the middle-aged owner of the shop, Jeni sat down on a red vinyl barber chair while Margarita pumped her foot on the lift. As Margarita clipped layers into Jeni's dark-brown hair and Ángela contentedly sucked a lollipop, I gazed around the dim front room, taking in the posters of once-popular hair styles, the faded plastic flowers decorating the counter, and the bottles of shampoo coated with dust. Two years earlier, Margarita had been Jeni's neighbor and had witnessed the worsening condition of both Jeni and her infant in the weeks after Jeni had given birth. Margarita eventually insisted to the municipal police and the *Demuna* (*Defensoría Municipal del Niño, Niña y Adolescente*, or the Municipal Ombudsmen for Children and Youth) that they intervene to remove both children from the kitchen of the restaurant where Jeni had been living and working. As Margarita expertly wielded a hairdryer and a cylindrical brush, styling soft curls around Jeni's face, she listened to Jeni chat about her life since she had been declared "morally and materially abandoned" by the Peruvian family court system and transferred to Palomitáy. Later, Jeni told me that getting a haircut was the least she could do for Margarita, who was the only person who had supported her during that difficult time in her life. "And now," she added, "my style is more up to date (*de modo*)."

• • •

This book explores how young women navigate everyday moral dilemmas, develop understandings of themselves, and negotiate hierarchies of power, as they endeavor to "make life better" for themselves and their children.[2] The encounters that I describe in these pages are drawn from sixteen months of ethnographic research conducted between 2009 and 2014 in Palomitáy, a residence for young mothers (aged twelve to eighteen years) and their children near Cusco, Peru. As they seek to create a "good life" and future for themselves, most often with their children but sometimes without them, young women like Jeni frame themselves as moral and modern individuals. Bringing attention to various dimensions of caring for, and caring by, young women illuminates broad social and political economic processes (global humanitarianism, systemic racism, deeply rooted gender inequalities, and precarious sociality) that shape girls' possibilities. At the same time, by closely considering the micro-politics of everyday interactions and creative expression in this transnational arena, I enrich understanding of the dynamic processes through which youth develop complex and changing senses of self.

While I begin with this moment of dialogue between Jeni and me, Jeni was not the only young mother at Palomitáy who expressed the desire to live "alone," "independently," or "just with my child." She and other young women voiced the sentiment both overtly and in more veiled fashion and in a variety of contexts—while watching television, doing schoolwork, or participating in workshops organized by international nongovernmental organizations (NGOs). They often intertwined their expressed determination to live alone with aspirations for a better life for themselves and their children. Figuring out just how one might care for a child, pursue an education, find a place to live, and earn enough money to survive independently were moral issues as well as practical ones, with material, social, political, and affective dimensions.

All of the young women who people these pages were placed in the home by the state, as I explain further below. Many of them struggled to come to terms with the various traumas they experienced before arriving, from the everyday violence of poverty, to sexual violence, to material abandonment. Young women also navigated the interventions of state and private organizations into their lives. This includes Palomitáy's requirement that each young woman make a conscious choice about taking on the long-term responsibility of raising a child or not, a decision fraught with emotional, moral, social, and economic complexities.

Yet not every young woman in the residence approached the question of how to live a better life in the same way. Some desired a boyfriend or imagined a future in a stable heterosexual partnership. Some aspired to finish high school or pursue professional careers. Some fostered a hope of closer ties to their natal families and communities, while others eschewed any connection. Some aligned themselves with the conceptual parameters and embodied sensibilities of motherhood fostered by the home, but others chose to give up their child for adoption or challenged Palomitáy's discourses and practices of care.

In the moment, I reminded Jeni of her youth and of the possibility that her life and circumstances might change. Looking back, I hear the ways my own more privileged experiences, and perhaps the possibilities I imagined for my own daughters, tinge this reply. (At eleven years old, my oldest daughter was just a year younger than some of Palomitáy's mothers.) I hear an echo of the hope—or perhaps the "cruel optimism" (Berlant 2011)—expressed by both the staff members and residents that personal aspirations, hard work, and a strong mother-child bond might enable poor young women to overcome pervasive obstacles and institutionalized oppressions.[3] But these are aspects of my response that I only considered much later.

Initially, Jeni's insistence that "just me and my child are enough" challenged me to think about how attention to single mothers, or young parents, might recalibrate understandings of relatedness and of gender in the Andes, and in Latin America more generally. That day, I reflected in my field notes that Jeni's emphasis on living alone seemed to contravene native Andean ideals of kinship and sociality. In recent years, several scholars (myself included) have shown that among many indigenous people in the Andean highlands, "relatedness" is created and maintained through everyday exchanges of food, material goods, and labor. Extended networks of kin and *compadres* (spiritual kin) may contribute to caring for children, valuing the affective, social, and material connections that such relationships entail.[4]

The often-fierce determination of Jeni and some other young women to raise children without marital partners also stood out against broadly-circulating discourses of gender and family. Both native Andean ideals of complementarity opposition (Harris 1978), in which married couples are equal and opposite halves,[5] and more generally hegemonic Hispanic values associated with patriarchalism envision women as the primary caretakers of children within heterosexual family structures.[6] Intertwined with a long history of Catholicism, women and girls are esteemed as mothers. However, single mothers, especially very young mothers, are stigmatized. In urban Cusco, public discourses characterize young mothers as "bad," failed, or immoral girls, often intertwining racial, class, and gendered discourses with moralizing frames. Of course, raising children "alone," without the committed collaboration of a male partner, is not a new phenomenon for women in Latin America (Dore 1997; Safa 2005). News reports in 2015 pronounced that families headed by single women were the "new norm" in the region.[7] In fact, recent studies estimate that a quarter of Peruvian households are headed by women. Yet for a young woman to aspire to raising a child alone—and to voice that desire or actively strive toward that goal—simultaneously may transgress and reinforce gender and kinship ideologies and other intertwined relations of inequality.

Thus, the longer I considered Jeni's words, the more I wondered just what Jeni meant by "me and my child are enough." How might Jeni's statement be an attempt to work out the possibilities for "a better life" for herself and her child? How might her voiced dream for the future reflect her current situation or her past experiences? At least in this instance, Jeni spoke about being contented to live with her daughter during a trip to the market to buy clothing for her daughter's baptism and her own. Within a week, she would extend her network of relationships through *compadrazgo* acquiring a *madrina* (godmother) and *compadres* (coparents) for herself and *padrinos* (godparents) for her daughter. She talked with me on the way to visit with an old friend who had cared for Jeni in a time of intense need. Understanding the meanings of raising one's child "alone" also, then, requires attention to Jeni's efforts to (re)establish connections and to position herself as a modern girl (with new clothes, a fashionable haircut, and a *gringa* anthropologist in tow.)

In the several years that have passed since my conversation with Jeni, I have come to write a book that is about the senses of self and moral encounter that emerge through peoples' efforts to care (for others and themselves) in contexts of insecurity. A home for young single mothers is the site of my research; however, the object of my analysis is not adolescent mother-hood, per se. Young women in Palomitáy do not always view themselves as mothers. Nevertheless, they produce understandings and enactments of a "good life" in a context where mundane activities and hopes for the future are directly and indirectly shaped by ongoing dialogues over care.[8] By using the phrase "moral encounter," I draw attention to the local contingencies of interaction that shape individuals' senses of self and of experience within broader hierarchies of power. I focus on young women's everyday practices and interactions, their voiced beliefs and creative expressions, as dimensions of creating a "good life" within a context that is constrained by inequalities and, at the same time, arcs toward possibility. The processes through which they endeavor to live a good life are dynamic and contingent and shaped by, not determined by, the insecurities and inequalities of contemporary life.

The story I tell in this ethnography draws on and contributes to ongoing conversations in anthropology and feminist theory about subjectivities and moral experience, reproduction and power, youth and social life. From an ethnographic perspective I argue that care is a significant arena of moral engagement in which young women navigate multiple and entangled dis-courses of power in contemporary Peru. Caring for themselves as well as their children, and positioned simultaneously as youth in need of care, these young women develop senses of self, deal with everyday dilemmas, and envision a future. At a more theoretical level, I emphasize that moral experience emerges in everyday encounters that are saturated by intertwined hierarchies of power. Integrating intersectional perspectives on inequality with an emphasis on ordinary moral experience allows for a more complex understanding of how individuals understand and engage in "living better." From a methodological perspective, I promote an analytical attentiveness to the dialogical produc-tion of moral experience, subjectivities, and sociality. The micro-politics of communicative interactions are as crucial as macro-historical structures of power for comprehending social life.

To lay a theoretical foundation for the ethnography, I draw together recent scholarship on ordinary ethics in cultural anthropology, feminist intersec-tionality theory, and approaches in linguistic anthropology that emphasize language as social action. I then introduce the setting of Palomitáy, a hu-manitarian organization in Cusco through which individuals circulate to care and be cared for. Finally, I discuss care as an aspect of relatedness, intimate labor, and moral experience and reflect on the methodology and ethics of my ethnographic research in twenty-first-century Peru.

Conceptual Foundations

Everyday Moralities

This book explores the ways in which individuals are engaged in reflecting on their own and others' actions, presenting themselves as good people, or striving to "live better lives," in ordinary interactions. Rather than viewing morality solely in terms of abstract norms, values confined to religious institutions, or regimes of power, I investigate the ways that moralities are emergent in ordinary situations among people and are personally experienced as well as entangled with broader structures of power. These young women may talk about being and becoming a (certain type of) mother, but they also laugh and argue, give voice to dreams, and act upon issues both momentous and mundane. Through these interactions, they produce understandings of the good or the proper. They navigate understandings of what might be hoped for in precarious circumstances. They transform and sustain relationships of power.

My approach draws on recent scholarship in the "anthropology of morality," which highlights ordinary experience as a ground for moral action and challenges anthropologists to go beyond investigating the diversity of moral systems throughout the world.[9] Jarrett Zigon and Jason Throop point out that a person-centered perspective on moral experience "leads us to examine how moral dispositions and ethical assumptions impact what we notice, how we react, who we love and hate, the attachments we acquire, the motives and desires that move us to act, the situations, relationships, activities, and orientations that we habitually take up" (Zigon and Throop 2014, 7). As people attempt to live a good life for themselves and for their children, they engage in habitual activities and face difficult dilemmas. Complicating any abstract standard of "the good," this analytical perspective opens up a space to explore just how individuals navigate the moralizing discourses (about young mothers, for instance) that circulate in public arenas without presuming that individuals tie themselves to a singular moral standard, ethical relationship, or affective attachment.

I explore moral experience as a significant dimension of everyday life, and of care more specifically. Anthropologist Cheryl Mattingly (2014, 4) recently has pointed out that the work of care is "a complex reasoning task that engenders ongoing moral deliberations, evaluations, and experiments in how to live." Care is an important aspect of young women's everyday practice in Palomitáy, and I discuss further below how my research contributes to the extensive scholarship on motherhood, kinship, and care. However, I first situate my exploration of Jeni's and other young women's talk and actions in terms of the moral dimensions of everyday activities (rather than single motherhood) to bring into the picture those girls who may choose *not* to care for their child or who do *not* understand themselves to be mothers (even though they have been placed by the state into a home for that specific reason). I closely attend to young women's shifting understandings of themselves not only as mothers but also as daughters, students, women, girls, youth, Quechua speakers, *mestizos, campesinos,* urban migrants, citizens, and as moral persons in the context of (extra-) state intervention into their affective and reproductive lives. In the process, I illuminate some of the contingencies and uncertainties, and the complexities and nuances, of young women's experiences as they interpret, reflect, and position themselves in relation to others and to a wider social and political sphere.

Intersecting Oppressions

I also extend this person-centered perspective on moral experience by integrating feminist and postcolonialist perspectives on the multiple and intermeshed oppressions that shape peoples' everyday lives. Young women at Palomitáy encounter publicly circulating moral discourses about girls and women, their sexual and reproductive practices, their education and decency, their willingness to work hard, their future prospects and presumed failings. If people live in and through understandings of the world in which moral discourses are inextricably intertwined with broad racial, gendered, sexual, and class hegemonies, then those who historically have faced multiple oppressions may also experience pressures to navigate social arenas, even supportive ones, in particular ways. To understand the on-the-ground complexities of moral experience, then, requires sensitivity to agency as "highly attenuated" in contexts saturated by hierarchies of race, gender, class, and imperial power (Lugones 2003, 6). In other words, attempting to do what's right or live a better life requires attention to social, political, and economic circumstances and individual subjectivities. To focus on moral encounters is to take seriously both the "active subjectivities" (Lugones 2003) of these young women and the complicated national and transnational arena in which they live and, more specifically, in which they try to "make life better" for themselves and for their children.

Like many feminist scholars in the social sciences and humanities, I take the perspective that categories of identity and inequality are "always permeated by other categories, fluid and changing, always in the process of creating and being created by dynamics of power" (Cho, Crenshaw, and McCall

2013, 297). Often called an "intersectional approach" (Crenshaw 1991),[10] this analytic sensibility developed in the late 1970s in the United States as scholars and activists, especially women of color, endeavored to expand analyses of the ways "systems of oppression are interlocking" (Combahee River Collective 1983[1978]). Feminists have used various metaphors to convey this concept. For instance, Marfil Francke (1990, 85) details the "braid of domination" of gender, race, and class that creates "a single structure that runs through all social relations, institutional and personal, public and private, production and reproduction, in the process of daily life and in the historical develop-ment of Latin America." Others have characterized these relations of power as "interlocking" or "intermeshed" or "entangled." These metaphors suggest a relatively unproblematic separation between these various strands. Indeed, Lugones (1994, 458) cautioned against this tendency and offered the image of an emulsion—mayonnaise—to think about a state in which substances mutu-ally saturate, where separate particles (of egg and oil) are not perceived as such (unless the emulsion "breaks" or "curdles"). These and other metaphorical images offer heuristic devices for understanding a complex reality and for methodologically managing the analytical complexities that an intersectional approach generates. Over the last several decades, this analytic sensibility has become dominant within feminist theorizing and has contributed to understandings of individual experiences as well as colonial and postcolonial institutions and structures of power.

Although I take the perspective that gender analysis is never simply about women, or even about the relationships between women and men, girls figure as the central characters of this ethnography. By orienting this discussion around how individuals position themselves in relation to moral issues, I illuminate "the enormously variegated ways of connection among people" and the multiple meanings that may emerge in social interaction (Lugones 2003, 6).[11] At times, deliberations about what to do in a particular situa-tion—how to take the best course—are tied up with the necessity to posi-tion oneself within a stratified world. I ask how certain situations become morally meaningful but not to every person or in precisely the same way. Highlighting the heterogeneous connections among people, I trace the ways these young women may represent themselves as mothers or not, establish or dissolve relationships, or negotiate just how they care even as their control over circumstances is constrained by broader structures.

In a postcolonial context such as this, young people navigate uneven po-litical, social, and economic terrain as they develop a sense of self. Children and youth actively engage in determining their life courses: they migrate from rural communities at early ages, pursue educational goals, labor in their family's agricultural plots or in the households of strangers, spend their earnings and pursue romance, and care for themselves and for others. By acknowledging that young mothers are social agents and asking how their "culturally mediated capacity to act" (Ahearn 2001, 112) (and their political and social status) may be constrained differently than that of adults, I forefront girls' engagement in producing cultural meanings, social and affective relationships, and moral experience. I also illuminate some of the locally specific constraints on young mothers and the processes through which they negotiate a changing self-concept and dynamic social relationships.

Dialogical Interactions

Of course, people everywhere elaborate understandings of self and social worlds, endeavor to create good lives for themselves and others, struggle to make sense of uncertain events, and enjoy the pleasures of the everyday. In this book, I draw on the stories and interactions of young women, including Jeni, to link the individual experiences to broader social and political economic structures. However, I also show how moral and affective experience emerges from involvement, from joint or dialogical interactions in everyday situations.[12] Zigon and Throop (2014, 1) suggest that attending to "the nitty-gritty complexity of actual persons interacting with one another, as well as other objects and beings, in relations of intersubjectivity" will enrich our understanding of moral experience more generally. I extend the insight that moral experience emerges through face-to-face embodied practices and everyday interactions by closely attending to the micro-politics of ordinary conversations and creative expression among young mothers.

As anthropologist Elinor Ochs (2012, 143) notes, "Experience no sooner comes into consciousness than it becomes penetrated by linguistic forms." If we are to understand "moment-to-moment thinking, feeling, and being in the world" (Ochs 2012, 144), then we must analyze on-the-ground interactions. This includes attention to the ways that talk relies on concrete situations and broad historical and social contexts for meaning. This seemingly simple idea takes on added depth when we acknowledge that talk (and other forms of communication) are social practices and social and political economic resources that occur in time and are unevenly distributed among people.[13]

Linguistic anthropologists argue that language is not simply an objective system that references objects out there in the world.[14] Nor do speakers rely on words or phrases as a "privileged entryway" to meaning. Instead, language has multiple dimensions and human beings have the capacity to evaluate multiple meaningful aspects of ongoing talk, often without being aware of doing so. We attend to loudness, tone, and rhythms of speech; performative style and audience; shifts in language or register; and the relation of what is said to the situation at hand. Social actors or "interlocutors" (speakers, hearers, eavesdroppers, bloggers) engage in pragmatic interpretation of meaning through different modes (face-to-face talk, radio broadcast, internet blog, printed text, text message) and in relation to the different publics in which language circulates (some limited and some quite broad). In other words, language is saturated by context.

Ordinary conversation and interaction is the primary location for "working out situated versions of who we think we are through clumsy propositions in the making and disjointed narratives of personal experience" (Ochs 2012, 153). Subjective experience and moral engagement are not necessarily formulated prior to talk but in the process of talking (and sometimes in the process of talking about something else entirely). Moreover, speaking subjects are always members of larger communities, and they play many different roles in a conversation (Goffman 1974, 1976, 1981; Irvine 1996).[15] In the course of talking, laughing, sharing photos, or acting in a play, people make sense of things—their understandings of themselves and their experiences—in coordination with others. In fact, participants in a conversation must work together to move an interaction forward.

Tracing the micro-politics of talk has potentially profound implications for understanding moral experience. In taking a perspective on language that is broadly dialogical, I argue for analysis of the dynamic and contingent processes through which people together create and transform social life through talk and other social actions. I bring analytical attention to an intermediary level, one that mediates between the circulating public discourses or institutional investments that shape young women's caring (and reproductive) practices and the self-understandings of young women as first-person subjects. Talk emerges in joint interactions that unfold in time, within particular situations, and across participants and audiences (some immediate, others far-flung). Meanings are not determined fully by any of these, nor can any single individual control what is said. Moreover, in the process of these interactions, people together act upon the situation, produce relationships, and sustain and transform culture.

Though moments of dilemma may produce bursts of moral engagement, even everyday conversation or unassuming habitual practices may be saturated with moral meaning. I invite readers to imagine the ways that the people whose stories I tell draw upon each other's talk, rely on previous conversations, or imagine future possibilities as they struggle to make sense of ordinary circumstances or unusual events. I bring attention to nonreferential aspects of meaning that are inextricably tied to context in order to enrich understanding of moral engagement and care as dynamic yet ambiguous, and as rendered through the "voices" of multiple others. I analyze young women's interactions and expressions to trace the layers of creative dialogue through which they navigate senses of self and relationship, doubts and desires, amid contingencies of daily life.

Ethnographic Encounters

Cusco as a Contact Zone

I ground my research in several months of fieldwork among young women who have been placed into an independent orphanage by the state, an orphanage specifically organized around caring for young mothers and their children. The broader setting for this unfolding story is the city of Cusco, Peru, located in the southern highland region of the country. This region, often called the *sierra* in Peru, is dominated by the Andean mountain range, which runs north to south from Colombia, through Ecuador, Peru, and Bolivia and into Chile and Argentina. Located at approximately 11,200 feet (3,400 meters), Cusco is surrounded by snow-capped mountains and lies adjacent to a fertile agricultural region, the Sacred Valley. The city and its surrounding region have been populated for millennia, but Cusco is perhaps most well-known for having been the administrative and religious center of the Inca empire.[16] After the city was invaded and sacked by Spanish forces in 1533, Cusco became an important center of colonial efforts to administer and convert the ethnically and linguistically diverse people of the Andes. Post-independence and into the twentieth century, Cusco was a regional center where local creole elites "paradoxically pursued authentic sierra modernization in the image of Peru's autochthonous heritage" (Hiatt 2007, 328; also see de la Cadena 2000) even as they maintained political, economic, and social control over indigenous people.

Cusco (population approximately 350,000 at the time of my fieldwork) has long been a transnational site through which commodities, ideas, and people circulate (INEI 2008, 63). In contemporary Cusco urban sprawl, low adobe houses, hotels, and highways meet ancient stone walls, cobbled streets, and colonial Catholic churches. Declared a World Heritage Site in 1983 by UNESCO, Cusco hosts one to two million visitors each year. In fact, Cusco's primary source of revenue is tourism, and the industry has grown at a faster rate in Cusco than in the rest of Peru since the early 1990s (Van den Berghe and Flores Ochoa 2000).[17] Many travelers simply pass through Cusco on

Cusco rooftops. Photo by Lawrence Kovacs

their way to the archaeological site of Machu Picchu, which was declared one of the "New Seven Wonders of the World" in 2007. Others remain in Cusco to work or volunteer in one of the many international humanitarian organizations that use Cusco as their base of operations.

Palomitáy is one of more than eighty organizations that support children and youth in or near Cusco. Founded in 2000, Palomitáy is an independent, secular orphanage run by a European nongovernmental organization. The specific aim of Palomitáy is to provide a safe space for young mothers to live with their children. The residence has a capacity for just sixteen young women (twelve to eighteen years) and their children (newborn to six years) at any particular time. Between its founding and the end of my research period in 2014, Palomitáy aided more than two hundred youth and children from all over Peru. In addition to food, shelter, and clothing, Palomitáy provides educational and co-curricular enrichment, parenting classes and childcare, job training opportunities, access to reproductive and early child health care, and psychological counseling.

Official flag of Cusco with a Catholic church, Iglesia de la Compañía de Jesús, in the background, Plaza de Armas

An Ethnographer's Arrival

Situated on an unnamed rutted dirt road, unmarked by a sign or number, on my first visit to Palomitáy, it was the door made of wooden planks tightly fitted together, stained a rich brown, and varnished to a dull shine that gave me the only hint that I might be in the right place. I walked past once, twice—that wooden door with curved iron hardware the only break in a nine-foot-high wall of unplastered adobe topped with barbed wire. Then I decided to press the button on the intercom that hung loosely by a wire. "*Quien*? Who is it?" queried a high-pitched voice. I introduced myself over the noise of a barking dog. The intercom buzzed, the lock clicked, and I pushed the door open.

Walking through the outer gate into the grounds of Palomitáy was a bit like stepping over the threshold into an alternate world, offering enough of a jolt to cause a momentary pause. From the gate, concrete steps curved downward to a building; the steps were flanked on each side by a struggling lawn and

Walking past Inca walls

Palomitáy's entrance

garden beds held up by stone retaining walls. Planted with pink and white cosmos and yellow chrysanthemums, the flowerbeds reflected the colors of the murals painted on the interior surface of the wall that I had just passed through. Immediately to the left of the gate, the image of a woman with long, flowing hair, a yellow star in her pregnant belly, decorated the wall. Other murals, both realistic and fantastical, covered the entire surface of the wall surrounding the property. Later I learned that the star woman was a favorite of the residents, and that all of the murals had been painted by various groups of volunteers. At the moment, however, I was being beckoned to walk down the stairs to the main building while a terrier, leaping madly at my legs, kept me cornered at the top.

On that first day at Palomitáy, I met with the director, Rosa. I explained the outlines of my project and requested permission to conduct research in the home. We talked in her office, a small room with a pair of angel wings painted on the wall behind her desk, as we drank Nescafe liberally sweetened with sugar. She explained that Palomitáy grew out of her experiences working in another orphanage, one that took in "so many infants." She wondered if supporting the young mothers of those babies might alter the lives of all of the children—the mothers and their babies—for the better. She emphasized that at Palomitáy the young mothers take part in caring for their children but also pursue an education so that they are better prepared for life once they leave the home. Rosa mentioned the traumas and structural violence that many of the residents experience before being placed in Palomitáy by the state. She talked about the importance of the beauty and aesthetics of the home, noting that when girls brought color into their bedrooms or added pictures to the walls, began washing their clothes and bathing their babies, she knew they were feeling better about themselves.

Rosa gave me a tour of the main building that day. Built around an open grassy courtyard, the ground-floor rooms were painted in bright colors: red, magenta, yellow, teal, blue, orange, green, and yellow. We peeked into the nursery, the lounge, kitchen and dining room, and two classrooms, and Rosa introduced me to some of the staff members. As we walked around the perimeter of the courtyard, I read the posters supporting women's rights and an end to violence, the weekly schedule of chores and workshops, and several bulletins and notices. The ground floor was the more public zone of the residence where the staff, residents, and volunteers spent most of the day, but we also visited the second floor, where the bedrooms for the residents, an office and classroom for the psychologist, and a small apartment for Rosa and her two young daughters were situated.

As we climbed the staircase, Rosa explained that each young mother was given a bed, mattress, pillow, sheets, and blankets when they arrived. "Most of them have never had their own bed," she explained. "We make sure they take the beds and bedding when they leave the home, and all of the things they have for their babies and themselves too." Painted in pastel hues, the residents' rooms each contained three or four beds and wardrobes; each resident shared a room with two or three young mothers and their children. However, the oldest resident, the one closest to eighteen, always moved into the one single room on the floor. "As she nears the time that she will need to leave Palomitáy, it's important that she has a chance to experience living on her own: sleeping in her own bedroom, cooking food for just herself and her child, and doing whatever she needs to do to manage their life."

Back downstairs, we leaned against the retaining wall, enjoying a few minutes of sunshine. Rosa smoked a cigarette. Four preschoolers played outside on the swing set. The bell on the front gate rang again, setting off another round of barking. Three college-aged women smiled and said hello as they passed down the steps and into the building. "All volunteers," Rosa nodded, once they passed. "We have a glut of volunteers right now." I suggested that I could perhaps offer a photovoice workshop or yoga classes as a way to interact with the young mothers. Rosa said, "Oh, it's fine for you to do the research. But it's just that they are so busy. I don't think we can schedule another workshop for several weeks. But if you want to start and spend time getting to know the *mamás,* you can help with the cooking."

Palomitáy's Residents

It was in the kitchen that I first met Jeni. She was standing on a small stool placed directly in front of the industrial stove. Reaching her arm over the top of a very large pot, she stirred the soup that would become the first course of that day's *almuerzo,* midday meal. The air was warm and moist from the efforts of Jeni and Ana, the other young mother who had kitchen duty that day. I had been conducting fieldwork at Palomitáy for only a couple of weeks and was slowly getting to know the girls. Jeni turned and smiled at my greeting, her head tilted to the side as she thought about what task to assign me. Ana prompted, "The onions! Have her chop onions!" Jeni nodded, pointing to a heaping pile of onions in a sizable basket on the floor. Ana left for the market to buy more supplies. I picked out a knife and cutting board from the shelf and set up my station at the concrete island in the kitchen's center. "What kind of music do you like?" Jeni asked, stepping down from the stool and walking over to the radio sitting on the shelf above the sink. "Anything," I said. Jeni found a station playing *cumbia.* I chopped onions, tears streaming down my face, while Jeni, now facing me across the island, peeled and chopped potatoes with a speed and confidence that inspired me to comment.

Although I did not learn many details of her life on that first morning, I did find out that Jeni had lived in the kitchen of a restaurant when she first arrived in Cusco. She worked eighteen-hour days, peeling and chopping potatoes for *papas fritas* (french fries), plucking and preparing chicken, washing dishes, and scrubbing pots to earn little more than room and board. Like many of Palomitáy's other residents, Jeni had begun working at a young age, first to help her family and later to survive on her own. Only later did Jeni tell me about how she ran away to Cusco from her home in a mining encampment, where she had been living with her mother, stepfather, and four (half-) siblings. Jeni suffered physical and sexual violence at the hands of her stepfather, and his abuse had only intensified as she grew older. Finally, two friends grew so concerned for her well-being that they helped her sneak away during school one morning. By the time the judge removed Jeni and Ángela from the restaurant and placed them in Palomitáy, they were both ill and malnourished.

As I came to know Jeni and other residents, I learned that each of the young women followed somewhat different routes to Palomitáy. Of course, their stories of arrival are more similar to each other than to mine. Jeni's story may serve as a touchstone for readers, for her story illuminates the collective patterns in the lives of Palomitáy residents even though particular individuals may not share all of her experiences.

All of the young women who arrive at Palomitáy's gate are either pregnant, or like Jeni, carry a newborn or, less frequently, a toddler. They come from various parts of the country, but most are born in rural highland communities or poor and working-class urban neighborhoods. Many speak Quechua as their first language. Several have migrated alone or with family members from rural communities to lowland agricultural regions or urban centers, such as Cusco, Puerto Maldonado, Arequipa, or Lima, before arriving at Palomitáy. Some have experienced exploitative labor conditions in the households of strangers or relatives, in mining camps, or in businesses. During their short life histories, the majority of these young women have endured the "everyday" or "structural" violence (Scheper-Hughes 1992; Farmer 1996) of poverty and of marginalization based on gender, age, class, race, and ethnicity. They also have suffered physical or sexual violence.[18] Some girls are survivors of sexual violence including rape by a relative, employer, schoolmate, or stranger or ongoing sexual abuse by a step- or foster parent, godparent, relative, or family friend. Others were involved in romantic relationships with partners who later abandoned them and were subsequently unable to access the support of natal families. Through the convergence of particular relationships—some social or interpersonal and others political or economic—young women enter into the state system.

Notably, the majority of young women living at Palomitáy at some point have spoken out or requested help from municipal or state authorities, or had a family member or friend do so on their behalf. Only the state may determine who lives at Palomitáy, but long before a young woman encounters a judge in the family court system or Palomitáy's director, she interacts with officials in the municipal police or the Demuna.[19] Most young women file a formal complaint—an official denunciation of rape (*violación*) or sexual violence. This initiates a process in which the state seeks a responsible adult, considers culpability, and determines a state of abandonment of the legal minor. Other young women seek help because they are unable to support themselves or their child. If state authorities are unable to locate an adult who is able or willing to take responsibility for the young woman and her child, she may be declared abandoned and transferred to an orphanage.

Thus, their lives are at least partially configured by state laws, judicial and administrative structures, and NGO policies. Their personal stories are read against legal frameworks pertaining to statutory rape, familial violence, sexual violence, and child custody. In Jeni's case, she went to the Demuna when she first realized she was pregnant. She had been living in Cusco for less than two months. Although Jeni told the Demuna about her stepfather's abuse, the official learned that Jeni also had sexual relations with someone else, a youth who worked at the restaurant in Cusco. The Demuna official sent her away, saying that they could not help her because it was impossible to know whether the pregnancy was the result of her stepfather's abuse or the consensual relationship with the young man. Until the birth of her daughter, Jeni continued working in the restaurant's kitchen, but afterward, she was unable to maintain the pace. Margarita, her neighbor, witnessed the worsening states of Jeni and her baby and went to the Demuna and then to the municipal police to voice her concern. On Margarita's third visit, the Demuna finally agreed to assist Jeni, and Jeni formally filed a complaint against her stepfather. Her purported abuser was not prosecuted, but her case did go to the family court, where Jeni was declared morally and materially abandoned and placed under the legal custody of Palomitáy's director.

Once individuals enter into this network of state and humanitarian organized aid, they may be subject to the definitions and procedures of these organizations, at least until they reach the legal age of majority: eighteen years old. For instance, only individuals who fit a home's "profile"—the official description of aims and policies created by the NGO and accepted by the municipal and federal governments—may remain in that particular residence. Palomitáy's profile establishes that the homes serve only girls between twelve and eighteen years of age who choose to keep their babies (and who comply with the rules and expectations of the home). The humanitarian efforts of NGOs and the state have both structural and interpersonal consequences, affecting how an individual enters and moves through the system, experiences daily life within any particular home, and eventually leaves the system.

In other words, being placed in Palomitáy may reshape young women's everyday practices and interpersonal and social relationships in predictable and unexpected ways. While living at Palomitáy, young women interact with other youth and adults who move in and out of the home. The organizational structures and explicit programming developed by directors and staff members and by foreign volunteers who circulate through the home may impact experiences of care and understandings of what a "good life" might mean. Interactions among young mothers, who initially are strangers yet come to rely upon each other, also shape relationality. Nevertheless, young women differentially navigate the structures of the organization, the various relationships with other residents, staff, and volunteers, and the opportunities and constraints of the home as they engage in the process of developing understandings of themselves as mothers, or not. Though the ethnographic context is a residence for unmarried, young mothers and their children, the ideas explored in this book revolve around the moral entanglements of youth who care for, and are cared for by, others.

Caring by (and for) Youth

This ethnography serves as witness to the practices, imaginings, and hierarchies of care that shape affective and moral discourses among young women and embed them in broader fields of power. As state and nonstate actors intervene into their intimate lives, these young women are positioned simultaneously as deserving of care and as responsible for care. As they navigate both the mundane demands and enrichment opportunities offered by Palomitáy, the material, affective, and embodied practices of care become interwoven with racial, gendered, and class hierarchies at multiple scales.

In addition to the theoretical and methodological perspectives already outlined, I engage with interdisciplinary scholarship on mothering and care. For many years, anthropologists have argued that kinship is "naturalized" (Yanagisako and Delaney 1995), or made to seem real or normal in relation to other structures of power.[20] Like many social scientists, I take the perspective that people within Palomitáy—or within any social and cultural context—"do mothering." Individuals actively perform particular practices and reinforce or transform specific beliefs in their everyday interactions, even as motherhood appears to be natural.[21] This has emotional, social, and material implications. When anthropologist Nancy Scheper-Hughes (1992) wrote that women in Brazil followed different trajectories of affective engagement with their children than did middle-class Brazilians (or North Americans), she disrupted the assumption that mother love was universally configured

A late breakfast in the dining room

and challenged us to recognize the oppressions that saturate emotional and social relationships as well as political economic relationships.

Others, like Evelyn Nagano Glenn (1992, 1), have focused more specifically on "reproductive labor" and promoted a broad view of reproduction that incorporates the embodied and affective interactions that support "social reproduction"—not only birthing and caring for children but also the "array of activities and relationships involved in maintaining people both on a daily basis and intergenerationally." From housework to elder care, from feeding children to managing the stuff of everyday life, everyday activities that may forge "relatedness" and promote the physical, affective, and intellectual needs of others are tied into broader political economic relationships.[22]

The affective practices that may produce relatedness also articulate with the "heightened commodification of intimacy that pervades social life" under neoliberal capitalism (Boris and Salazar Parreñas 2010, 1). Moral discourses and structures of race and ethnicity, class and nationality, and of course, gender and sexuality are imbricated and mutually shape how care, and other forms of intimate or affective labor, is performed. Economist Nancy Folbre (2002) has shown that moral discourses at multiple levels demand altruism from women so that they supply "caring labor" that is unpaid, undervalued, and often unacknowledged as essential to the reproduction of families and society. Just as significantly, individuals may frame their actions as moral as they negotiate social relations and labor regimes. Elana Buch (2013) complicates understandings of care and moral discourse by pointing to the ways home health-care workers construct themselves as moral persons as they alter their own sensorial worlds in order to support their clients' needs.

Most of this research on motherhood and care has focused on adults. The ways that youth themselves contribute to the (economic, social, ideological) production of relatedness and care for others who may, or may not be, "their own" children has mostly remained obscure.[23] I attend to ways caring by young women is governed, and, at the same time, I forefront the processes through which individuals come to understand themselves as mothers, and more particularly, as modern mothers. In other words, rather than focusing on "adolescent motherhood" as a "social problem" (for example, Alfonso 2008; Shepard 2006; UNICEF 2007), I reflect on the dynamic ways girls establish subjectivities as mothers. Like many girls and women in Peru, the young women in Palomitáy support the bodily and affective needs of others, engaging in intimate forms of labor that are reinforced through locally- and globally-circulating discourses. In contrast to those who already consider themselves to be, or desire to be, a mother (for example, Roberts 2012a), the individuals in this book struggle to develop a sense of whether, and how, care and mothering may be integrated into their own sense of self and their efforts to live well.

This ethnography also illuminates distinctive aspects of youth experience in twenty-first-century Peru by bringing attention to the processes through which young women come to understand themselves and navigate state and civil institutions that impact the distribution of economic responsibilities, affective labor, and imaginative opportunities for living a good life. Through their efforts to imagine and enact themselves as mothers, these young women mobilize widely circulating discourses of "modernity" that are embedded in national racial distinctions, neoliberal sensibilities, and feminist and humanitarian perspectives on human rights. Jessaca Leinaweaver (2008a, 2008b) has compellingly shown that for children and parents in Arequipa, Peru, the goal of advancement places poor people in an especially difficult position. Many, like the young women at Palomitáy, endeavor to increase their educational access, hold down scarce jobs, and navigate structural and everyday violence, even as they nurture their own and others' lives. Heeding the experiences of these young women illuminates patterns of social, political, and economic encounter that extend beyond the walls of the residence.

Fieldwork as Faithful Witnessing

In *Pilgrimages/Peregrinajes: Theorizing Coalition against Multiple Oppressions*, Lugones (2003) offers the notion of "faithful witnessing" as a way of accounting for what one sees and does within a broader context of power, a way of naming those relationships of domination or inequality and one's place in it. She notes that *seeing* domination is itself a subversive act: "To witness faithfully one must be able to sense resistance, to interpret behavior as resistant even when it is dangerous, when that interpretation places one psychologically against common sense, or when one is moved to act in collision with common sense, with oppression" (Lugones 2003, 7). The concept of faithful witnessing offers anthropology a standpoint from which to detail and analyze the ordinary and extraordinary ways that social actors are engaged in resisting and reproducing hierarchies of power. Faithful witnessing also points toward a mode of doing and writing ethnography that clarifies the anthropologist's position in relations of power (for example, Berry et al. 2017; Goldstein 2009).

A Note on Methods

To understand moral engagement among youth, through the lens of care and other practices that are emergent in everyday interactions, I conducted long-term qualitative and ethnographic research in Palomitáy. My aim was to understand young women's lives and the processes through which they expressed and enacted understandings of self in the context of an independent humanitarian NGO-run residence. I collected data in a variety of forms, including participant observation, open-ended interviews and informal conversations, photographs and video-recordings of daily life and events, documents related to the home itself, and popular-press media focused on children and youth, women, and humanitarianism in Cusco. I was able to work closely with the young mothers for many reasons including the generosity of staff and residents and their willingness to share ideas about their lives and the organizational structure of Palomitáy, which facilitated my presence in various contexts.

One of the primary methodologies that I used was participant observation. I spent hundreds of hours in the residence, engaging in more-mundane

practices of daily life (cooking, watching TV, caring for children) and in
specific events or activities (tutoring sessions with Peruvian teachers, workshops run by foreign interns and volunteers, and special events of the home
that included staff). Young mothers do not attend school daily (owing to
the policies of public and private schools barring pregnant teenagers), but
their children do attend school once they are old enough. Thus, the young
mothers spend a great deal of time at the residence, engaged in a variety of
activities. In particular, the workshops organized by interns and staff were
important sites for observing and interacting with young women and with
staff and interns. Although my research focused on the youth in Palomitáy,
I also interacted with younger children and babies. Because the day-to-day
running of small, privately funded organizations such as Palomitáy is tenuous at times, I was often called upon to "help." I held infants and played
with toddlers in the nursery. I taught preschoolers for a month when their
teacher had emergency surgery. I chopped vegetables and washed dishes
when girls were overwhelmed by kitchen duty. I accompanied children to
the local playground or young women on fieldtrips in the neighborhood or
to more distant locations in the city. All of these interactions have deepened
my understanding of the relationships among individuals and the possibilities of, and constraints on, care in the home.

I also conducted open-ended ethnographic interviews with young women
who are figured as mothers by the state but who often see themselves in ways
far more complex. Although many of these were conducted in a one-on-one
fashion, some of the young women requested that they do their interviews
in pairs. Many but not all were recorded, according to the preference of
the interviewees. The interviews between two subjects and myself offered
opportunities to consider the mutual structuring of interactions. Typically,
interviews focused on young women's experiences as girls and as mothers and
their expectations for the future. I did not ask young women to ruminate on
their past experiences, although some spontaneously told me their stories.
To supplement my understanding of individual cases, I analyzed orphanage
documents, including more than 150 case histories taken upon the admittance
of each client to the home (between 2000 to 2012). These documents included
information about each girl's place of birth and family of origin, educational
background, and events leading up to her admittance to the home.

I employed visual methods including photography and videography in my
research. I took photographs and digital videos to document events in the
home and to situate Palomitáy in a broader ethnographic context. Using a
collaborative "photovoice" approach, young women also took photographs

and documented aspects of their lives and then talked with me about them. Analyzing the arrays of images that young women produced has substantively shaped my discussion in chapter 5. A video recording that young women requested I produce of their theatrical performance was crucial to my analysis in chapter 6. Young women gave me permission to use their photos in this book, and I have included a handful of those that maintain the anonymity and confidentiality of participants while conveying aspects of their daily lives.

Finally, to gain an understanding of the history and structuring of the home, the goals of the institution, and the changing configuration of state policy and humanitarian work around children, I interviewed Palomitáy directors and staff and interns. Additionally, I observed monthly meetings in which staff and interns reviewed the status of each resident. I also conducted research in six other institutions for children and youth in Cusco and the Sacred Valley to gain a sense of the array of institutional priorities, organizational structures, and everyday practices in Cusco. By the last six months of the fieldwork period in 2010, I focused on Palomitáy owing to the depth of relationships I had established, the intellectual aims of my project, and the structure and mission of the home.

Representational Ambiguities

To write about care, or intimate labor, in the context of ethnographic fieldwork among poor and working-class, indigenous, and mestizo youth in an international NGO requires some reflection on dimensions of transnational and interpersonal power. Several anthropologists also have written about the power relationships implicit within ethnographic research, from the privileged position of the scholar embedded in a "field" of cultural "others" to anthropological representations of often marginalized places and individuals for audiences back home (for example, Asad 1973; Goldstein 2009; Kovats-Bernat 2002). Lugones (2003, 2) offers a view from "within the matrices of oppression" that emphasizes the simultaneity of resisting and reproducing hierarchies of power and challenges those who are more privileged to integrate the ambiguities of this into substantive interpretations of events. More recently, literary critic Walter Mignolo (2011) has reflected on the scholarly tendency to write as if we are floating above interactions or the broad institutional structures that maintain certain longstanding inequalities (also see Berry et al. 2016; Lugones 2007; Mignolo and Schiwy 2003). My fieldwork in Cusco relied on and reinforces particular structures and relationships of privilege even as it illuminates the lives of individuals who are often marginalized. While I do not play a prominent role as a subject in this ethnography, I am embedded in broader social, political, and economic relationships and hierarchies, just as are my interlocutors.

Yet a simple rendering of positionality, drawing on identity categories, is insufficient to the task of addressing the uncertainties or ambiguities of power in fieldwork and "at home." It is not only that, as Jennifer Robertson (2002, 788–90) notes, the anthropological turn toward reflexivity had the unfortunate effect of essentializing complex subjectivities and personal histories and making the anthropologist's positionality more significant than the discussion of on-the-ground relationships. It is also that in spite of a reflexive and critical perspective, research may be shaped—in sometimes unexpected ways—by our embeddedness in broader fields of power. For instance, many of my interlocutors in Cusco regarded me as a tourist or as a volunteer more than as a researcher or a scholar. Like tourists and humanitarian workers, my nationality as a U.S. citizen and my social class allowed me certain privileges, including the relative ease of my movements into and out of places or situations.[24]

Another aspect of my positionality and privilege was my ability to engage in caring practices unmoored from relatedness and tied more to a global circulation of care. Unlike other volunteers and interns at Palomitáy, I was in the midst of raising my own children and had long-term and stable employment as a professional anthropologist and college professor. I had spent substantial time living in Bolivia (with a family in a rural community and in cities) and could understand a great deal of Quechua (even if my accent and the Bolivian dialect I speak mostly caused laughter) I brought ideas and presumptions, social and economic resources, and material objects into my interactions with young mothers and other interlocutors in Cusco.

In an arena where multiple discourses (of gender, for instance) circulate while national and global political economic and social inequalities remain entrenched, I do not claim a position of neutrality or innocence, as an ethnographer or as a feminist. However, I do follow both feminist and decolonial scholars in efforts to hold in tension the focus on dynamic subjectivities and the broader context of power in which multiple relationships of domination shape experience. I focus attention on the interactions between social actors, on the situations in which they (and, of course, I) were caught up, situations that no one person could control on their own. Individuals become involved with each other, often below their level of awareness, to maintain ongoing social interactions. Ordinary instances of talk may be arenas where social actors collaboratively sustain ongoing relationships of power. To argue that social actors collude with each other in ways that maintain dominant power structures is to illuminate the micro-politics of what Lugones calls "resisting/oppressing" and to ground her philosophy in the empirical world, thereby extending it.

As will become evident in the pages that follow, I try to balance my discussion between attention to individual people and broader structures of power, between the ethnographic details of place and moment and the more general questions that shape our lives as human beings. I offer readers stories of real people's practices and interactions without presenting these young women as victims, as passive subjects, or conversely, as free agents, completely certain in their actions. I also invite readers to reflect on the ways they are themselves caught up in local and global structures of power even as they consider these young women's efforts to live better for themselves and their children. In other words, I aim to reflect on individual subjectivities of young mothers in Peru with some degree of complexity and without losing sight of the ways in which structural relationships shape their lives.

Simultaneously, I strive to maintain the confidentiality and protect the identities of the people with whom I worked. While I incorporated collaborative approaches to collecting information during my fieldwork in 2009–2010 and 2013, I have mostly analyzed data independently of the residents, staff and interns, and the director of Palomitáy. The home does not keep records on young women after they leave. When I returned for follow-up research in 2013, only two participants remained living in the residence. For this reason, gaining a sense of subjects' views on my preliminary analysis or of their ongoing circumstances proved mostly impossible. However, I also analyze data independently to protect the identities of the residents who may use first names or other identifying terms in recorded interviews. In addition to using pseudonyms for the names of individuals and institutions, I sometimes use composites of individual stories. All draw on a combination of ethnographic interviews, institutional documents (including case histories), personal interactions, and fieldnotes. I may alter identifying details (when those details are not substantive to the more general point) but aim to faithfully depict patterns of relationship, interactions among individuals, and perspectives expressed by the young women who have lived at Palomitáy, while allowing greater anonymity for these young people.

Finally, I do not offer readers all of the details that I know about individuals' lives, either prior to their arrival at the home or during their stay. In part, this is because the young women do not necessarily define themselves in terms of these experiences (even though the state and NGOs use these particular experiences to place them in Palomitáy). I interweave facets of the stories of individual residents or encounters between individuals (drawn from institutional entrance interviews, personal interactions, ethnographic interviews, and fieldnotes) with more general descriptions to enrich a sense of the broad ethnographic context in which people live. My aim is to write beyond any individual's story in order to situate care, insecurity, violence, and motherhood in a more extensive landscape—one that incorporates Peru's recent history and national and transnational structures of hierarchy but also attends to the ongoing dialogical interactions in which we all participate.

To link global and national structures to everyday relationships and more specifically the individual lives of the girls at Palomitáy, I trace the heterogeneity of discourses of care, and of "living a better life," in Peru. By focusing on moral engagement and the hierarchies of care, I resist an analysis that presents an opposition between (a lost) indigenous sociality and (an acquired) modern (international humanitarian or national urban) maternal practice. Such a dichotomy obscures the ways in which young women may act upon complicated webs of relationships when they say, "just me and my child are enough." Such a dichotomy reproduces representations of (native Andean) women as either inextricably linked to traditional practices or as ambivalently involved in contemporary social and political economic worlds. It is undeniable that these young women are engaged in mothering in ways quite different than they might have been if they were living in extended families, in rural communities, or on their own in cities. At the same time, they are neither individual aberrations nor members of families that have somehow failed. Their relationships are inextricably entangled with longer historical processes and broader global and national structures of inequality. The cases of these young women at Palomitáy, thus, illuminate more general issues of insecurity, care, and ordinary morality in Peru and elsewhere.

Chapter Overview

Thus, this book focuses on moral engagement among youth, through the lens of care and in a context thoroughly saturated by inequalities of power. In the following chapters, I trace young women's dilemmas and desires, victories and vacillations, as they care and are cared for by others. My attention to the ways people live in and through their interactions, positioning themselves in the dynamic and often ambiguous events of ordinary life, is balanced by attention to the contours of this particular social and historical context. Because many readers appreciate an overarching sense of the organization of the book, I end this introductory chapter with a brief outline of the remaining chapters.

Here in chapter 1 I have introduced theoretical perspectives on caring by, and caring for, youth. Beginning with Jeni's statement that "just me and my child are enough," I have described how I came to conduct research in Palomitáy and explained how I orient my ethnographic research to broader methodological and ethical discussions in anthropology. Not simply an ethnography about adolescent mothers, this introductory chapter sets the stage for reflections on care and moral experience as emergent in the dialogical interactions of individuals.

The next two chapters delve into the ethnographic context of my research. Chapter 2, "Dimensions of Precarity and Possibility in Peru," details the broader structural hierarchies of gender, race, and class that shape girls' sometimes fierce determination to "advance" for themselves and their children. Most of the book focuses on a limited case—of young women in Palomitáy. This chapter traces a confluence of social, political, and economic relationships in neoliberal Peru that impact girls and women generally, including migration, sexual violence and reproduction, and humanitarianism. The chapter explains why Peru is an important location for reflecting on the aspirations and insecurities of youth. Chapter 3, "Shaping Modern Mothers in Palomitáy," explores the more specific context of the residence and offers glimpses of everyday life among the girls who live there. The chapter argues that Palomitáy governs the care of young mothers in ways that unevenly laminate affective relationships between mother and child with long-standing racial and gendered discourses.

The final three chapters explore the ways social actors become actively involved or entangled with each other as they develop senses of self that may, or may not, integrate mothering. Chapter 4, "Dynamic Selves, Uncertain Desires," shifts the level of focus from institutional parameters to individual efforts to mobilize, resist, and remake understandings of themselves as mothers. Drawing on the voices of three young women, the chapter shows that individuals refract dominant discourses of motherhood through their own experiences and toward their own ends. Chapters 5 and 6 reflect on the partial and interpersonally mediated processes of care and moral engagement by analyzing creative expression in Palomitáy workshops. More specifically, chapter 5, "Making Images, (Re)Visioning Mothers (a Photography Workshop)," explores creative expression through photography. Analyzing how young women use cameras in proscribed and creative ways, the chapter demonstrates that individuals imagine themselves as "just girls" (explicitly, not mothers) as well as mothers. In chapter 6, "Moral Dialogues, Caring Dilemmas (a Theater Workshop)," I explore the overlapping moral dilemmas that emerge in the production and performance of a play, *Natasia's Story*. The play offers a multilayered arena in which social actors collaborate with each other to work out the "hierarchies of care" (Buch 2013) or the problem of just who should be cared for. I explore how these creative dialogues may reinforce or reshape racialized and gendered discourses, tying care to broader hegemonies.

Throughout the book, I forefront the ordinary imaginings, mundane practices, and creative expressions through which individuals aim to create a good life for themselves and their children. At the same time, I shed light on the moralizing discourses about young mothers and the convergence of racial, gendered, and class inequalities tied to caring labor in contemporary Peru. Grounded in the interactions of young mothers in one institution, this ethnography illuminates more general questions keyed to the emergence of subjectivity and moral experience in everyday life.

CHAPTER 2

Dimensions of Precarity and Possibility in Peru

Girls in Contemporary Peru

That young women take on the material, social, and emotional labor of care is part of a wider pattern of youth who may delay, opt-out, or hopscotch over expected life course events, not always voluntarily, in the face of entrenched inequalities and the contingencies of daily life (Mendoza-Denton and Boum 2015, 300). In the late twentieth century, anthropologist Sharon Stephens challenged anthropologists to explore how late capitalism and globalization affect the experiences of children, and asked how "children themselves experience, understand, and perhaps resist or reshape the complex, frequently contradictory cultural politics that inform their daily lives" (1995, 375). A surge in scholarship on youth has demonstrated that the very boundaries of the category of "youth" (or "child") are culturally variable and also situationally fluid. Moreover, scholars have asked how the lives of youth in the early twenty-first century are patterned in particular ways.[1]

This book illuminates distinctive aspects of youth experience in twenty-first-century Peru by bringing attention to the processes through which young women come to understand themselves and navigate state and civil institutions that impact the distribution of economic responsibilities, affective labor, and imaginative opportunities for living a good life. To make sense of young women's subjectivity, moral experience, and the contours of care in Palomitáy requires a broader understanding of the political, economic, and social context of Peru. The young women who figure in these pages are individuals who have found themselves in situations of insecurity, but the precarities they face are not the isolated "failure" of an individual or the breakdown of local community relationships. The potential relationships or opportunities they build are not isolated from more general possibilities and aspirations of youth in Peru.

Peru is a multilingual and ethnically diverse South American nation with a population which is, on the whole, quite young. Just over 45 percent of Peru's almost thirty-two million people are under the age of twenty-five years old.[2] Spanish, Quechua, and Aymara are the official languages of the nation, but Spanish is the hegemonic language. Almost 83 percent of the population speaks Spanish, compared with approximately 13 percent who speak Quechua. Moreover, as I explain below, language is entangled with gender, ethnic, and racial discourses and keyed to long-standing structural inequalities that exclude some individuals and collectivities from rights and opportunities and constrain some peoples' lives more than others. Bordered to the west by the Pacific Ocean, to the north by Colombia and Ecuador, to the east by Brazil, and to the south by Bolivia and Chile, Peru is rich in natural resources. The world's second largest producer of copper and silver, the economy relies on metal exports, fisheries, agriculture, and increasingly, remittances from Peruvians living elsewhere. Between 2009 and 2019, more than two million Peruvians emigrated, mostly to Argentina, Spain, and the United States.

In this chapter I take a wide-angle view and describe the complex networks of historical and contemporary social, economic, and political relationships that shape peoples' lives in twenty-first-century Peru. To highlight the confluence of relationships that shape young people's efforts to survive and thrive, I organize the chapter around three dimensions or arenas, including migration, sexual violence, and humanitarianism. Within each of these dimensions, discourses of identity and inequality (especially, gender, race, and class) are mutually entangled, and relationships along multiple scales—local, national, regional, transnational—are intertwined. My description of the place of Peru is necessarily partial and arcs toward a rendering of those facets of context that are significant to Palomitáy as an ethnographic case. Nevertheless, my discussion also provides a foundation from which to discern how the talk and actions of residents might illuminate the lives of girls and women in Peru, and the Andes, more generally.

This chapter ties contemporary discourses and practices to a longer history of colonial relationships and to a broader global political economy. I do not argue that an unbroken or unchanging set of understandings or structures of gender and race, ethnicity or nationality exists from the colonial period to the present in Peru. (In fact, the region's histories of encounter between people of multiple ethnic and linguistic backgrounds span millennia, not

Map of Peru with major cities, including Cusco, which is indicated by a star. Map compiled by Abigail Gonneville

centuries.) However, I use the concept of coloniality to frame my understanding of contemporary oppressions as embedded in historical processes.
The expropriation of lands, decimation of populations, homogenization of
diverse languages and ethnic groups into a singular category (of "indians,"
for instance), and disenfranchisement of diverse groups of people emerged in
novel ways during and after the European invasion (for example, Mannheim
1991; Silverblatt 1987; Stern 1982). The economic, social, and political systems
established at that time have implications for not only racial and class-based
oppressions but also gender and sexual oppressions that extend into the
twenty-first century.[3] At the same time, neoliberal political and economic
reforms and discourses and global circulation of media, people, finance, and
ideas overlay these historical inequalities.

Neoliberalism, sometimes referred to as late capitalism, is a global or transnational set of relationships and projects. A central feature of neoliberal
capitalism is the idea that economies will grow when market forces are left to
"self-regulate."[4] Proponents of neoliberal policies argue that opening markets
to free trade and privatizing state-owned businesses, rather than protecting
weak national industries, will enable countries to compete on the global stage.
The theory behind this notion is that "privately owned businesses are more
likely to rein in excesses and inefficiencies and are able to respond to the fluc-
tuations and demands of markets and allocate resources in more productive
ways than publicly owned enterprises" (Kohl and Farthing 2006, 105; cited
in Tapias 2016, 7–8). Neoliberalism has local histories and permutations. In
Peru neoliberalism is tied to fiscal policies and austerity measures promoted
by the World Bank and the International Monetary Fund and undertaken
by several Latin American governments in the midst of economic crises of
the late twentieth century.

Additionally, neoliberalism impacts the relation between a state and its
citizens. An ideology that emphasizes individual responsibilities (Brown
2006; Freeman 2014; Rose 1990) along with sometimes stringent fiscal imperatives legitimated the state's reduction or outright removal of social services from its citizens. From a neoliberal perspective, state intervention or
interference is viewed as a negative limit on freedom (of the market and of
the individual). Autonomy and flexibility and choice are valued. Yet when
individuals are viewed as self-sufficient, enterprising, and responsible for
helping themselves rather than relying on the state for support, states shift
the burden of assembling a safety net for the livelihood of its most vulnerable
citizens to private enterprises such as NGOs or to individuals themselves.

Intermeshed Inequalities in Peru

Before exploring various dimensions of social life, I explain Peruvian structures of hierarchy, especially gender, race, and class. The young women who I
came to know, like girls and women in Peru more generally, navigate everyday
relations of inequality that articulate with the political economic context of
neoliberal Peru. Throughout this book, I use categories such as gender in a
strategic and provisional way to trace the currents of inequality that structure
interpersonal relationships and institutions within Peru. From an analytical
perspective, gender, race, and class (and sexuality, ethnicity, and nationality)
are constructed and situated in specific cultural contexts. Moreover, these
aspects of identity and inequality are performative; they emerge in interactions among individuals and through habitual (and often unnoticed) acts.[5]
Taking this perspective requires a degree of provisionality because just how
subjects identify themselves is dynamic and always in process. At the same
time, these trajectories of identity and inequality are structured by enduring
institutions and intertwined with social, economic, and political relations
at multiple scales (local, national, regional, amd global). The residents of
Palomitáy, and other individuals in Peru, including me, also encounter het-
erogenous discourses of identity, some that circulate globally. I concentrate
here on discourse of gender, race, and class as they are configured locally.

Gender Hegemonies and Countercurrents

In Peru gender discourses are shaped by institutional structures of the state,
religious ideologies, public media, and local cultural ideals and practices. In
urban and Hispanic gender discourses, social relations and cultural values
of patriarchalism are pervasive (Alcalde 2010, 1995; Miles 2000, 63; Franke
1990).[6] As Rosana Vargas Valente (2010, 11) points out, this generally hegemonic ideology enables a "double standard for sexual behavior, control over
women's sexuality and motherhood, and an emphasis on virility, strength and
lack of interest in domestic affairs." Although masculinity is partly defined by
the ways a man supports his family (Paulson and Bailey 2003), these values
are intertwined with long-standing political, legal, and economic structures
and religious ideologies based in Catholicism that position men as dominant
and women subordinate.

Patriarchy is not simply about men being heads of households, as historian
Elizabeth Dore (1997) has noted. This model of gendered status and privileges has long been entangled with racial and class hierarchies, reinforcing
differences among men of different classes, castes, and ethnic groups as well

as between men and women. Men's social and political authority was institutionalized in the colonial period through *patria potestad* (the authority
and power of the father), which made the father into the guardian and legal
representative of every member of the household. The honor of the father
and household was linked closely with the sexual morality and respectability
of mothers, wives, sisters, and daughters.[7] Well into the twentieth century,
Peruvian civil codes legally bound children to obey their fathers (not mothers), wives to obey their husbands, and all those attached to the household
(employees, serfs, and so forth) to obey the patron. The father was empowered to enter into contracts and control all the property of the household,
and the legal authority of the father extended to legal statutes and political
institutions that made men the legitimate citizens of the nation.

Women and girls are positioned as responsible for the reproduction and
care of the family and for their own and others' respectability and moral
decency through religious ideology as well as state policy and procedures.
In fact, the Catholic Church has played an important role historically in the
promulgation of cultural and social values related to gender and family and
the implementation of state policy.[8] Families are presumed to be heterosexual,
monogamous, and Catholic (or Christian), and the Church as well as the state
police women's gender and sexual identifications (Guy 2000, 15). From the
official Church's perspective "sex should be confined to marriage and only
for the purposes of extending the family" (Cáceres et al. 2008, 143). A young
woman is, ideally, a virgin until marriage and presents herself in a modest
way that does not incite the desire of young men (Yon 2014, 92). Girls' and
women's moral standing is tied to controlling their sexual desires and being
respectable (*digna, decente*), as I discuss further below.

Other discourses of gender also have circulated in both urban and rural
regions of Peru (see, for example, Silverblatt 1987). As I have already noted,
gender ideologies and hierarchies in indigenous communities in the Andean
sierra position men and women in ways that are "complex and related to
context" (Harris 1978, 21). Ideals of complementary opposition overlay a
gender division of labor. Primarily women care for children, but women also
control the distribution of household resources (in a subsistence economy),
travel independently, maintain individual relationships of exchange, and
own property, among other things. Relationships within these households
and communities may not be egalitarian; however, in native Andean communities (as compared to mestizo urban ones) political, economic, and social
authority is more broadly distributed between men and women (Allen 2002;
Van Vleet 2008). Finally, while most people are Catholic, Andean Catholics
mobilize a cosmovision that incorporates saints and virgins, *Pachamama*

Catholic churches dominate the urban landscape

(Earth Mother), and multiple sacred places (such as mountains), all of whom act upon peoples' lives. Native Andeans interpret women's sexuality and desire through a schema that positively values fertility more than virginity (Allen 2011; Van Vleet 2008).

In neither rural nor urban communities do people's lived experiences align neatly with social ideals. The culturally specific practices and concepts of gender in a Quechua-speaking native Andean collectivity are intertwined with national hegemonic gender and racial formations that reinforce a particular coloniality of power. These are also entangled with more recent global circulation of media, commodities, and ideas. Children, even those who grow up in small rural communities, encounter urban discourses of gender hierarchy in their daily lives through various forms of media (television, radio, internet, school textbooks, music), interactions with adults (family members, teachers, doctors, and clergy), and encounters with peers. Their connections extend beyond local communities or neighborhoods to other places and people in Peru or elsewhere in the world. As anthropologist Ana Yon (2014, 108) notes of young women in Ayacucho, a city in the southern sierra, girls draw aesthetic ideas from famous Latin American and North American singers and actresses (Shakira, Rihanna, Katy Perry, and Dulce María Espinoza and Ahahí Puente from the Mexican telenovela *Rebelde*). They aspire to wearing beautiful and modern clothing, such as tight jeans shorts, miniskirts, and high-heeled boots, rather than track suits and sneakers.[9] Moreover, some girls identify with these female artists and especially value the "rebellion, audacity, eroticism, transgression or disinhibition" (Yon 2014, 108) in celebrities' performances. Virginity is a religious value and social ideal, but not one always attained in practice. To maintain social prestige and present oneself as modern and beautiful, girls must navigate sometimes contradictory discourses in which gender is saturated by race and class as well as religion.

Race, Class, and Discourses of Modernity

Before exploring how gender and other aspects of identity become entangled in different social arenas in Peru, I first explain the parameters of racial and class discourses. As Marisol de la Cadena (2000, 4) has argued, many Peruvians hold a "belief in the unquestionable intellectual and moral superiority of one group of Peruvians over the rest." However, racial (and racist) distinctions rely on "cultural" differences more than on purported biological differences. In the Andes, and much of Latin America, race is not assumed to be phenotypically obvious through variations in skin color, for instance, nor are racial categories organized predominately through hypodescent. Racial difference is instead keyed to educational achievement, access to commodities, modes of work, social networks, language, residence, religious affiliation, and importantly, manners, decency, and respectability.[10] Early twentieth-century intellectuals in Cusco, in fact, rejected biological categories of race (de la Cadena 2000). Establishing their own racial credentials in contrast to the Lima elite, these individuals argued that one might acquire language (Spanish), education, and "culture" to become *gente decente* (literally decent people, and figuratively "whites").

At the same time, as Weismantel (2001) and others have demonstrated, in the Andes race rests on a symbolic opposition between "indian" and "white."[11] By this, Weismantel means that the categories rely on each other for meaning and point to (or index) each other. In her formulation, "white" operates as a normative or unmarked category (as it does in the U.S. system). In Peru the term "mestizo" may be substituted for "white" because "mestizo" functions, symbolically, to represent the standard or unmarked racial norm. "Being white" or "being mestizo" or being "decent" is the unmarked, hegemonic racial category.

Thus, in contemporary Peru and other Andean nations, race may appear to be "malleable," that is, alterable through "changes in body and comportment" (Roberts 2012b, 229), education, and opportunity. The notion that individuals might move from one category, "indian," to another unmarked, standard racial category, "mestizo," is partially shaped by the emphasis on "culture" as a racial indicator. Peruvians emphasize the possibility of transforming oneself from the subjugated (indian) to the more powerful (white or mestizo) through key social practices. At the same time, they maintain a socially constructed distinction between the categories of indian and mestizo (for example, García 2005; Goodale 2008; Stephenson 1999). What is significant in Peru is the relative *positioning* of one individual or collectivity to another.

Racial distinctions and hierarchies, built on long-standing historical relationships, are continually reinforced and negotiated in ordinary interactions. As linguistic anthropologist Margarita Huayhua (2014, 2401) notes in her analysis of social interactions aboard a Peruvian *combi* (minibus), Peruvians do not simply assess each other's racial position in terms of categories such as "indian" or "mestizo." They also evaluate each other's racial positioning tacitly through a variety of signs. Peruvians use visual cues (such as wearing certain clothes or holding oneself in a particular way) and linguistic cues (such as whether a person speaks Quechua rather than Spanish) to evaluate each other. These index, or point to, an individual's position in the social hierarchy.[12] If cues do not match stereotypes, participants rely on linguistic perception to assess other participants. Quechua is tied to "primitiveness, backwardness, and ignorance" (Huayhua 2014, 2401), and how one speaks Spanish—whether one speaks "standard Spanish" or not—is also linked to determinations of individuals as ignorant or *motosos* (Huayhua 2014, 2401). Often without being aware of it themselves, people perceive differences in vowel systems, rhythm, and other aspects of articulatory style and make evaluative judgments about others.[13] This suggests that social actors may reinforce racism and racial opposition through interactions that may not necessarily *seem* to be about race at all (Huayhua 2014; for example, Sue and Golash-Boza 2013).

The material embodiment of race is always constrained by intertwined relations of power. In Peru the emphasis on racial malleability is part of an overarching racial project in which people emphasize the possibilities of (class) "advancement." Quite often, Andean women's (and men's) struggles to live dignified lives put them under intense pressure: to attain a "better life" one might pursue education, professional jobs, urban residence, and a modern presentation of self that require constant attention (for example, Leinaweaver 2008a, 60; Berg 2015, 46). When individuals mobilize ideas of "getting ahead," "advancing," or "civilizing" in urban neighborhoods and rural communities, they position themselves in ways that draw together discourses of modernity with race and social class.[14]

Not surprisingly, particularly given the imbrication of culture and language in institutional and interpersonal racism, education is often a key mode through which parents engage in a process of aspiration and advancement for their children and through which youth attempt to get ahead themselves.[15] As Carlos Ivan Degregori (1991) has argued, since the middle of the twentieth century, education has been viewed as key to social, political, and economic advancement and modernization. Access to public schools has expanded tremendously, but schools in rural communities are widely viewed as offering low-quality education. Secondary schools may be simply unavailable or require students to travel hours by foot in rural areas. Schools in both rural and urban areas also emphasize mestizo models of knowledge and are often arenas of exploitation that reinforce hegemonic values (Oliart 2003, 2010; Yon 2014, 55; García 2005).

Especially those living in poverty in Peru's cities and rural communities face social, political, and economic barriers to any movement in status. Entrenched structural hierarchies offer little real opportunity for poor people to attain a different class position. Moreover, many young people find that education does not contribute significantly to social mobility through formal employment. From this perspective, the notions of racial malleability and class advancement are part of the racial formation that promotes a social lie that one simply may acquire the educational and intellectual characteristics, or demonstrate the proper manners, decency, and respectability, or mobilize the language, commodities, and social relationships, to attain a higher status or claim belonging in an equally just nation.

Anthropologist Jeanine Anderson points out that "the people normally relegated to the categories of 'poor' and 'subordinate' do not, as a rule, focus their lives or build their identities around the issues the categories pretend to index. They, like anybody else, are involved with projects that reflect their own definitions of what a good human life is all about" (2010, 83). She goes on to note that one of the "bitterest of injustices" faced by the poor is "denying them the possibility of their own diverse visions of transcendence" (Anderson 2010, 85). Like the families in a Lima squatter town with whom she has conducted research since the 1970s, many individuals in Palomitáy develop strategies to accomplish things, compare themselves to others, and envision their life histories in terms of progress (Anderson 2010, 83). Delineating just how racial and gendered hierarchies are produced and challenged on the ground contributes to broader projects of accounting for peoples' efforts to establish identities, claim rights, affirm their humanity, and pursue their dreams in small and large ways.

Migration and Youth Mobility

To make the mutual saturation of relationships of power more concrete, and to demonstrate how these ideologies impact people's bodies and lives, I consider various dimensions of social life. In this section, I focus on patterns of migration among youth, and adults more generally, in Peru. As I have already noted, many of the young women who are subjects of this ethnography had already moved from their natal homes or between rural communities, urban neighborhoods, and lowland regions months or years before entering into the state system and being placed into Palomitáy. Jeni, for instance, migrated with her mother and younger brother from a small community in the southern highlands to a mining encampment when she was eight years old. Her father left the family two years earlier to work in Argentina but had never sent money or returned home. Eventually, she escaped her stepfather's abuse by going to Cusco on her own and finding a job. Both insecurity and aspiration figure in the movements of youth, alone or with relatives, to different households, cities, or regions of Peru. To better understand this aspect of the individual life histories of residents, I detail a brief history of internal migration and the patterns of mobility among youth and women, more generally, in contemporary Peru.

A Brief History of Internal Migration

People of all ethnic and linguistic backgrounds have traveled within the country and the region for centuries as they traded and marketed agricultural goods and other commodities; sought jobs in distant cities, agricultural regions, or mining centers; pursued educational opportunities or social justice; and endeavored to maintain relationships or develop new connections (Larson and Harris 1995). Almost half of Peru's population lived in rural areas, mostly in the sierra, in the mid-twentieth century, but this is no longer the case. In 1950, 59 percent of the population lived in rural regions and 41 percent in urban areas. By 2010 the balance of the population living in urban areas was far greater, at 72 percent (UN 2011).[16] This trend has continued, with 78.6 percent of Peruvians living in urban areas according to 2015 estimates.[17] Adults and children—traveling alone, with companions, or as families—increasingly migrate to Peru's regional cities from rural communities. However, almost one-third of the country's population lives in the capital city of Lima.[18]

Rural to urban migration is partially shaped by the ways understandings of place are tightly intertwined with racialized distinctions between "types of people." From public school textbooks to guidebooks and internet sites for tourists, Peru is characterized as a country distinguished by distinct ecological zones—the sierra, coast, and lowlands—and each of these regions is characterized in ways that reinforces particular sets of power relationships.[19] The sierra is characterized as a primarily rural (and backward) area populated mostly by Quechua-speaking peasants, referred to as *serranos* or *campesinos*. Sometimes romanticized as the indigenous descendants of the Inca, many urban mestizo and elite Peruvians habitually describe serranos as dirty, uncivilized, and "still living in the eighteenth century." Layered symbolic oppositions—between city (*ciudad*) and countryside (*campo*), modern and traditional, civilized and uncivilized, present and past, wealthy and poor, coast and sierra—saturate Peruvian public discourses. These categorical distinctions conceal the heterogeneity (demographic, ecological, or otherwise) within each region, the embeddedness of both urban and rural communities in national and global political economies (for example, Mayer 2002), and the interconnected cultural, linguistic, social, and economic ties people maintain (for example, Berg 2015; Paerregaard 2015). Further, these stereotypical characterizations displace indigenous (or poor, or disenfranchised) people from the contemporary moment and obscure the political, economic, and social inequalities and precarities of the present.

Both internal and external movements of people are configured also by political and economic processes at national and global scales. In Peru, and Latin America more generally, the 1970s were years of social and economic transformation, including social and political movements for land reform and democratization. The left-leaning Revolutionary Government of the Armed Forces under the leadership of President Juan Velasco nationalized mining and railway industries, dismantled haciendas, dispersed land, and instituted an education reform that encouraged bilingual education in support of the poor and most disenfranchised of Peru. In practical terms the dismantling of haciendas and the redistribution of land in the 1970s caused major economic, social, and political upheaval in Peru (Seligmann 1995; Smith 1991; Mayer 2009). Migration to urban areas increased when indigenous people were freed from the exploitative labor conditions on haciendas yet offered scant financial support to strengthen agricultural production. Some were drawn by educational opportunities in cities. Although primary schools were established in rural communities, few children could access secondary education outside larger towns.

By the end of the 1970s, a severe economic crisis intensified social, economic, and political turmoil in the country. In the following decade, expanded processes of globalization facilitated the circulation of goods and subjects internationally. Political and economic elites continued to lose their monopolistic hold over land, labor, and businesses as foreign capital, transnational corporations, and entrepreneurs entered the scene. However, many working-class and poor families relied on both subsistence agricultural production and labor in the informal economy to survive. Often women remained in rural communities as men migrated seasonally for work. The temporary and permanent migration of individuals from rural communities has fundamentally altered those communities as well as provincial towns and urban centers.[20]

During the 1980s, another major factor pushed people from rural communities to urban centers, especially Lima. People began fleeing the violence that erupted between the Sendero Luminoso (Shining Path) insurgency and the government's scorched-earth campaign.[21] Poor and mostly Quechua-speaking migrants left areas of concentrated violence in the rural southern highland departments of Ayacucho, Apurímac, and Huancavelica and arrived in Lima, only to be excluded from "decent" city centers. Forced into marginal zones, migrants created shantytowns on the outskirts of cities (Berg 2015, 4; Larsen 2005).[22] The internal conflict fragmented families and disrupted community life in ways that have continued to have repercussions decades later (for example, Theidon 2012; Leinaweaver 2008a). The flow of migrants that began years before the conflict has continued long after the end of the war.

Inequality and Mobility

While many involuntary migrants became permanent residents of Lima, children and youth in addition to adults continue to swell the population of regional cities as well as large urban centers. Women make up an increasing percentage of internal migrants, moving to cities in pursuit of opportunities for work and education. Some migrants rely on connections to relatives or compadres to orient them to a new location, but others arrive in a new location without support. Women migrants are less likely to be underemployed or unemployed than men since the turn of the twenty-first century (Altamirano 2003), and the numbers of households headed by women has increased from about 15 percent in 1992 to about 26 percent in 2012, according to the World Bank.[23] Few poor and working-class Peruvians traveled internationally in significant numbers through most of the twentieth century (Berg 2015, 6–7). In the late twentieth century, individuals and families across the spectrum mobilized resources (genealogical connections, wealth, education, government documents, and so forth) to travel to Argentina, Spain, Italy, and the United States. The country's more recent economic growth has been partially supported by remittances sent by emigrants.

In general, the mobility of native Andean folk, poor and working-class Peruvians, and children and young women was and is far more constrained than that of middle-class and elite Peruvians (or foreign tourists, humanitarians, educators, administrators, or missionaries). The majority of residents at Palomitáy experienced mobility as a mode of familial survival or individual survival and as a strategy for success.[24] The earliest residents of Palomitáy were born during the internal conflict, but the young women I knew were born in 1996 or later. They are part of a wider pattern of children, especially poor children, migrating with relatives, or circulating between their natal family home and the homes of relatives, compadres, and strangers, or moving into and out of institutions such as orphanages, or living on the street to support themselves and their families.

Some girls move to find work and pursue educational aspirations. For instance, when Faviola was nine years old, the teachers from her primary school had approached her mother and father and asked if the little girl could live with them. Faviola had been attending school, and the teachers appreciated her quiet smile and willingness to work. A married couple, the teachers needed extra help in the house to care for their baby, prepare food, and wash laundry. Her parents agreed, and during the first year, Faviola lived with the teachers but still saw her parents and four brothers. The community was small and in moments between carrying water or going to school, she could stop by her house, where her mother would give her a snack or some small treat. At the end of the year, the teachers accepted a different teaching post in another department. Faviola's mother might have refused to let her young daughter travel so far away, but the family was struggling. Faviola's father and mother subsisted by planting potatoes, oca, and barley. Her father drank alcohol often and at times hit her mother. The teachers promised that Faviola would attend school and that they would treat her as their own daughter. When her mother asked whether she would go with the teachers, Faviola said that she would.

Faviola began primary school again in the new town and studied until the second grade. Then the teacher had a second child, and Faviola began staying home from school to care for both children and do the housework. "No one made me study, so I lost my matriculation." She entered yet another primary school when she was eleven years old, completing the second and third grades. When she was thirteen, the teacher and her husband enrolled her in a different school, one with a basic alternative education program that offered classes on Saturdays. Faviola said she did not have close friends. Shy in disposition, her responsibilities in the household and movements into and out of various schools made it difficult to get to know other girls. Faviola referred to the teachers as *patrones* (bosses) in her conversation with me, indexing their relative power and authority in the relationship. The teachers did not treat Faviola as they had promised her mother, for they would have made a daughter study and pursue certain aspirations.

These kinds of movements both reflect and create conditions of insecurity. Individuals and families may lack extensive social or political connections or economic resources in the new place. Their conditions may be so precarious that unexpected events—a death in the family, a prolonged illness, loss of a job, a daughter's unexpected pregnancy—may have a profound impact on family configurations and dynamics. Migrants may be taken advantage of by those who are supposed to help them. Youth, women, indigenous Peruvians, rural migrants, and/or those who speak Spanish as a second language may be paid less, made to work long hours, or mistreated physically or emotionally. Even those who go to work in a relative or compadre's home are vulnerable to exploitation and violence. For young women in particular, migration from rural to urban communities, on their own or with their families, may shift the ways gender, class, and racial discourses impinge on people's bodies and lives.

Sexual Violence and Maternalism

Another dimension of experience that is key to understanding the kinds of vulnerabilities young women face is sexual violence and (unexpected) pregnancy. Many Palomitáy residents become pregnant unexpectedly and in violent or coercive circumstances. Having a child and raising a child—motherhood or, more broadly, reproduction—is valued by people in Peru. However, especially very young mothers are stigmatized, and raising a child on one's own is often fraught with social and financial insecurities (for example, Bant and Girard 2008). Considering sexual violence and reproduction within the same dimension illuminates state policies and public discourses that constrain young women's possibilities and unevenly affect rural, indigenous, and poor youth.

Sexual Violence Patterns and Policy

Palomitáy residents' experiences of violence tie them to many other girls and women in Peru, as indicated by statistics from the period of my fieldwork. According to the Peruvian Ministry of Women and Social Development (MIMDES 2008), rape and sexual violence rank as the third most frequent crime in Peru.[25] The United Nations Children's Fund (UNICEF) estimates that in Peru six out of ten pregnancies in girls (aged eleven to fourteen) result from incest or rape, and eight out of ten cases of sexual abuse are perpetrated by a member of the family environment (Vargas 2010, 5; UNICEF 2007). More generally, approximately 50 percent of women claim that they have suffered physical violence by an intimate partner; that statistic climbs to 70 percent if emotional or psychological abuse is included (Boesten 2010; INEI 2008). As in many other places, sexual or gender violence is underreported; however, women are the vast majority (93 percent) of those reporting such crimes. Adolescents between fourteen and seventeen are the most affected group among women (44.5 percent).

As in many parts of the world, physical and sexual violence against women is normalized. Although Peruvians went to the streets in 2017 to publicly protest violence against women with the slogan "*Ni una mas!*" (Not one more!), long-standing institutional structures enable intimate violence and impunity.[26] In Peru sexual violence is difficult to prosecute because of legal institutions and prevailing assumptions. In her analysis of the rape trial of Mercedes Ccorimanya Lavilla, historian Laura Bunt examined 250 cases filed under the rubric of rape in Cusco from 1909 to 2001. Ccorimanya Lavilla's case was one of only five that ended in a conviction (Bunt 2008, 286). Until

Handmade poster ("Women should be treated with respect by all public employees") hanging on the courtyard wall

the late twentieth century, cases under the rubric of rape were evaluated under the 1924 Penal Code and could involve a range of issues from statutory rape to broken marriage promises (Bunt 2008, 290). Since then, the state has passed laws against familial violence and instituted several procedures, including the stipulation that victims younger than eighteen years of age or those who could not afford legal counsel should be aided by the district attorney's office. However, Bunt (2008, 290) argues that, in general, plaintiffs must "strategize against judicial and cultural bias, rather than maneuvering within the letter of the law." Most women who pursue legal action actually collect evidence and develop a case on their own or with a privately hired lawyer.

Based on a set of cases of sexual violence that occurred during Peru's internal war, Jelke Boesten (2014, 5) has argued similarly that the "judicial and broader political neglect of sexual violence" is the result of generally accepted ideas about violence against women, perhaps especially sexual violence. The

Handmade poster ("Express your thoughts and feelings, woman!") hanging on Palomitáy's courtyard wall. The speech bubbles read (left to right): "I will finish studying," "I am a little girl but I will be a woman," and "I want to be happy"

Peruvian Truth and Reconciliation Commission (Comisión de la Verdad y la Reconciliación, CVR), which investigated Peru's internal armed conflict (1980–2000), found that the rape of women, especially indigenous women, was widespread and perpetrated primarily by the army and the police.[27] Perceptions of girls' and women's class and racial backgrounds shaped how they were treated by military, police, and Sendero forces, and sexual violence reinscribed alterity on their bodies (Boesten 2015; Bueno-Hansen 2015; Theidon 2012).[28] However, none of the 554 cases of rape documented by the CVR, including sixteen cases for which evidence was raised, have proceeded to trial (Boesten 2014, 5). The state has prosecuted other human rights violations but refused to punish human rights violations related to sexual violence.

Moreover, when women decide to speak out against abuse, they become caught up in multiple ways in powerful systems of hierarchy. Women often face "humiliation and discrimination . . . even at the hands of the state agents designated to aid" them when they make formal complaints of sexual violence (Bunt 2008, 290). The intense social stigma is tied in part to the particular ways that violence, including rape, is linked to moral discourses about women's decency. For instance, to obtain a court hearing (much less a conviction), a woman had to prove three things: her virtue (or, virginity), her age, and her "honor" (Bunt 2008). In the case of Ccorimanya Lavilla, it was only by demonstrating that she was of a better class standing than her assailants that she was able to move her case to court. This was in spite of the fact that all six of the accused men confessed to the police, and a medical examination of Ccorimanya Lavilla provided confirmation of the rape.

Maternalism and the Precarities of Unexpected Pregnancy

The social relations and political structures that make sexual violence difficult to prosecute overlap with a maternalist framework and moral regime. Girls and women are valorized as mothers in Peru and other Latin American countries, as I have already noted, and *not* being a mother is stigmatized (for example, Roberts 2012a). During the CVR hearings, even as women testified about being brutally raped, state representatives positioned women as suffering and self-sacrificing. They applauded women for their "maternal expressions of unconditional and selfless love" for the children born of these encounters (Bueno-Hansen 2015, 94).[29] Such framings obscure potential relationships (such as paternity), state responsibilities (criminal investigation of sexual violence, protecting the human rights of citizens), and pervasive structural inequalities.

It is not insignificant that in Peru abortion is illegal even in cases of rape. Only when the life of the mother is in danger is abortion legal; even so, doctors may refuse to perform the procedure.[30] Peruvians attempted to decriminalize abortion, in some cases, during a broader reform of the 1924 Criminal Code in the early 1990s. Feminist organizations such as Centro de la Mujer Peruana Flora Tristán, Movimiento Mauela Ramos, Colectivo de Derechos Reproductivos, and Latin American Committee for the Defense of Women's Rights, among others, aligned with several congresspersons and the Peruvian College of Physicians to press the legislature to decriminalize abortion in cases of rape. These organizations stressed the "discriminatory nature of illegal abortion for women in poverty . . . and called into question the meaning of motherhood imposed by violence" (Cáceres et al. 2008, 136). However, the Catholic Church and other more conservative leaders succeeded in preventing this change. Moreover, they successfully argued for legislators to reform the constitution in 1993 so that the "unborn child" is recognized as "entitled to all the rights that may benefit them" (Cáceres et al. 2008, 137). In subsequent constitutional interpretations, the state reinforced the view that life begins at the moment of conception.

The Catholic Church and the state are actively involved in shaping policies that affect reproduction, even when they are seemingly at odds with each other (Ewig 2006, 2015; Htun 2003; Morgan and Roberts 2012). Another well-documented example of this is the Fujimori government's clandestine and coercive campaign to reduce fertility through permanent sterilization of mostly poor and indigenous women. Instituted in the mid-1990s and revealed by Peruvian journalists by the end of the 1990s, the Church used the scandal to promote its own agenda—immediate end to all family planning services (Boesten 2010; Cáceres et al. 2008, 143; Ewig 2006, 2010). In fact, in the first decade of the twenty-first century, two successive ministers of health who belonged to conservative Catholic orders (of Opus Dei and Sodalitium Chritianae Vitae) dismantled much of Peru's reproductive health services. More recently, human rights and women's activist groups campaigned to make emergency contraception freely available in public clinics. They were successful in 2006, but by 2009 authorities banned distribution of the Pill in the public health system.[31]

These policies point to the fraught debates around reproductive health and politics, and significantly, to the potential consequences for the lives of some individuals (indigenous, poor, and working-class women and girls) more than others. Because 68 percent of the individuals who use contraceptives are reliant on the public health system, banning the Pill, and emergency contraception more specifically, disproportionately affects rural and poor women, adolescents, and rape survivors, who otherwise have little access to private pharmacies. In addition to accessibility, young women's sexual practices, response to sexual violence, and use (or not) of family planning services are shaped by the dearth of robust information, fear of stigma, concerns about privacy, and shifting state policies.

In this context, it is unsurprising that most of Palomitáy's residents seek assistance from state or municipal authorities only when they realize that they are pregnant. Their official accusations (*denunciación*) of sexual or intimate violence, whether a single incident of rape or ongoing sexual abuse, mostly are not pursued in the legal system. As Rosa explained in an interview, "Look, we know that Peru has a big problem with violence, sexual violence, violence in the family. But very few will report violence. . . . And you have to understand that officials in the Demuna, the National Police, the family court system, and even their family and friends give very little weight to violación unless the young woman is pregnant." In other words, rape is problematic because of an ensuing pregnancy (and an effort to establish paternity) rather than because of the physical, emotional, and social suffering of an individual survivor of violence.

To illustrate her point, she told me about Lydia, who was a resident at Palomitáy until December 2008. Lydia was an orphan from a rural community in southern Peru, and after her parents died, she went to live with relatives in a provincial town. After a year, she and one of the sons of the household (her second cousin) fell in love. When his mother realized that the two teenagers were romantically involved, she threw Lydia out of the house. She sent her to Lima to find a job because she "did not want any problems at home." Eventually, Lydia did find a job as a maid in a wealthy household. Within a few weeks, Lydia suffered a brutal rape by the son of her *patrona* (employer). "In all of my years doing this work, it is the worst case I have ever heard of," said Rosa. Lydia told no one; the young man had threatened to kill her if she did. She was frightened, and she had nowhere else to go. When her patrona's uncle visited a few days later, he cornered her and made sexual advances. Lydia was too terrified to resist him. Worried about getting pregnant, ashamed of what had happened to her, and fearful of further abuse, she confided in a friend but did not report the abuse. Two months later, when Lydia realized that she was, in fact, pregnant, she was inconsolable. Fearful that she would not be able to work and support a child, she worked up enough courage to go to the Demuna and seek help. Authorities offered her scant protection. Lydia could not show physical evidence of violence. She could not name one specific perpetrator as the "father of the unborn child." No formal complaint was filed and no actions were taken against either of the men, and officials sent Lydia to a state orphanage until a space opened up at Palomitáy.

Demuna and other state officials may not dispute the details of Lydia's or other girls' stories, but view the violence as impossible to address through legal or official channels. Only when a girl is younger than fourteen years old—and the violence considered under the legal framework of statutory rape—do the courts give more weight to accusations of sexual violence. In 2007 the age of statutory rape was lowered in Peru from sixteen to fourteen years of age. From Rosa's perspective, one consequence of this is that girls may be considered sexual agents and also "provocateurs" (Bunt 2008) at a younger age. Men accused of rape by girls fourteen years and older may argue that the sexual relationship was consensual. Moreover, if the accused mobilizes greater social or financial resources to deny the claim, a young woman may not be able to demonstrate her lack of consent.

Many ordinary people in Peru draw on moralizing discourses that police the reproduction of girls and women, including unexpected pregnancy in contexts of violence. Hegemonic mestizo (and Catholic) ideologies emphasize abstinence and view sexual activity prior to marriage as improper and as a moral failure. Young women who find themselves pregnant after romantic encounters, or coercive or violent ones, are held to a different standard than young men. They are often also racialized through reference to their sexual and reproductive practices. Although many urban mestizo and rural indigenous youth engage in active sexual relationships (for example, Yon 2014), especially poor, working-class, or indigenous girls are assessed according to more stringent standards than their mestizo counterparts. If a girl remains silent until she realizes she is pregnant, she likely will be unable to press charges. Many families do support their daughters' efforts to raise and care for children. In other cases, the state may determine that the young woman, as a legal minor but not a sexual minor, is in a "state of abandonment."

Youth and Humanitarianism

Diane Hoffman notes that the idea of child vulnerability "has its roots in international discourses of children's rights that reflect an idealized, universalized child, whose immaturity creates dependence and innocence, and whose proper maturation demands adult protection and intervention" (2012, 156). This notion of vulnerability may contradict local understandings of children's roles or agency and at the same time "facilitate cultural moral and political processes of globalization" (Hoffman 2012, 157). In an arena such as Palomitáy, residents may be characterized (by the state, by staff, by volunteers, and so forth) primarily in terms of vulnerabilities. In particular, young women may be portrayed as victims (or survivors) of violence within a wider context of Peruvian patriarchy. The social and historical relationships related to sexual violence and maternalism comprise one dimension (among many) of these young women's lives. In what remains of this chapter, I elaborate on a final dimension of social life in Peru: the day-to-day insecurities of neoliberalism and the florescence of humanitarianism in Cusco.

Among the broad social, political, and economic relations that shape Cusco—and that make this particular place an important site for considering youth and caring labor—is the expansion of humanitarianism at the turn of the twenty-first century. In Cusco, international NGOs promote political, economic, and social agendas for women and indigenous political movements, provide health and educational services, and offer rural development and poverty relief. The increase in number and kinds of humanitarian organizations is linked to broader transformations in the national and global economy, including the circulation of people, ideas, and commodities.

Neoliberal Transformations

In the late twentieth-century Peru became increasingly embedded in a global neoliberal economy. In Peru, as in other parts of Latin America, an economic crisis of massive proportions developed in the 1980s. The crisis was addressed by the World Bank and International Monetary Fund through austerity packages, free-trade agreements, funding cuts to social services, privatization of state-owned mines and businesses, and debt refinancing. Then President Fujimori instituted neoliberal reforms in 1990, widely referenced as "Fujishock" and regarded as "drastic, cruel, and excessive" (Mayer 2002, 314). Public services, including health and education programs, were cut back or abandoned, and the government embarked on structural readjustment programs to control inflation (Mayer 2002, 314). While many Peruvians welcomed the end of hyperinflation, daily economic conditions and the aftermath of the internal conflict made conditions difficult for many (Berg 2015).

Inequality grew after Fujishock, but the GNP began to grow by the end of the decade. Although Fujimori's government was highly centralized, authoritarian, and corrupt, it did rebuild infrastructure and institute a short-term poverty alleviation program. In the first decade of the twenty-first century, the country began experiencing an economic boom (with a 5.6 percent average annual growth rate). The percentage of Peruvians living in poverty shrank from more than 55 percent in 2004 to fewer than 30 percent by 2006 (Vergara and Watanabe 2016, 150–51). However, when poverty rates are considered by region, ethnicity, or class group, neoliberalism's uneven benefits are more evident. For instance, during this period, the city of Cusco had a poverty rate of approximately 28 percent but the surrounding region stood at approximately 51 percent (WEF 2013, 2). In general, Peru's urban and coastal communities seem to have benefited more from recent economic growth than rural, Afro-Peruvian, indigenous, and poor populations. The economic growth is balanced in part on high international prices for Peru's metals and minerals (which make up about 55 percent of the country's total exports) and cash transfers from Peruvians working in other countries, especially Spain and Italy. The benefits from GDP growth impact certain groups more than others, and changes in the international market may have a profound impact on Peru's GDP.

Moreover, the forms of economic production fueling the country's economic growth are based on a historically entrenched disavowal of the rights to land and survival, and the humanity, of indigenous people. Foreign resource extraction has spurred economic growth but mining and oil companies have offered few formal jobs. Meanwhile, in these areas of gold mining and oil

Shopping for groceries. Photo by Palomitáy resident

extraction, environmental damage (of water and land), exposure to pollution, and loss of territory without compensation are layered upon a dearth of formal jobs, poor working conditions, and the flow of money out of communities. All of this exacerbates intertwined relationships of insecurity and inequality. More generally, in Peru the availability of formal jobs has declined even as the rate of economic growth has remained strong. Formal jobs are important because these provide some benefits, including pensions. As Vincent (2016, 387) notes in her discussion of elderly pensioners who support their children, Peru's informal sector has expanded from 48 percent in the 1980s to 58 percent in 1990 to more than 74 percent of economically active individuals in 2012 (INEI 2014, 113). Younger adults who are unskilled have few opportunities to enter into formal employment (Vincent 2016, 382). However, families increasing rely on children to help contribute to their economic sustainability (Campoamor 2016; Vincent 2016).

Humanitarian Expansion

It is in this context that the presence of humanitarian organizations has grown rapidly in Peru. Humanitarianism relies on certain forms of structured in-equality and expands along with crisis and its aftermath (Fassin 2006; Fassin and Das 2012; Tichkten 2011). Although the humanitarian presence began to increase in the 1970s, it was after the end of the armed conflict between the Peruvian state and Sendero Luminoso in 1992 that the number of NGOs pro-liferated (Andolina et al. 2009; Boesten 2010; Oliart 2007, 295). The Peruvian government's increasing reliance on humanitarian organizations (Boesten 2010) also follows a more global pattern. Funding models for humanitarian aid and development projects shifted at the end of the twentieth century so that financial support was funneled through private organizations rather than state governments (Andolina et al. 2009). As governments instituted neoliberal fiscal policies that reduced state support for their most marginal populations, NGOs stepped in to fill the gaps.

As I have noted, Palomitáy is one of several independent and public in-stitutions that care for children in Peru. Former minister of the Integrated National Program for Family Wellbeing (INABIF) Ana Vásquez de Velasco (2009, 5) notes in an internal report that the majority of the eighteen thou-sand children institutionalized in the country were housed in private orphan-ages. Only one-fifth of institutionalized children were placed in orphanages run by the state at that time. Nearly half of the public orphanages were in a state of emergency at the time of her 2009 report. Few orphanages provided special services for disabled children, young mothers, or survivors of sexual or physical violence.

The large number of children's homes relative to Cusco's population is also part of another larger pattern, the growth of tourism in Cusco. In other words, the large number of independent orphanages is at least in part a consequence of the ways in which the international community views Cusco as a favorable location for their bases of operation (Valverde, personal com-munication, March 30, 2010). In the 1990s, tourism, especially cultural tour-ism (which promotes a reverence for an often-romanticized Inca past), was targeted as an important trajectory of economic development (Babb 2010, 2012; Van den Berghe and Ochoa, 2000). The vast majority of Peru's tourists spend some time in Cusco and Machu Picchu (WEF 2013; Steel 2008; Ypeij and Zoomers 2006). Humanitarian and development organizations rely on many of the same amenities (from restaurants to internet access) that attract national and foreign tourists.

In Cusco, orphanages vary widely in their organizational structure, programming, physical space, financial status, and even their ability to provide food and basic necessities. Humanitarian and development organizations may offer services for children and youth that are unavailable otherwise. However, because they are privately funded, organizations and programs may appear (and disappear) in relation to the concerns and efforts of individuals. Many of the independent orphanages in Cusco are founded and run by individuals: an evangelical Protestant couple who responded to "a call from God," a nurse who recognized that physically disabled children needed targeted support, a wealthy woman seeking to memorialize her grandson's death by helping other children in need. Some private orphanages are established by large international organizations, such as the Methodist Church. In 2009, orphanages were required to register with the municipality and with INABIF-MIMDES, but only two staff members stationed in Lima oversaw all of the country's private orphanages. Both municipal and federal governments provided more oversight of orphanages and children's programs in 2014 (the end of the data collection period) than in 2000 (when Palomitáy was founded) or in 2009–2010 (when I conducted the majority of my fieldwork).

Palomitáy may be the only institutional setting in which a young woman (and her child) will ever live, or it may be just one in a series of institutional settings in which she and her child will live. Yet most of the residents of Palomitáy are not orphans in the way that North Americans tend to understand the term. Many of the residents, including Jeni and Faviola, have living relatives. This is true, more generally, of children and youth in orphanages in Peru. Some poor families in Peru, as elsewhere in Latin American (for example, Fonseca 2003), may use orphanages as temporary shelters from the contingencies of life. When a family member dies or becomes ill or loses a job, the family may have little recourse. Living relatives, sometimes parents, may be unable or, in some cases, unwilling to take custody of the mother and her child. Parents or guardians may be deemed (by the state) to be unable or unfit to do so; the family is not always the safest place for children. In the vast majority of cases, the young women at Palomitáy, and the children and youth in orphanages throughout Peru, have little access to resources or assistance outside the state or NGO.

Palomitáy is embedded in a context that draws together projects of aid with broader relations of inequality in postcolonial contexts. Like many poor children and youth, many of the young women had inconsistent access to education, housing, and nutrition before living at Palomitáy. Yet in their efforts to request help from the state, and in many cases, to denounce abuse, they become enmeshed in a network that at least for a time alters the contours of their everyday lives and the lives of their children. They are put under the protection of the state or removed from their parents' or guardians' custody if the judge determines that incident(s) of sexual or familial violence occurred or ascertains that the custodial adult(s) is unable or unwilling or unfit to care for the girl and her child. The circumstances might range from the poverty of a family to the withdrawal of support by relatives because a young woman is pregnant, to an already established dearth of care (for example, because the girl has already been living without her parents).

As I have already noted, Palomitáy, like many orphanages in Cusco, incorporates foreigners into the programming and staffing of their institutions, drawing on the large numbers of tourists and students traveling to and through Cusco. The directors (from Spain and Peru) and full-time staff (mostly from Peru) most directly shape the policies, procedures, and curricula that impact the girls' and their children's routines. The young mothers attend classes within the residence, which are supported by tutors (from Peru); some attend weekend public school classes. Additionally, the young women attend workshops run by interns (mostly undergraduate students from Europe who remain for four to six months) or by other staff from other independent NGOs. Volunteers (primarily from North America and Europe, who remain for periods of just a few hours to several weeks at a time) may contribute to the home's operations or organize activities and events. Volunteers support nursery staff, paint murals, tend the garden, donate supplies, do clerical or technical work, or offer occasional entertainment or enrichment opportunities, among other things. I describe the context of the residence in the following chapter.

Conclusion

In this chapter, I link long-standing structures of inequality with recent neoliberal political-economic transformations and patterns of social relationships keyed to reproduction in order to sharpen understanding of uncertainties of everyday life for young women in Peru. As much as this book focuses on young women's moral engagement through on-the-ground interactions, this chapter sets the stage by outlining the broad discourses that circulate within and beyond Palomitáy. Entangled hierarchies of race, gender, sexuality, social class, ethnicity, nationality, and age saturate the everyday life of children and youth in neoliberal Peru, within the walls of Palomitáy and well beyond them. Consider the complexity of an arena in which individuals from multiple communities, both within Peru and internationally, work and live, eat and talk, play and study and care for children and mothers for a relatively short time (from a few months to a few years). Multiple aspects of inequality impact the experiences of individuals. However, the complexity of an intersectional approach develops from an effort to recognize the cultural construction and historical situatedness of categories (of race, gender, sexuality, class, and so forth) in various contexts and simultaneously to recognize the long-standing, often national and transnational relations of power shaping these.

All of the young mothers who live at Palomitáy, along with their children, are legal minors; they were removed from the custody of their parents (or guardians) by the state and transferred (temporarily or permanently) into the custody of the director(s) of the home. Their personal stories may be read against legal frameworks, social structures, and recent histories. For many, however, the insecurities of poverty intertwine with the vulnerabilities of being young and being girls. By attending to the intersection of inequality at multiple scales within various dimensions of social life, I have established a broad foundation from which to trace the specificities of interaction in Palomitáy.

As Veena Das has pointed out, "to be vulnerable is not the same as to be a victim, and those who are inclined to assume that social norms or expectations . . . are automatically translated into oppression need to pay attention to the gap between a norm and its actualization" (Das 2000, 209; cited in Theidon 2013, 173). Moreover, just as public discourses on respectability and decency are gendered and racialized in the national context, so too are discourses that stress young women's vulnerability. To recognize intermeshed oppressions or structures of power is part of an effort to understand individual acts, discourses, and beliefs in relation to a broader context. In subsequent chapters, I turn to a more finely grained analysis of the parameters of Palomitáy and young women's talk and actions as they navigate these relationships and position themselves as good people.

Young women's life experiences point to a consistent tension that permeates neoliberal, postcolonial Peru in which claiming exception, implicitly or explicitly performing indigeneity or marginalized subjectivity, consistently results in sanction or in the reinforcement of racialized boundaries at multiple scales. This impacts the contingencies through which subjectivities of motherhood are developed and the creative and conventional ways that young women navigate hierarchies of care and endeavor to live a good life. This work interrogates how the girls differentially take up these discourses, drawing on personal experiences, claiming for themselves positions from which to resist negative stereotypes, and incorporating positive images and ways of being in the world as gendered and kinned individuals. However, first I explore the governance of reproduction in Palomitáy and especially the everyday life in the home.

CHAPTER 3

Shaping (Modern) Mothers in Palomitáy

Governing Care

"A la lay! I'm so tired," Mónica groaned. Noelia, the education coordinator, was yelling from the courtyard that it was time for everyone to wake up. I had just poked my head into Mónica's room from the second-floor corridor. It was Saturday morning, and much earlier than I typically arrived at the home, but Mónica and I had planned an interview. Unfortunately, she was nowhere near ready. Mónica had just asked Eli, one of the girls who shared the bedroom, if she would watch Reina, her nine-month-old daughter, for a few minutes. Eli went over and sat her one-year-old, Carlitos, on the bed next to Reina. Mónica admonished, "Don't move. Stay right there," as Reina watched her with big eyes. "I'm coming right back," Mónica said as she scooted out the door and ran down the stairs to the bathroom.

By 7:30 a.m., Mónica had showered and dressed, dressed Reina and fed her breakfast, and carried Reina down to the cuna, the nursery. The playroom was the largest part of the L-shaped space and painted bright purple and green. Children from infancy to three years spent most of the day in the cuna, playing and eating in the sun-filled playroom or napping in the small, constantly dim sleeping room. Laura's daughter, Violeta, who was just four days old, was already wrapped tightly in a blanket and sleeping in her basket in the darkened room. Katia, one of the caretakers on the Palomitáy staff, settled her own infant, bundled in a white crocheted cap and sweater into a nearby crib. His fat cheeks and bright eyes peeked out from the blue blanket she had wrapped firmly around him. In the playroom, Mónica squatted down next to Reina for a minute and handed her a squeaky rubber cow. She watched out of the corner of her eye as Sebastian, a toddler of three years, grabbed a car from Angelica, another toddler, who burst into tears. Franklin, who was not yet crawling, sat on the mats chewing on his fist. Katia spread another thick mat onto the floor and brought out a basket of toys for the toddlers. She left the two low tables and several tiny chairs stacked in a corner while she waited for the arrival of the other children and for Yaneth, who would take a turn working in the nursery along with Mónica.

The surveillance and control of intimate relationships—of romance, reproduction, child rearing, and concubinage—are crucial to the ways colonial
and postcolonial states govern.[1] Yet, as Lynn Morgan and Elizabeth Roberts
(2012, 243) point out in their discussion of "reproductive governance," not
only states but also other collectivities might "produce, monitor, and control
reproductive behaviours and practices." Certainly, NGOs, religious organizations, and various other institutions mobilize discourses that embed young
mothers into broader moral regimes and ideological formations that govern
care and reproduction.[2] This chapter offers a glimpse of daily life in Palomitáy
and illustrates some of the mundane tasks, implicit inducements, and overt
constraints, as well as the unexpected opportunities, empathetic encourage-
ment, and commonplace pleasures through which Palomitáy governs caring
for and caring by young women.

If governance depends on making social relations legible, then Palomitáy
clarifies the relation of young women *as mothers* to their children. A resident
of Palomitáy is encouraged to engage in the mundane labor of caring for children and to establish an intimate connection between herself and the child to
whom she has given birth. Young women are expected—if just implicitly—to
develop a corporeal knowledge and affective orientation in which her child
is central to her everyday activities. At the same time, Palomitáy requires
residents to develop a sense of care that extends into the future. Residents
are offered opportunities to "better themselves" through education, urged
to comport themselves in particular ways, and inspired to envision a better
life for their children. As mothers, young women are responsible for their
child's well-being in the present and in the future.[3] By bringing into the same
analytical frame caring *for* young mothers and caring *by* young mothers, I link
ethnographic description of "affective economies" (Richard and Rudnyckyj
2009) in the home to broader gender and racial hierarchies and modern
sensibilities that extend beyond the home in this global neoliberal context.

I also amplify Morgan and Roberts's focus on governance by drawing on
Mattingly's (2014) concept of "moral laboratories." In her long-term study of
families with very sick children, where women and men were tied to medical
and scientific communities through their children's (and their own) experiences of trauma, Mattingly explored the temporal and contingent ways that
people constituted their actions as moral. I refigure her metaphor to evoke
Palomitáy as a "moral workshop," a place of fleeting and long-term relationality in which care and affective social relationships are facets of apprenticeship.
In this moral workshop, care is explicitly taught and implicitly crafted. Young
women explore, normalize, and transform ethical and affective engagements
and subjectivities. In subsequent chapters, I contemplate young women's

View of the balcony. Photo by Palomitáy resident

creative expression and experimentation in photography and theater. In this chapter, I concentrate on the broader parameters that configure care in the residence.

I begin by describing the broader structural aspects of care in the home. From an institutional perspective, caring *for* young mothers encompasses myriad practices and perspectives. While living at Palomitáy, these young women learn practical and emotional aspects of infant care, pursue formal education, and develop embodied sensibilities and styles of comportment that are tied to more broadly circulating discourses of maternity and modernity. Framed around the social arenas of the cuna, the classroom, and the workshop, this chapter illustrates some of the mechanisms and discourses through which care is governed. Young women simultaneously are positioned as mothers (who care for others) and as youth (who need care).

Structures of Care in Palomitáy

Before continuing, I note here that I often refer to Palomitáy as a singular organization, but to say that *Palomitáy* cares for young mothers may obscure the diverse set of individuals who provide the residents with childcare and education, psychological support and nutritious food, and job training and a safe and stable place to live. In a general sense, I conceive of Palomitáy as a "community of practice" (Eckert and McConnell-Ginet 1995) in which administrators, staff, volunteers, researchers, and residents participate in the endeavor of care. The members of Palomitáy are not a community *because* they share a set of attributes; Palomitáy is far from homogenous. Moreover, people who live and work and encounter each other in Palomitáy also belong to other groups, organizations, and communities beyond the residence; Palomitáy is not bounded. Nevertheless, in Palomitáy people of different ages, nationalities, cultural backgrounds, languages, marital statuses, and genders (among other things) jointly participate in an endeavor "and in a set of social practices that grow around that endeavor" (Eckert and McConnell-Ginet 1995, 472). That endeavor is care.

The sense of care that I explore in this book follows anthropologist Lisa Stevenson's definition of care as "the way someone comes to matter and the corresponding ethics of attending to the other who matters" (Stevenson 2014:3). Care, as I noted in chapter 1, is an aspect of the reproduction of families and communities, but not only that. Care may be conceived of as an array of practices and affective orientations that connect one individual to another affectively—but also socially, morally, and economically. Care emerges in the interactions among people in Palomitáy and simultaneously produces a heterogeneous community of practice.

For instance, on the first day that I toured Palomitáy with Rosa, I encountered many individuals engaged in the intimate labor of care. We stepped into the cuna and greeted Katia, one of two staff members in charge of childcare. She was busy overseeing a midmorning snack. Toddlers seated in tiny chairs circling two low round tables eagerly dipped their spoons into *mazamorra morada*, a deep-purple pudding. Two volunteers and two young mothers spooned the snack into the eager mouths of the babies. Out in the courtyard, Yaki, the humanities teacher, a tiny, dark-haired woman in a maroon pantsuit and black pumps, directed several young women to set up tables and chairs in the open patio. Minutes later, when Davíd, the math and science teacher, arrived she explained that after almost two solid weeks of rain, the girls needed to be in the sun while they did their studies. We peeked into a small classroom where a teacher and four preschool-aged

Laundry hanging to dry

children (who were "too old for the cuna but too young to go to public school") worked on jigsaw puzzles. We passed by the lounge, empty at the time, but often the space of encounters of care from family visits to enrichment workshops, from staff meetings to television breaks. We entered the large kitchen, interrupting a conversation between Noelia, the educational coordinator, and the two young women who were in charge of preparing lunch that day. "It's a big job, so they rotate kitchen duty. But when they finally live on their own, cooking just for themselves and their children, it will seem much easier." Walking through the open door at the rear of the dining room, we greeted Ana. She hung wet towels on the line and kept one eye on the washing machine as it vibrated violently through the spin cycle. "The girls do their own clothing and their child's clothing by hand," noted Rosa. "But Ana does the household laundry and diapers. She's been here for as long as Palomitáy has existed."

All of these people, of course, support and care for the young women and children in the home, as do other staff members and volunteers. Various individuals may engage in different practices and view their care of young mothers in various ways. However, Palomitáy is also characterized by general institutional structures and patterns of discourse. As Elizabeth Povinelli points out, "To care is to embody an argument about what a good life is and how such a good life comes into being. Thus, the arts of caring for others always emerge from and are a reflection on broader historical material conditions and institutional arrangements (Povinelli 2010:19–20). Especially significant is the way the home encourages young women to care *for* their children (and monitors the material production and affective engagement of young women) while simultaneously producing desires for a "better life." Palomitáy as an institution governs care, especially the care of young mothers for their children, and in this way shapes the lives of those young women who reside in the home.

In fact, the very structure of the organization rests on the connection between mother and child. Palomitáy is a residence specifically for adolescent mothers and their children: a young mother cannot remain at Palomitáy without her child, and vice versa. During their time at Palomitáy, each young woman goes through a process of reflecting on the responsibilities of raising a child. She is required to decide whether or not she will keep the child she gave birth to—with the expectation that she will continue to care for the child even after she leaves the residence. Various factors play into this decision: the conditions under which she became pregnant, her prospects for returning to relatives, concerns about how her child will be treated by adoptive parents, her sense of belonging or opportunity at Palomitáy, and her prior experiences of family and community life. Young women consult with the director and psychologist as they consider this sometimes very difficult choice. Most, but not all, of the young women choose to remain in the home until they reach the age of eighteen. Should a young woman decide not to take on the long-term task of care, both minors (the young mother and her child) will be transferred to different orphanages, no matter how long they have lived at Palomitáy. Similarly, if staff members become seriously concerned about an infant's safety and well-being or a mother's capacity to care or her adjustment to the home, the director may bring the case again before the court. The state may determine an alternative situation for the care of each minor, including transferring legal custody of each "child" to another individual or institution.

For those who remain in the residence, the home's daily routines, as well as organizational structure, reinforce the position of a young woman as a mother. A young woman and her child are treated as an ontological and social unit. Staff members always refer to the residents as mothers, calling them "*mamás*" even though the young women themselves always refer to each other as girls, "*chicas*." Each infant's medical history and case documents are filed along with the mother's file. At least in part, this is because the director and most staff members (and the state) view the relationship of motherhood in fairly straightforward terms: the "biological facts" of sexual reproduction and the embodied materiality of pregnancy condition their understanding of just who is a mother. Many young women also take this perspective, as I describe in the next chapter. Palomitáy additionally approaches mothering as a set of skills, an affective orientation, and a long-term obligation. Palomitáy cares for young women by teaching them just how to care for their children.

In the Cuna

Palomitáy normalizes and reinforces the relationship between a young woman and her child through expectations about the ways each girl cares for her child's physical, emotional, and social well-being on a daily basis and (perhaps more significantly) express affective involvement with her child. This is especially evident in the nursery. Routines of bodily care and the development of emotional attachment are seen as fundamental to developing each girl's "capacity" and "potential" as a parent. In the cuna, young women are trained to particular sensorial contexts, embodied practices, and social relationships.

• • •

Mónica, who had been at the residence for almost a year, had forgotten her rotation in the nursery when we scheduled our interview. She asked me to join her in the nursery since Yaneth did not yet know the ropes. Yaneth had only been at Palomitáy for two weeks, and was eight-months pregnant. Mónica and I both knew that Yaneth's already-round belly would expand even more in the next month while she awaited the birth of her child, but neither of us knew that Yaneth already had substantial experience taking care of babies.

With all of the children present, and an extra volunteer (me) in the nursery, Katia decided that they could begin the process of bathing the children. Mónica sat on the floor of the playroom keeping an eye on toddlers and chatting with me. Yaneth followed Katia to the nursery's changing room, which connected the playroom and sleeping room. With a long counter, deep sink, and a wall of cubbies to hold each child's diapers and extra clothing, the room was used throughout the day for diaper changes and potty-training. Katia filled the deep sink with a few inches of warm water and showed Yaneth how to test the temperature by using her elbow. Then Mónica picked up Franklin from the floor of the playroom and brought him over to Katia, who undressed the baby. Katia then showed Yaneth how to hold Franklin's head while resting his bottom in the shallow water, how to wash his legs, torso, arms, hands, and feet, and finally how to hold the head of the squirming and slippery child. One by one, Katia and Yaneth situated a clean and freshly diapered and dressed infant in the playroom and retrieved another for their turn in the washroom. "You can talk to them while you bathe them," said Katia. "It makes them feel safe." Reaching into the deep sink to bathe the babies was difficult for Yaneth, her round belly creating extra distance between her body and the edge of the counter. Her back ached. Katia smiled and said, "Well done. Go on and grab the next one."

• • •

Overt statements and habitual routines naturalize intimate labor and stress the significance of forming a relationship of intimacy with a child. In the nursery, young women (residents, but also volunteers and interns who gener- ally have scant experience caring for children) learn the mechanics of tending to infants and toddlers. In addition to bathing children according to a par- ticular schedule and method, caregivers teach young mothers how to change diapers following the home's rules of hygiene, prepare and feed solid food to the babies, engage the children with toys and books, and put the children to sleep in their own baskets or cribs. All of these practices unevenly overlap the caring practices that young women may have encountered in their own households. The staff occasionally explain the methods as commonsense or authoritative (medical, psychological) knowledge if asked by myself or a volunteer, but more often they simply model the appropriate actions for residents to follow.

Young mothers learn the home's practices from the beginning of their residence. The mothers of newborns generally spend the most time in the nursery. They remain in the cuna or close at hand to breastfeed their infants, learn how to respond to an infant's cries, and recover from labor and delivery. If a young woman begins her residence with an older baby or toddler, she also initially has a longer rotation in the cuna. Once young women have lived at Palomitáy for a few weeks and have learned to care in appropriate ways, they enter into a cooperative rotation and work in the cuna once every week or two. Longer-term residents, like Mónica, model the appropriate modes of caretaking that all the young women—residents and volunteers—are ex- pected to learn and use.

Staff members may explicitly coach, or scold, residents in order to shape their practices. If a young woman struggles with the material or emotional aspects of caretaking, she will be assigned more time in the nursery, not less. In other words, she will spend time in the cuna daily until she "learns how to interact appropriately" with her child.

A peek into the nursery

This was the case for Norma, who was transferred to Palomitáy when her child was already three years old. I first met Norma in one of Cusco's public orphanages. Her more masculine gender presentation caught my attention, initially. I soon realized that Norma was often embroiled in conflicts with the other young women in that institution. I was surprised when I arrived at Palomitáy one day and saw her sitting in the cuna. Later I learned that the social worker in the public orphanage had discovered that Norma had a child. Norma had no interest in raising her child, and in fact, had left her daughter with her mother when the child was still an infant. Nevertheless, the social worker began to explore various options for transferring Norma to another residence. In the family court, the social worker pointed out to the judge that the state had removed Norma from her mother's custody because of a history of sexual abuse from her stepfather; Norma's daughter might also be at risk living in a household with the same man. The judge removed Norma's daughter from the care of her grandmother (Norma's mother) and placed both minors in Palomitáy.

The staff members in charge of the nursery attempted to teach Norma, as they had taught Yaneth and others. Although Norma was not the first young woman uninterested in procedures and routines of caring for babies (diapering, bathing, feeding, and so forth), the caregivers, Katia and Teresa, admitted to being at their wits' end. Norma had no interest in her own child or any other; she refused to touch or make eye contact with her daughter, ignored her crying, and sometimes even antagonized her child and the other babies. The caregivers continually reiterated to Norma that she must show patience with the children. They demonstrated how to hold and feed the babies. They encouraged her to interact with the toddlers and pay special attention to her own daughter to try to get to know her.

During a staff meeting Rosa admitted, "It's a tough case. Norma's poor child never saw her mother at all. She doesn't know Norma or any of us. And," she continued, "she's old enough to miss her grandmother, the only mother that she's ever known." When other staff members raised additional concerns about Norma, Rosa reminded them that Palomitáy had little choice but to follow their own procedures because the state had placed Norma and her daughter in the home. "The little one is starting to get accustomed to us. We have to be patient," Rosa reminded the staff. "I know that Norma steals. She lived on the streets for a long time. She is hardened. But right now, we need to give her time." Like other young women, Norma met with the psychologist and social worker and was in the process of deciding whether or not she would keep her child and remain in Palomitáy until her eighteenth birthday. In the meantime, the live-in staff and the residents would have to support Norma's care of her daughter even when the cuna was closed (from six in the evening until seven in the morning and all day on Sundays). Typically, young women are expected to take primary responsibility for their own children during those periods. In this case, staff members recognized that ensuring the safety and well-being of all of the children in Palomitáy required joint effort.

In the Classroom

The relation between mother and child is set apart, or made exceptional, through an emphasis on the close emotional bond between mother and child. That connection is established and expressed through a young woman's attentiveness and sensitivity to her child. Staff view the moments in which girls mobilize the mundane practices learned in the cuna as sites for the production and enactment of social and affective connection between mother and child. When a young woman does not establish an emotional bond with her child, the young woman may be positioned as aberrant. Simultaneously, Palomitáy stresses the long-term responsibility of a young woman for her child, a responsibility that is conveyed through a future-oriented imaginary. Mothers should think beyond the day-to-day care of babies and toddlers to anticipate the financial demands of feeding, clothing, and educating children, to support their social and emotional development, and to ensure their well-being in the present and in the months and years ahead.

Explicitly and implicitly, Palomitáy encourages young women to develop educational and professional aspirations that are tied to a sense of obligation and determination to support themselves and their children. Palomitáy provides and promotes formal education tied to public school curriculum as a resource for the residents. Entrance interviews indicate that the vast majority of residents had not completed their primary education before being admitted. Some began caring for siblings within their natal family, or for children or elderly adults in the households of wealthier relatives or strangers, in order to ease the financial burden on their own families. Others did not have consistent access to public schools owing to distance, work obligations, or lack of money to pay for uniforms or supplies. Marina also left home at an early age, traveled to Cusco, and found work as an *empleada* (domestic worker), caring for an infant and doing household chores. Marina left home to continue her studies because the nearest secondary school was a 2.5-hour walk each way. But she found herself too tired during the evening classes and unable to keep up with the homework. She sometimes skipped school in order to complete her chores, and as she fell further and further behind in her coursework, she became ashamed to return to class. "I lost hope of ever catching up," she explained.

In a practical sense, Palomitáy does not simply encourage but requires that residents participate in both formal and informal educational endeavors. Most children living in public and private orphanages in Cusco attend public or private (usually Catholic) schools; however, most schools do not allow pregnant teens or mothers into regular classrooms. Palomitáy provides certified public-school teachers to tutor the residents and sends the children of residents to the local public schools once they are old enough. Because the residents vary in their preparation, and in their motivation, the teachers work with them individually and in small groups. Some of the young women are taught basic literacy and numeracy skills and others are supported in the middle- and high-school curriculum.

All of the residents begin by doing schoolwork within the home, but a handful also attend classes once per week in an alternative public-school program. For the girls, attending school on Saturdays is a reward that allows them the opportunity to make friends outside the home and "experience life normally," as one put it. They continue working with Palomitáy tutors, but further their education by moving through material more quickly and maintaining matriculation in a public school. Whether or not they eventually graduate, the girls spend several hours each day engaged in formal educational activities.

The residents are encouraged to view their own educations—and that of their children—as crucial to their futures. For instance, Yaneth was placed in Palomitáy's primary group at about the third-grade level once Yaki and Davíd assessed her writing, reading, and computational skills and talked to her about her educational background. Yaneth preferred to stay in the cuna. She did not attend the tutoring sessions even though she was encouraged to do so. "In another month, it's going to be harder for you to sit in class. You should take advantage of it now, before your baby is born!" said Teresa, the other staff member in the nursery. Because she was adjusting to Palomitáy and was due to give birth soon, the teachers and the rest of the staff allowed her some flexibility. However, Yaki, the humanities teacher, pointedly told Yaneth that she needed to "catch up." "The others [in the primary group] are going to leave you behind. You have to work to improve yourself!"

Other young women excelled at school and quickly moved through the curricula. The teachers, staff members, and director offered positive reinforcement through verbal praise and additional opportunities. For instance, Melisa, who was seventeen at the time of my fieldwork, began attending courses in a two-year nursing program that fall. Palomitáy paid for her tuition even after she turned eighteen and had to move out of the residence. She found a room to rent nearby, and her four-year-old son, Marcos, continued to attend the preschool in Palomitáy. The next year, her son went to public school, and a staff member would pick up Marcos when school ended in the early afternoon. Marcos would remain at Palomitáy until his mother could retrieve him in the evening. From the perspective of the director and most staff, acquiring an education meant that young mothers might one day get a (professional) job that would enable them to materially and financially support themselves and their child and thrive in the national urban context of Peru.

Palomitáy encouraged girls to look toward the future. To take "better care" of one's child, a mother needs to enact individual responsibility and motivation beyond caring for the everyday material needs of a child. Part of being a mother (as opposed to an unrelated caregiver) is pursuing an education so that one might support oneself and one's child financially. The normalization of the mother and child unit is thus tied to a logistical and conceptual tension: to care in the long term, young women allow others to care for their children in the short term.

In the *Taller*

Palomitáy additionally creates various opportunities for residents to explore new ideas and relationships, develop life skills, and comport themselves within and outside the home in spontaneous and planned interactions. The most ubiquitous of these opportunities are educational and recreational workshops (*talleres*) that are developed and run by staff, interns, and volunteers. Workshops vary in form and content, but all are framed as enrichment opportunities that support youth who are endeavoring to "succeed in life." While the individuals and groups who organize these events may figure participants in various ways (as vulnerable girls, at-risk children, survivors of violence, adolescent mothers, or less often as emergent adults), the director emphasized that all of the workshops, trainings, and opportunities help young women develop a sense of themselves as individuals and strengthen their self-esteem.

Whether occurring just once or transpiring over several weeks, workshops are an integral part of Palomitáy's mission to support and care for residents. During my fieldwork, some workshops incorporated explicit instruction about reproductive health and wellness. Young women learned about the anatomy and physiology of reproduction and forms of family planning. They also considered strategies for requesting birth control from a pharmacist (as well as responses to accusations of prostitution). They rehearsed ways of telling a potential boyfriend that they already had a child. Some workshops encouraged young mothers to gain broader perspectives on the social, economic, and political arenas in which they are enmeshed. For instance, in a workshop run by the staff psychologist, young women discussed "human rights," reflected on their experiences of familial violence, and practiced controlling their own anger. Other workshops offered opportunities to relax and have fun, foster relationships with each other, develop confidence, learn self-care, and gain skills that might be mobilized in work or home life. Sports, massage, cooking, photography, theater, and crafting workshops often round out the days of residents. These humanitarian efforts to support young women are entangled with unspoken assumptions of modernity and ensue through empathetic engagement, pleasurable activity, and play as much as overt instruction.

The form as well as the content of a workshop may allow for the development of sensibilities of modernity by offering an arena for structured and informal interactions among residents and between interns and residents. Workshops provide explicit and implicit lessons on how to carry oneself and how to be in a relationship with others (staff and volunteers as well as other residents and children). For instance, in their interactions with the young college-aged foreign-born women who were interns and long-term volunteers, young mothers expressed playfulness, curiosity, and intimacy. On the afternoon I have in mind, I walked into the TV lounge just as fourteen-year-old Sandra yelled, "*Pesa, chicas, pesa!* Weigh her down!"

• • •

Sandra wrapped her arms around Miranda, an intern, and knocked her sideways. Mónica and then Jeni began tickling Miranda until they all collapsed onto the floor. Faviola, Laura, and Nilda piled on as well, giggling and squealing. The sun shone through the windows of the small TV room where the girls met with Miranda and Daysi for their workshop on Monday and Wednesday afternoons. The walls of the room were painted magenta and the wide built-in wooden benches were topped with rectangular cushions covered in bright yellow and orange vinyl; the room glowed with soft, rose-suffused light as the girls rolled, laughing, on the floor.

As she extracted herself from the bottom of the pile, Miranda adjusted her glasses, saying, "We need to get started, girls!" Looking quite pleased with themselves, the girls got up from the floor and moved to join the others already sitting on the benches that lined the edges of the room.

"First, we will do a game like you all asked before," Miranda said. She had the girls split up into pairs. In each of the pairs, one girl was blindfolded; the other girl was to lead her partner around inside the house and outside on the grounds of Palomitáy for five minutes. "Then you can switch! Make sure you each get a turn being blindfolded!"

As the girls began the trust walk, Miranda told me that last week they had asked to play a game at the start of the next session because it was feeling too much like school. "They were bored," she said, raising an eyebrow. She and Daysi were college students near the end of a four-month internship. "All right. Now it's time to switch," Daysi called as Faviola led Nilda around the courtyard and into the dining room and Jeni led Laura up the steps, holding her by the elbow.

While the girls continued the trust walk, Miranda and Daysi filled me in on the activity they had planned for that morning and the previous session of the workshop on reproductive health and sexually transmitted disease. "Maybe we could not do this workshop in other

Reproductions of the Madonna and Child for sale to tourists

Madonna and Child on parade during Corpus Christi. Photo by Lawrence Kovacs

orphanages, but since these girls are mothers already, Palomitáy supports it. We give the girls information. Even if they cannot have boyfriends while they are here, they will need to know after they leave."

• • •

Workshops sometimes provide particular kinds of information (for example, about birth control or human rights), enable moments of spontaneous inter-action (trust walks, "tickle fights"), and incorporate planned collaborations that are also part of a wider constellation of practices that normalize mo-dernity in a broad sense in Palomitáy. The residence is constituted as a very particular arena—one in which such intimate connections of empathy and play may occur among residents and interns. At the same time, in workshops and other everyday contexts, social actors establish and reinforce tacit agree-ments about the relative value of certain embodied and sensorial practices and hierarchical and authoritative relationships.

In other words, young mothers experience various interventions into the intimate and bodily aspects of life, many of which reinforce certain long-standing relationships of hierarchy and coloniality. Interns and volunteers like Miranda and Daysi emphasize enriching the lives of girls, increasing their self-esteem, deepening their understandings of gender or human rights, or encouraging bonding with their children. They are not attuned to discourses of advancement as racialized and gendered even as they promote various experiences and ideas, aspirations, and sensibilities as a form of care and a collaborative effort toward helping others live a better life.

Caring Hierarchies and Modern Comportment

Social theorists working in other cultural contexts have pointed out that modernity might be understood "as a project, as something that is always being made or kept or defended, feared or desired" (Ortner 2003, 13–14; also see Dickey 2012). In Palomitáy caring becomes linked with being modern. Broadly circulating discourses of modernity and incitements to advance for one's child entangle affective orientations (of love for one's child) and caring practices with formal education and enrichment opportunities. It is not only that the home promotes certain forms of feeding or bathing a child, aligned with mestizo or cosmopolitan understandings of best practices. More generally, residents are encouraged to shape themselves to the "sensorial landscapes" and "moral worlds" (Buch 2013, 639) of Palomitáy which are intertwined with broadly circulating national and global discourses of gender and race.

Palomitáy's emphasis on mundane practices, affective connections between mother and child, the responsibility of ongoing care does not happen in a vacuum. A close relationship between mother and child overlaps native Andean understandings of gender and kinship. Indeed, the image of an indigenous woman carrying a child on her back is iconic of the region even though a birth mother is not understood to be solely responsible for caring for a child. Hegemonic mestizo ideologies of gender frame motherhood as a significant facet of femininity, as well. A closely bonded mother and child is linked to discourses of maternal sacrifice and mother-child love that circulate in soap operas, school celebrations, and newspapers and magazines. Catholic ideologies of family and images of the Madonna and Child are ubiquitous throughout public spaces of Cusco. Political discourses that frame the responsibility of the state for Peru's children are also keyed to notions of the bond between mother and child (Luttrell-Rowland 2012; Theidon 2015). That mothers (not fathers) are primarily responsible for the care of children is a view tied to these and other broadly circulating discourses in Peru, and more generally in Latin America.

At the same time, Palomitáy's emphasis on both formal education and enrichment emerges from and reinforces the pervasive notion of *superarse*

(Leinaweaver 2008b, 2007), or progress, that I described in chapter 2. To "advance oneself," or to become "more modern," is embedded in racial and class distinctions and tied to urban residence, religious affiliation, language, access to commodities, and significantly, education. Jeanine Anderson (2010) has shown that parents and children articulate aspirations for advancement but that these goals may be constrained by long-standing circumstances or unexpected events, such as a death in the family or a child's unplanned pregnancy. Pregnancy usually disrupts young women's possibilities for education and professionalization. In Peru as in many parts of the world, young parents are often less socially and financially mobile than their childless companions. When a young woman gets pregnant, parents may react with anger and frustration (Leinaweaver 2008a, 111–15). One of Leinaweaver's young informants in Ayacucho acknowledged that her parents would kick her out of the house if she were to get pregnant—and she would understand. "Your parents sacrifice themselves so that you can study, and for you to repay them like that . . . ?" (Leinaweaver 2008a, 116). Palomitáy, thus, enables residents to pursue goals that otherwise might be unattainable for young women.

At the same time, residents acquire particular behaviors or demeanors in Palomitáy, a context in which Hispanic forms of knowledge rather than rural Quechua forms of knowledge are normalized.[4] Girls realize that speaking Spanish dominates the space of the home. They find out that only certain kinds of dishes, especially the Peruvian specialties (*platos típicos*) typical in the city, are cooked for the main meals of the day. When in need of something more familiar, they may covertly cook and share small amounts of food (like *ch'uñu,* freeze-dried potatoes) that are commonplace in native Andean households. How to present oneself and one's child and interact with authorities such as a child's doctor or teacher are among the many forms of self-presentation, comportment, and care taught implicitly and explicitly. Wearing jeans and shoes rather than full-skirted *polleras* and sandals may be described by staff as indicators of a young woman "gaining self-esteem" or "improving herself" or knowing how to be "acceptable in public." These practices and perspectives are also, of course, part of a network of intermeshed oppressions that Quechua speakers navigate daily, both within and outside the walls of Palomitáy.

A rather mundane example of the significance of comportment occurred one day while Mónica and I were in the kitchen cooking the midday meal together. Mónica asked me if I would take a photograph of her. When I agreed, she rushed up to her room. "Where are you going?" I called.

"I'll be right back!" she said. Several minutes later, she appeared wrapped from the waist down in a bath towel. She led me over to the garden where the magenta dahlias and yellow chrysanthemums were in full bloom. Positioning herself in front of the new-age mural, she took off the towel to reveal her pollera. "I used to have really nice polleras," she reminisced. "But the social worker always criticized me. I gave them away to my cousin when she came to visit me last year." Although all of the other girls were in class, and the courtyard was deserted, Mónica covered herself with the towel again before she headed back upstairs to change into her gray sweatpants.

Later I asked Rosa whether the home had rules related to dress. She was surprised, and insisted that the home does not have formal or informal rules about young mothers' self-presentation. "The girls simply choose to wear more Western clothing after living here for a while." Yet other girls told me that they had become embarrassed to wear polleras after the social worker, Elizabeth, scolded them. Not all of the staff members would have concerned themselves with Mónica's outfit. Moreover, the pressure to shift to a different style of clothing (or to develop styles of mothering) deemed appropriate in the home also emerged in interactions among the girls. Throughout most of their time at Palomitáy, the mothers dress and undress, chat and argue, watch their own and each other's children, play games and attend classes, do chores and watch television together. To suggest that the residents "simply choose" obscures the more general context in which Palomitáy encourages certain senses of gender, care, and relationality while it discourages others.

Anthropologist Elena Buch (2013, 639) explores the ways that power hierarchies permeate contexts of care through embodied practices and moral orientations. Her research among home health-care professionals in Chicago is very different from the context I describe here. Yet her analysis speaks to the governance of care. She shows that the home health-care professionals, who were mostly poor women of color, "saw themselves as moral persons precisely because their embodied performances of social hierarchies enabled them to sustain their older, often wealthier clients' ways of life and, thus, their independence." These women would reconfigure their own routines, experiment with different ways of being in domestic and social worlds, and sometimes incur bodily discomfort to support a client's "independence" and sense of self. Yet the clients were uninterested in allowing the workers' "sensorial landscapes" (Buch 2013, 639) to enter into their social and moral worlds. Buch points out that the labor of home health-care workers allowed the "independence" of clients but obscured the ways that independence was "deeply relational" and founded upon hierarchical relations.

It is the residents (clients, young mothers) more than the workers (staff, interns, and so forth) who must develop an "embodied knowledge" of the "material and sensorial worlds" (Buch 2013, 643) in Palomitáy. I do not

Making posters during a Palomitáy workshop

suggest that the staff ignore girls' differences of experience or personality. However, rather than empathetically orienting knowledge toward individual needs, or endeavoring to strengthen a client's sense of self by mediating between the sensorial and material world in which a client grew up and the world of Palomitáy, the staff expect young women to accommodate to the organization.[5] While girls are recognized as individuals, in general, neither their preferences—in food or learning style, for instance—nor their cultural knowledge and beliefs are sought out. The staff assist girls in becoming accustomed to Palomitáy and create an arena in which girls may recognize themselves and remake a sense of self, and of care, also in terms of wider hegemonic sensibilities and material relationships.

Laura Disrupts

Young women become involved in projects of living better as they orient themselves around the expected parameters of care in Palomitáy. A Fou-

Palomitáy residents on an afternoon fieldtrip

caultian perspective emphasizes that individuals may become amenable to specific modes of discipline and governance (Richard and Rudnyckyj 2009, 58–59). However, they do not always comply in the same way. Some young women, depending on their subjective inclinations, histories of experience, or familiarity with national or urban institutions easily accommodate to Palomitáy's temporal structures and physical spaces, internalize sensibilities of care, or take pleasure in the opportunities offered. For other girls, attuning to the governing practices of the home creates contradictions. Tensions develop even as their reproductive lives are shaped through material inducements and educational opportunities, practical requirements, and expressed hopes for the future. I previously described Norma's lack of interaction with her child and the explicit attempts by staff in the cuna to reshape her relationality. Laura's case also challenges further reflection on governance as it emerges in the interstices of daily life in the home.

In Laura's case, "too much" bonding with her infant daughter caused staff to reinforce relational boundaries. Laura arrived at Palomitáy in November

2009 just hours after having given birth to her daughter, Violeta. Unlike the other mothers in the home at that time, Laura still wore a full-skirted pollera and sandals, kept her hair in two long braids, and spoke primarily Quechua. I remember meeting Laura one cloudy February afternoon when her daughter was just four days old. The girls' teacher had canceled their tutoring session that day, and when I arrived, Noelia asked if I might lead the mothers on a little walk outside town, a field trip. A few minutes later, a group of fifteen girls headed out of the gates with me, although they were clearly leading the way, walking up the hill along the muddy dirt road.

· · ·

When we arrived at the fields, Laura exclaimed at how beautiful all the green plants were, and Sandra pointed out the tiny berries in the trees surrounding the fields. "They're ripe," she said. The girls tried pulling the pods off the lowest branches of a small grove of trees, but the trees had mostly been stripped clean already. "Let's go over there! I'll climb up over there!" Suddenly excited, the group hiked across the edge of a field, and leaped over an irrigation ditch, headed to another row of trees. After some negotiation among themselves, one of the girls passed a pair of shorts to Sandra; she put them on under her skirt and then removed the skirt, ready to scale the tree. Mónica spread a llik'lla (carrying cloth) on the ground to collect the rain of small berries that came down as Sandra shook the upper branches. Laura refused to give up her llik'lla, in which newborn Violeta was sleeping. "You can hold her in your arms! She's still so little," the others encouraged. "She'll be fine!" But Laura refused.

· · ·

On that day and for the first several weeks, Laura carried Violeta in a carrying cloth on her back as often as possible. Like many women in rural communities in Peru and Bolivia, she rarely set the infant down, but the staff—especially the teachers and caregivers in the nursery—began to frown on Laura's attempts to maintain constant contact with her child. By the time Violeta was two months old, the staff alternated between encouraging Laura to leave the child in the nursery to sleep in a bassinet so that Laura could take classes and participate in workshops and chiding her for her frequent visits to the nursery to nurse. In the classroom, Laura showed little enthusiasm for workshops and tutoring sessions, often falling asleep. She puzzled out the ongoing conversations in Spanish, only occasionally asking another girl to translate for her.

By the time her daughter was six months old, Laura was sneaking from the classroom into the nursery to check on her daughter and spend time with her. These aspects of Laura's caring practices overlap Palomitáy's emphasis on establishing strong affective connections and demonstrating clear engagements with an infant. Laura's love for her daughter and her willingness to care for her infant (on a daily basis) were not in dispute. Nevertheless, the tension between Laura and the staff continued to grow over the next few months. In informal conversations and staff meetings, the teachers and Noelia explained their frustration with Laura by saying that Laura's efforts to care for her baby hindered her ability to take classes and participate in workshops. How can she develop skills necessary for supporting her child if all she does is sit in the cuna and nurse her? Staff members emphasized that Laura should allow her infant to be fed solid food so that she would fall asleep more easily in her basket rather than on Laura's back or in Laura's bed. They argued that Laura, like the other mothers, had to learn to trust other caregivers to attend to her child's needs.

Laura's other actions displaced other facets of Palomitáy's moral and sensorial framework of mothering: developing a long-term sense of responsibility and obligation to increase one's capacity to materially, emotionally, and financially support oneself and one's child. The very existence of the nursery speaks to the significance of this aspect of Palomitáy's landscape of care. To be a mother, young women cannot constantly care for their children but must pursue modern aspirations. If a young mother arrives from a rural community where women typically carry infants on their back, breastfeed on demand, or incorporate babies and children into routines of labor, she must accommodate to a new set of expectations about childcare and development. The normalization of a close mother and child connection is thus tied to a logistical and conceptual tension: to care in the long term, young women allow others to care for their children in the short term.

Staff and volunteers earnestly attempt to support young mothers and their children in a variety of ways. By enhancing the girls' identification as mothers while supporting their development of social and affective caring practices and encouraging the girls' continued education, they aim to help two generations—the young women and their children. When staff members at Palomitáy encourage girls to continue their education or feed their children with bottles or present themselves through their clothing, language, and taste as "not-indigenous," they may do so because they assume these practices are "best for the girls." Some staff members contend that young women will have an "easier time" navigating life outside Palomitáy if they present themselves in particular ways.

Yet as the case of Laura indicates, these efforts are saturated by racial, national, gendered, and class hierarchies. I never heard a staff member or volunteer disparage a young woman as indigenous. However, in this and other instances, micro-aggressions connect mundane practices of care or comportment to racial discourses in ways that impinge on girls' lives. Explicit and implicit corrections to caring practices or to comportment may mark Quechua or native Andean ideas and practices against the unmarked background of normalized mestizo or cosmopolitan ideas and practices.[6] To acknowledge that staff in Palomitáy were uninterested in other modes or configurations of caretaking, or unaware that residents' practices may be grounded in salient cultural schemas, is to figure Palomitáy as a social space in which Laura and other girls were compelled to operate according to hegemonic social, linguistic, and affective cues.

Young women may be framed as incompletely formed and as having the ability to shape and monitor their own behavior, to redeem themselves, to become adults, parents, citizens who are "better." Anthropologist Bonnie McElhinney has argued that analyses of the interestedness of states or civil institutions in the intimacies of everyday lives of citizens are not simply about how colonial practices *affect* children, or women, or potentially *alter* practices of parenting or sociality but also about "how notions, images, ideologies, and presumed scientific truths *about* children and child-rearing help elaborate notions of rationality and modernity in colonial and postcolonial theories and practices" (2005, 184; my emphasis). The overarching orientation of the home is to support young women in *becoming* modern (and moral) mothers, so that they may (better) care for their children once they leave the home. And girls must *rely* on the support of the home to become a modern mother (in the ways expected by Palomitáy).

Conclusion

While living at Palomitáy, young women access opportunities and information as well as material benefits and relationships, which many other girls and women in both urban and rural communities in Peru cannot access. They are encouraged to work toward goals and to hope for things like education and professional jobs; they are praised when they care for themselves and others (even in small ways) or express aspirations for the future. Structural, economic, and political conditions of insecurity under which these young women—and many others—live their lives remain. But while at the home, efforts to support self-esteem and survival intertwine with discourses of racialized modernity and transnational and national class inequality. After they leave the home, the support available to them as "children," as wards of the state, and as clients of an international humanitarian organization are no longer accessible in quite the same way.

Drawing the digestive system during a workshop on nutrition

In short, *as mothers* at Palomitáy, these girls access material opportunities and imagined possibilities that they could not have otherwise. Certain caretaking practices are promoted as being more modern, and young mothers are encouraged to aspire to professions that may be unattainable once they turn eighteen and leave the home. To pursue educational and enrichment opportunities that are crucial to "advancement," then, girls learn to allow others to care for their children. Although the concept of moving forward is not exclusive to Palomitáy, the home explicitly encourages girls to pursue their own educations, develop aspirations toward professionalism, change their modes of dress as means to advancement, and strive to have a better life for their child. Often what they learn in Palomitáy and how they integrate a broad range of acquired understandings with an evolving sense of self makes returning to "normal" life in rural communities or urban neighborhoods challenging. However, it remains very difficult for most young mothers to survive and thrive outside of the home because of the myriad economic, social, and political constraints that shape their lives.

Palomitáy mostly obscures the relational and hierarchical aspects of care within the institution. From Rosa's perspective, Palomitáy fills a need created at least in part by the patriarchal structures of the Peruvian state. Palomitáy receives mothers and their children, declared abandoned by the courts; they house, feed, and protect all of these minors. They do not aim to integrate girls back into relationships with the biological fathers of the children or help them maintain relationships with natal families or communities. Sometimes, Palomitáy is legally (or ethically) prohibited from doing so. Sometimes, Palomitáy is unable to develop the logistical, social, and financial resources necessary to support visits from relatives who may live far away, have little time or money to travel, or view young women as having behaved badly, fraying relational bonds. Thus, Palomitáy aims to make the bond between the mother and child as strong and as empathetic as possible.[7]

In an interview Rosa explained to me that she and three friends had started the home after having volunteered in an orphanage and witnessed many young mothers having to "abandon their children." Many of those babies were left at the orphanage because their mothers had been kicked out of their homes or abandoned by boyfriends or husbands; unable to sustain the financial, social, and emotional obligation to care for children on their own, they turned to private and public institutions for help. By supporting a young woman so that she is able to reinforce her own self-esteem and deepen an emotional bond with her child, Rosa reflected, both mother and child may live better lives. Although the young mothers are their primary focus, by reinforcing a positive, emotional bond between mothers and children, Palomitáy aims to make lives better across generations.

The staff, volunteers, and director do challenge public discourses of "bad girls" and question neoliberal efforts to withdraw social services from poor women and children. Yet Palomitáy's emphasis on a young woman and her child becoming an affective, social, and economic unit also reinforces the idea that caring labor is an individual responsibility. Peru increasingly relies on women's organizations and international NGOs to provide social services to poor and indigenous communities and urban neighborhoods (Boesten 2010). The state "outsources" care; the staff, volunteers, and residents of Palomitáy are embedded in this more general individualization and feminization of caring labor.

Palomitáy, and other humanitarian organizations, may not explicitly promote the "benevolent assimilation" (Rafael 2000) of colonial contexts, in which indigenous mothers' caring practices were portrayed as the cause of illness or the reason for a society's inability to modernize or in which children and youth were removed from their homes and communities in order to civilize them.[8] Nevertheless, care entails governance of reproduction and incorporates the racial and gendered terms of the wider postcolonial context.[9] Of course volunteers, staff, and ethnographers are shaped by governing practices and national and transnational systems of inequality and coloniality, just as residents are.[10] An aspect of my fieldwork was providing care according to Palomitáy's frame (and in terms of a broader humanitarian sensibility that views care as desired, ethical, transformational, and pleasurable); thus, I also participated in the project of creating a modern mother or shaping the ways in which one might "do mothering."

In the next chapter I focus on the ways young women who are residents of Palomitáy experience and enact themselves as mothers. I examine the ambiguities of developing a sense of self as a mother amid broader relationships of hierarchy. Young women navigate this sensorial and moral world, but exactly how they are positioned as caregivers or in need of care themselves—as mothers or as daughters, as emergent adults or vulnerable children—requires further exploration. Moreover, the individuals and organizations who interact in this community of practice engage in talk and actions that frame certain actions as "good" or "proper." Bringing together the shifting ground upon which residents are positioned as caregivers or as children in need of care with understandings of "living better" may clarify our understanding of the moral dilemmas that young women face and the embodied practices through which they express themselves.

CHAPTER 4

Dynamic Selves, Uncertain Desires

Subjectivities in Process

Imagining and enacting oneself as a mother requires particular shifts in desires, obligations, and attachments through a process that may occur before, and long after, the birth of a child. This may be true more generally, of course. In chapter 3, I argued that the very structure of Palomitáy as an institution, as well as its programming, influence young women to show an active willingness to undertake the daily material care of, express affective engagement with, and develop a sense of long-term responsibility to support a child. However, not every resident comes to see themselves as a mother in precisely the same way or through the same temporal processes or conceptual schema. The experiences and self-understandings of these young women cannot be explained solely through the governing practices and structures of this institution or the broader social, political, and economic context in which Palomitáy is embedded.

In this chapter I reflect on the variable and contingent ways that a young woman may come to understand herself as a mother. I use the idea of subjectivity to represent the dynamic process of identifying oneself, of establishing a "sense of self."[1] I thereby write against the notion of an obvious or natural identity as a mother. An individual's sense of self may "partially or completely, temporarily or permanently" occupy an extant social category, or "subject position" (Boellstorff 2003, 229). Just how one "fits into" a category such as "mother" may vary. Moreover, a subjectivity is always in process. Thus, we may consider young peoples' efforts to shape or produce their own lives, to develop a sense of themselves as *particular kinds of* mothers (or not), even as they are constrained by social and institutional parameters (such as presumptions of the primacy of biological reproduction).

In bringing attention to young women's subjectivity, I recognize the enduring structures of inequality, the ways that individuals at times collaboratively reinforce those—even when they do not intend to do so—and significantly the "slippages in reproduction, the erosions of long-standing patterns, the moments of disorder and of outright 'resistance,'" in the words of Sherry Ortner (1996, 17; also see Anderson 2010, 84; Holland et al. 1998). Although Palomitáy and broader state and popular discourses may shape young women's talk and actions, I also open up a space in which young women are recognized as cultural agents. I highlight the voiced sentiments of young women at different moments in their tenure at Palomitáy to bring attention to the diverse ways that people may claim, refuse, reimagine, or refigure hegemonic sensibilities of modernity and maternity.

I ground my analysis in three moments of interaction, each of which highlights a particular young woman: Jeni (whose words, "Just me and my daughter are enough!" figure in the opening pages of this book), Laura (whose refusal to put down her baby appears in the previous chapter), and Marina (whose fraught decision about raising her son emerges here). I focus on individuals—on their perspectives, experiences, and actions—as one current of analysis that converges with others in this book to create a nuanced representation of moral experience, subjectivity, and care. Each of these young women aspires to and retreats from various practices of caretaking and sensibilities of mothering. Jeni ruminates on the potential adversities she will face raising her child independently; Laura perseveres in mobilizing familiar practices in spite of growing pressures; and Marina grapples with interpersonal constraints and unwanted choices while relishing unexpected opportunities. Their stories point to the tensions that ensue as individuals develop subjectivities, aligning with or veering from (aspects of) the framework promoted by the home. While all of these young women are embedded in the discourses that circulate daily in Palomitáy, and in Peru more generally, they do not conceive of or "do" motherhood, or mothering, in exactly the same way.

The stories of Jeni, Laura, and Marina point to the heterogeneous, and sometimes circuitous, routes through which individuals develop self-understandings in ordinary interactions. Refiguring one's subjectivity to incorporate a sensibility of modern motherhood is not a straightforward project for many of the residents. Most young women in Palomitáy experiment with various practices: they adjust, contemplate, ignore, and speculate about various routines, mechanisms, and concepts. It is not simply that these young women encounter unfamiliar practices or ideas in their interactions with other young mothers, with staff and volunteers, and with state officials and community members. It is not simply that some of the beliefs, practices, images, and commodities are incommensurable with those that have framed their significant social relationships in the past. As they try to do their best for their children, and themselves, these young women encounter situations that are ambiguous or uncertain, that have no clear path forward yet require them to work out as best they can what to do in the process of living *through* a situation.

Incorporating the ways individuals negotiate the social relationships, everyday practices, and moral worlds of Palomitáy does not mean that these young women are free agents. I reflect on an individual's talk and actions around mothering to extend understanding of the ways that subjectivities are developed, reconsidered, or framed under specific regimes of power. As these young women put forth effort to survive and thrive, they engage in and simultaneously resist constraints and opportunities. The everyday talk and actions of Jeni, Laura, and Marina demonstrate that to forge a self-understanding as a mother is to take part in a broader set of discourses that intertwine the obligation to care with the obligation to choose. Although mothering is naturalized, the framework of care in Palomitáy is at least partially tied up in discourse of neoliberal individualism and responsibility (Brown 2006; Freeman 2014). Neoliberalism is not simply a set of free-market economic policies but a "political rationality" (Brown 2006, 693). As Nikolas Rose suggests, people "are not merely 'free to choose,' but obliged to be free, to understand and enact their lives in terms of choice. They must interpret their past and dream their future as outcomes of choices made or choices still to make" (1999, 87). I reflect on the ways that young women may come to see themselves as mothers through dynamic and contingent enactments, including ones that resist or synchronize with the practices and sensibilities of a neoliberal self. I also keep in the picture those residents who choose, in the end, *not* to care for children, *not* to be mothers.

I begin by recounting a conversation that Jeni had with another young women near the end of 2010, when both girls were contemplating their upcoming eighteenth birthdays and their possible futures living outside the home. By the time I knew her, Jeni had lived in Palomitáy for three years, and in many ways, she aligned herself with Palomitáy's caring framework. In contrast, Laura consistently pushed against the home's daily practices, especially those aspects keyed to modernity. While Jeni's words point to the moral and affective, social, and economic risks young mothers will face outside the home, Laura's refusal to leave her child in the nursery points to the interpersonal uncertainties and institutional distrust within the home.

Finally, Marina's struggle to decide whether or not to raise her son illustrates the contingent construction of self-understanding, as a particular kind of mother and as a moral person. Though all three of these young women were born in rural Quechua-speaking communities, each navigates the constraints and opportunities of the home in ways distinct from each other and in ways that may shift in time. I trace both the uncertainties of their aspirations and their sensibilities of autonomy as they position themselves as good people, and as good-enough mothers.

Jeni's Uncertain Aspirations

I remember the afternoon when Daniela burst into the room and collapsed onto Jeni's neatly made bed, groaning, "I'm so tired!" Daniela had kitchen duty that day, which included cooking three meals for more than forty young mothers, staff members, volunteers, and children; she had just finished cleaning up after the substantial midday meal. Jeni and I had been audio recording an open-ended interview, and Jeni invited Daniela to join our conversation. I had been working in the home for almost nine months, and although the young women were accustomed to me, they also enjoyed doing interviews with a partner, talking together with me about particular issues or experiences. In this case, Daniela and Jeni turned the discussion to a topic that was much on their minds: what would happen when they celebrated their eighteenth birthdays a few months into the future? Lounging on Jeni's bed, the only place to sit in the room apart from the desk chair that I occupied, the girls expressed the tension between a sense of possibility and of trepidation about the relative independence of life outside Palomitáy.

Some young women, frustrated by daily chores, orphanage rules, and mandatory attendance at school and in workshops, expressed impatience for the day they would turn eighteen. With that birthday close at hand, Jeni and Daniela lamented that their lives would soon be very different. "I wish I could stay in school!" exclaimed Jeni. Daniela nodded in agreement. They would have few educational opportunities in the coming year. A job would likely mean long hours of work, extending from six a.m. until eight p.m. The girls commiserated with each other about the tasks ahead of them: finding a place to live, working to support themselves, locating a school and childcare for their daughters. Jeni, in particular, worried about the logistics: how could she work until eight p.m. and simultaneously ensure the safety of Ángela, whose preschool day would end at two p.m.? How would she earn enough to pay for school fees and materials, clothing and food, and rent and transportation?

Both young mothers emphasized that for each of them, "being a mother" meant materially providing for their children, and they recognized that this responsibility carried consequences. Providing for a child meant that their lives would be different from the lives of other young adults. As Daniela stated,

> It's just not the same for someone who has a daughter and for someone who doesn't. The one who doesn't have a child can work normally, return to his room, and choose to eat. If he doesn't eat, he doesn't eat. But I have to cook no matter what so that my daughter doesn't get sick. If I don't feed her well enough, she's not going to grow or stay healthy.

Daniela recognizes that having a daughter fundamentally reshapes how she will operate on a daily basis. She did not critique the social, political, and economic inequalities in which she was situated or question the assumption that the primary responsibility to care for a child belongs to a mother. However, when she shifted to a male pronoun while describing a person who can "work normally," eat or not eat as he chooses, she at least implicitly points to the gendered hierarchies that structure caring for children.

Daniela indexes her own modern sensibilities, knowledge, and skills when she points out that infants and toddlers need food, even specific kinds of food, to stay healthy. She also recognizes that just *knowing* your child needs food is not enough. When they leave the home, young mothers may have the skills to cook platos típicos or understand the nutritional requirements for a child's growing body, but they may not be able to provide those foods for themselves or their children.

Not only will their experiences be different from those of single (yet childless) young women or men, but their opportunities and future possibilities may be more constrained. The availability and conditions of paid work, adequate shelter, transportation, health care, and childcare are among the political, economic, and social conditions that shape young mothers' ability to care for another. As Janet Jacobs and Stephanie Mollborn (2012, 931) note in their research on early motherhood in the United States, adults in particular "fear for their daughters' future and loss of social mobility" when they find out their daughters are pregnant. Even where broad social networks offer material and emotional support to young mothers, harsh economic conditions may have devastating consequences on the future life circumstances of young mothers and their children.[2]

As much as she internalized the ideal of the modern mother and child, Jeni also talked about the ways that caring for her daughter was an aspiration, one that was tenuously balanced on her ability to navigate economic, political, and social circumstances. In our conversation, Jeni repeated several times,

"I'm going to be able to do it. Even if I don't have the support of my child's father or of my family members, I can do it! I will be able to raise her on my own." Of course, Jeni's insistence in a different moment that "just me and my child are enough" and her aspiration to raise her child on her own are shaped by her particular life history in conjunction with Palomitáy's ideals and broader social discourses and structures. In our interview, Jeni referred back to her experiences of sexual and physical abuse when she explained to me why she had decided to keep Ángela rather than put her up for adoption. In a barely audible voice, Jeni recounted how she managed to escape with the help of two friends, leaving in the midst of the school day so as not to arouse suspicion at home. Once in Cusco, she found work in the kitchen of a small restaurant. She realized that she was pregnant several weeks after she arrived and sought help, unsuccessfully, in the Demuna.[3] Only after Jeni had given birth and her neighbor, Margarita, went to the police as well as the Demuna to demand that the state step in did Jeni and her baby receive help.

Jeni and Ángela were eventually transferred to Palomitáy, and after three months of counseling, Jeni decided to keep Ángela. "More than anything, I was afraid that someone would mistreat her." She was determined, she said, to raise Ángela on her own because she did not trust a stranger or even her own family to keep her daughter safe. According to the director, Jeni had made tremendous gains in her self-esteem and her ability to connect intimately with her daughter during that time. Rosa viewed Jeni's decision to have her hair styled as an indicator of her increasing self-esteem, a contrast to her early days in the home when she refused to shower or to wash her own clothes or those of Ángela.

For Jeni, and for other mothers at Palomitáy, the home's discursive emphasis on the unit of mother and child provides a context in which they may establish ties of tenderness with and attention to their children, strengthen their sense of self, and garner some of the social and cultural capital necessary for supporting themselves and their children. She reiterated several times, to herself, Daniela, and to me, "I can do it. . . . I will be able to raise her on my own." Jeni claims a sense of self tied up with her long-term care of Ángela. At the same time, she acknowledges (at least implicitly through repetition) that to guard the material, emotional, and physical well-being of her daughter is an uncertain endeavor. She seeks reassurance from us as she embarks on this path.

Finally, Jeni's sense of herself as part of a connected unit of mother and child is overlaid with a sense of her continuing bond with her own mother and her aspiration to "do better" than her own mother. After Jeni voiced her determination to raise Ángela without the support of others, she then tempered her vision of her future with reflections on the practical considerations of raising a child. She reflected on her memories of her own childhood and somewhat wistfully said, "If my mother couldn't own a home, I'm going to have one. If she couldn't have something, I'm going to have it. If she couldn't enjoy life, I'm going to enjoy it. I'm going to work for everything because that's what my mother said, 'Don't be the same as me. Be better than me.'" Entrenched social, political, and economic inequalities constrain Jeni's ability to raise her daughter on her own (as they constrained her mother's ability to raise Jeni and her siblings). However, Jeni frames her desire to move forward in terms of her mother's experiences as well as her own. Her mother's advice, "Don't be the same as me. Be better than me" reflects a sense of failure and optimism for the future. Jeni's understanding of herself *as* a mother is intertwined with an individualized and gendered sense of responsibility to care for a child, but extends beyond Palomitáy. Not only does Jeni aim to avoid those alternatives fraught with potential danger, but she aims to *have* something. To *enjoy* life.

The ways that Jeni talked about and enacted care of her child are indicative of how girls navigate the institution's emphasis on producing "modern" and educated mothers with their own complex subjectivities and sensibilities. From one perspective, Jeni's emphasis on caring for her daughter on her own reinforces a discourse of the modern mother and child, in which neoliberal selves take responsibility for themselves. At another level, Jeni's decision to raise Ángela on her own is imbricated with a sense of moral action, a sense of ensuring that her daughter has a better life than she did herself. Jeni's insistence on caring for her daughter autonomously reflects both her sense of responsibility and of hope.

Jeni and other young women embark on a path to challenge their circumstances within a situational and national context that is highly constrained. They elaborate a sensibility of mother and child, at least partially, while they are at Palomitáy. Jeni's determined words also, however, hint at recognition that her aspirations for herself and Ángela may exceed possibilities. The governing framework of the home may scaffold Jeni's developing subjectivity and enable her emotional, social, and economic survival. Yet, the underlying conditions of violence and impunity and of poverty and economic marginalization remain. Taking on the subjectivity of modern mother does not mean that a young woman will achieve as much as she hopes, or in quite the ways she envisions.

Laura's Unspoken Autonomy

Jeni's story does not offer the only illustration of the ways young women actively produce themselves as mothers or engage in efforts to create better lives. Residents approach the parameters of parenting in the residence—including bodily care and self-presentation, conscientiousness around chores, pursuit of an education, and affective attention to a child—in various ways. Some girls may embrace and aspire to the project of becoming a modern mother, while other girls might retreat from it. Some may struggle to articulate their experiences of care or their understandings of exactly who they hope to become. Laura, whom I introduced in the last chapter, developed a close bond with her daughter from their earliest moments together. Yet Laura contested aspects of Palomitáy's organization.

As I reflect on the actions of Laura and other young women in the home, Maria Lugones's characterization of how one might *sense* resistance frequently came to my mind. She writes,

> Sometimes you are stuck in a chair and the tiny movements in your hands are a level of intense resistance that requires a closeness of understanding to sense tactually the forcefulness of the motility. Sometimes you walk miles in a closeness of people giving birth to an intention that was not in any of us alone, with banners and other crafted signs of our impudence. (Lugones 2003, 2)

Lugones uses pilgrimage, traveling, and movement metaphorically to witness and convey—and encourage her readers to witness and convey—the activeness of subjectivities and the simultaneity of oppressing/resisting in worlds saturated by intermeshed (not interlocking) relations of power.[4] She also explores the possibilities for cultivating an understanding of agency as diffuse (across individuals). Incorporating a sense of the unspoken, unobtrusive, or ambiguous expressions of autonomy may open up a conceptual arena for discussing people's struggles to define the parameters of care in a hierarchical context. Who is deserving of care, who will provide this emotional, social, and material labor, and how often caring is performed are practical and ethical issues that impinge on agency and personhood.

Laura's actions, though mundane and often unspoken, were not invisible. By refiguring "autonomy" as an analytical lens, we might deepen understandings of youth as much as motherhood, and of the ordinary ethics of self-care and survival as much as care for others. Palomitáy is a social space in which mestizo or cosmopolitan ideas are unmarked and assumed and Quechua or native Andean ideas and practices are marked. Laura was immersed in a situation in which she was forced to operate according to hegemonic social, linguistic, and affective cues. Thus, when Katia, one of the caregivers who worked with the infants and young toddlers, scolded Laura for breastfeeding Violeta immediately before the cuna's scheduled lunch time, Laura remained silent. "When you feed her right before, she's not hungry enough to eat. And then she's very hungry later when we are all done. She needs to learn how to eat food!"

While Laura's caring practices pushed against Palomitáy's framework, she also experimented with and occasionally practiced a modern mother-and-child approach. Laura played with her self-presentation, occasionally projecting a more "modern" or "mestizo" face. Although she most often wore a pollera and sandals, Laura also tried different styles of clothing. During Palomitáy's anniversary celebration, for instance, Laura squeezed into a pair of jeans and a camisole, brushed out her braids, and enjoyed the party while her daughter was cared for in the nursery. Her experimentation with clothing might be understood as part of a process or negotiation of subjectivity that incorporates both motherhood and modernity. Rather than moving from one racial/ethnic category ("serrano") to another ("mestizo"), wearing particular clothes may point toward an active project of claiming class positioning, or of enhancing propriety, or of negating racist and sexist assumptions about a woman or girl's sexual availability.

Of course, her perspectives, like those of other young women, are complicated by her previous experiences and future aspirations, including the structural constraints that shape the lives of native Andeans in Peru, and by the interactional politics of situation. I say more about what I mean by the interactional politics of situation in the subsequent chapters. Here, I simply note that in her initial entrance interview with the director, Laura responded to a question about how she became pregnant with an iconic representation of Andean courtship: she said that a young man accosted her while she was herding sheep. Laura did not elaborate upon the relationship with the young man (in that interview or later over the course of her stay). According to court records, the youth in question refused to marry Laura even after her father visited the provincial judge to demand recognition of paternity. Months later, a judge in the family court system determined that Laura's parents, who had nine children of their own, lacked the financial resources to support Laura and an additional child. The court removed her from her natal family and transferred custody of Laura and her infant to Palomitáy.

Eventually, Laura disrupted the running of the home to such an extent that the director asked to have her transferred to another institution or returned to the custody of her parents. The crucial moment came several months after I had returned to the United States. The director and staff decided that infants and young children should no longer sleep at night with their mothers but instead sleep in their own cribs.[5] Laura and a few other young women consistently removed their children from the cribs to sleep with them each night. Because Laura also continued to ignore, reinterpret, and refuse other procedures and policies of the home, she was eventually asked to leave Palomitáy. The judge overseeing the case determined that Laura could return home, because she had been removed from her natal family because of their poverty rather than outright neglect or abuse.

Rather than relying on identity categories (campesino or urban, Andean or mestizo) as a way to draw boundaries around practices or ideologies of care (or yet a singular definition of motherhood),[6] we might imagine autonomy with enough analytical openness to bring into focus young women's moral, affective, and social experimentation. Laura never talked about raising her child alone. Unlike Jeni, she did not aspire to caring for her child on her own, independently. Nevertheless, she and other young women actively chose activities, and navigated moments of interaction, or inhabited certain attributes of the mother-and-child frame at various moments in time. Whereas Laura's actions reinforce Palomitáy's emphasis on a close affective bond between mother and child, her experiences also point to the consistent tensions that permeate Palomitáy and broader contexts within neoliberal and postcolonial Peru.

For these young mothers, the ability to "move forward" requires types of cultural capital (Bourdieu 1986) beyond the right clothes or shoes, the ability to speak Spanish, or the attainment of a secondary school education. To internalize the bond between mother and child yet leave an infant in the care of others rather than carrying her on one's back, to feed solid food to a child who does not yet walk rather than nursing her, to pay attention in school and participate in workshops enables—and requires—a particular kind of subjectivity and a particular notion of what motherhood entails. Here, claiming exception—in this case, implicitly or explicitly performing indigeneity or marginalized subjectivity or a marked form of caring—results in sanction. Understandings of maternity, or care more generally, might not align completely across social and cultural contexts, and tracing such divergencies or gaps may consistently reinforce racialized boundaries. At the same time, by reflecting on the autonomy, or active subjectivities, of these young women, we might gain further insight into the senses of self—as mothers and daughters, adults and youth, students and laborers—that they deploy.

Marina Rejects the Choice

As Andrew Hostetler and Gilbert Herdt argue, "Only by paying attention to how individuals balance cultural demands, political commitments, and deeply socialized life-desires—some concordant, others discordant with cultural norms—can we arrive at a deeper, more complicated conceptualization of individuals' subjectivity and agency" (1998, 261). Of course, the emphasis on modern mother and child does not exist in a vacuum, and neither do the young women who enter through the doors of Palomitáy. They are in dialogue with others and with themselves, with remembered experiences and future possibilities. They are exposed to broad discourses of gender, race, and class that reinforce or challenge their understandings of themselves, and they claim for themselves positions from which to resist negative stereotypes and incorporate positive images and ways of being in the world. In the process of negotiating their subjectivities, their understanding of themselves, these young women also imbricate broader ideological concerns with mundane demands of daily life and desires to live "better" lives.

In juxtaposing these stories, I do not suggest that one person's behavior is more "moral" than another person's behavior. Rather, my aim is to draw attention to the attempts and false starts, ambiguities and diversities of perspective that emerge as these individuals take on the project of becoming mothers. Just how subjectivities are constituted in process cannot be understood solely through attention to broad governing structures. Individuals balance competing demands, emerging moral frameworks, and sometimes contradictory desires in these (and many other) circumstances. The discourses and practices of the home may be contrary to or reinforcing of (some aspects of) parenting, propriety, or sociality. An individual may rely on habitual practices or experiment with less familiar ones, shifting their understandings across different moments in time. Bringing attention to these cases adds texture to our understandings of the way subjectivities are refracted through broader governing discourses and shaped by the contingencies of everyday life.

Like Jeni and Laura, Marina was born in a rural Quechua-speaking community and navigated multiple discourses of care and of appropriate mothering before and during her tenure at Palomitáy. Marina had black eyes that sparkled with mischief and a broken front tooth that gave her smile a rakish air. In contrast to Jeni and Laura, Marina did not initially bond with her infant son, Adrián. In fact, the process of coming to understand herself as a mother—and incorporate the affective and material practices of care in the home—was fraught with ambivalence. Over the course of time she lived at Palomitáy, Marina wrestled with the decision of whether or not to keep her child. Her case offers another glimpse into the moral and material contradictions faced by youth who balance the labor of mothering with the labor of "improving oneself" in neoliberal Peru.

I met Marina in the late fall of 2009. I remember Marina alternating between sitting silently on the mats of the play area in Palomitáy's nursery and scolding the young toddlers with a high-pitched stream of recriminations. At the time, she was fifteen and her son was several weeks old. In spite of the efforts of Katia and Teresa (the nursery staff members) to teach Marina how to interact appropriately with her child, Marina did not exhibit the attentiveness and affection for her own baby, or for the other infants and toddlers in her care. After the entire staff reviewed her case at a monthly meeting, Marina was placed on an extended rotation in the nursery so that she could become more comfortable caring for the babies. Throughout the time that she worked in the nursery daily, she was verbally reminded by staff to show patience with the children, make eye contact, and listen for their cries. She was encouraged to mimic the interactive style of other caregivers, including other residents. Marina endeavored to maintain equanimity in the face of these daily caretaking demands.

During this period and into the spring of 2010, Marina was preoccupied with figuring out whether or not she would commit to raising Adrián. The Palomitáy director, psychologist, and social worker insist that every young mother carefully (re)consider their decision, whether the young woman arrives assuming she will raise her child or not. Most young women decided within two months of living at Palomitáy whether their mothering would encompass hands-on involvement and care of the child at the home and well into the future, or whether their mothering would incorporate allowing a child to be raised by someone else. Rosa, the director, acknowledged that in prevailing public opinion, the best person to care for a child is the child's biological mother. Nevertheless, she emphasized to young women that either choice could be an act of love. She encouraged her staff to provide a neutral sounding board to young women even as they maintained oversight on the health and well-being of both mother and child.

Marina vacillated for months as she attempted to make her decision: would she take on the responsibility of raising Adrián on her own? The director and staff believed that Marina initially had difficulty bonding emotionally with Adrián because he was born with a cleft palate. He was otherwise a healthy, bright-eyed, and alert baby boy. As Theidon (2015) has noted, many Peruvians view children born as the result of rape or assault as carriers of that violence, and marked by it. Adrián's disfigured face stigmatized him *and* Marina and made feeding and caring for him more difficult. The staff at Palomitáy decided to give Marina more time, waiting until after the baby's surgery, to make a final decision. After Adrián's surgery, Marina seemed to engage more fully in the mundane practices of care. She began making eye contact and exhibiting affection for Adrián. She was participating consistently in tutoring sessions and workshops, and the teachers, at least, recommended that she be able to attend weekend public school classes.

Yet, still she remained unsure. Some of her ambivalence emerged in a conversation with another young mother, Yesenia. While showing me photos of her two-year-old daughter, Yesenia had emphasized how much she liked caring for her. Yesenia—like most of the other residents—acknowledged that caring for a child was exhausting: "It makes you old," she groaned.

"It's ridiculous how tired you get," agreed Marina.

"But," Yesenia elaborated, "being a mother means someone will accompany you, through the good and bad; she is with you." At least to some extent, the practical and imaginative work of mothering enriched Yesenia's conception of herself. She found rewards in parenting. Like Jeni, she professed a desire to live independently, without a spouse or boyfriend, saying, "You just don't know what people can do to each other in this life." Her boyfriend had abandoned her after she realized she was pregnant. Although Yesenia was in contact intermittently with her ex-boyfriend's mother, she had not seen or heard from him in over a year. She received no support from him, financial or otherwise, and she had no plans to return to her natal community. Still, Yesenia quite directly insisted, "I believe that it is for the mother to maintain the child; it's her responsibility, not his."

At that point Marina broke in, "It's unjust!"

"What do you mean?" I asked.

"Because [the fathers] should have to give at least a little bit of money to help support the child!"

Yesenia shrugged.

"If they don't, they should go to prison," Marina concluded emphatically.

Like many individuals at Palomitáy (and in Peru more generally), Yesenia viewed raising a child as primarily a woman's obligation. Although Marina acknowledged the role of women, she countered Yesenia's perspective by pointing out that fathers are also responsible for the pregnancy as well as for the child. Marina emphasized that if fathers do not contribute to the financial obligations of raising a child, at least, the state should punish them.

Marina's perspective may have diverged from Yesenia's in part because of the different experiences that led up to their placement in Palomitáy. Unlike Yesenia, who became pregnant during a consensual relationship, Marina had been raped by her godfather. According to her entrance interview, Marina was ten when she was sent by her mother to live with her godparents in Cusco, where she attended school in the evenings after doing domestic labor (cleaning, laundry) for her godparents during the day. Marina was thirteen when her godfather first abused her sexually, and he threatened to kill her if her godmother found out. When she realized she was pregnant, Marina confided in a friend, who reported the situation to the municipal authorities. When the police arrived at the house to question her godfather, Marina's godmother accused Marina of seducing her husband. Marina's case could not be considered under statutory rape laws because by then she was already fourteen. Mobilizing greater financial, social, and cultural resources and presenting a unified front, her godparents characterized Marina as promiscuous and argued successfully that they should have no responsibility for the pregnancy, or for Marina. With no one to support her in court and no signs of physical violence, Marina could do little to defend herself. Although Marina's mother was still alive, the judge determined that her mother did not have the means to support her. The judge placed Marina in Palomitáy on the basis of "moral and material abandonment." Marina gave birth to Adrián while in the home.

Even after the successful surgery to correct Adrián's cleft palate, Marina could not choose. Thus, with Marina's permission, the director invited Marina's mother to the home, paying for her bus fare so that she could visit and participate in a meeting about Marina's and Adrián's futures. Rosa hoped that with the support from her family, Marina could finally make a decision about whether she would keep Adrián—now nine months old—or not. A few days later, Rosa admitted to me in an interview that the meeting had been a "disaster." Marina's mother criticized Marina for the difficulties she had caused for her compadres: "They were right to kick you out." She told Marina that because the baby was a boy, Marina should raise him. "Of course you should keep him," she said. "Boys at least will take care of you. Girls always are trouble."[7] If Marina decided to give up the baby, she continued, "I will adopt him, but you will not be allowed back into my house. You will no longer be my daughter."

Weeks later, the director remained troubled by the woman's explicit offer to care for her grandson even as she refused to care for her own daughter, Marina. By then, Marina finally settled on a decision to raise Adrián and remain at Palomitáy. She reconciled herself with the routines of the home and demonstrated more interest in her son's daily care (washing his clothing, feeding him, and cuddling him). By the time I returned to the United States in July 2010, Marina had developed a close relationship with Noelia, the educational coordinator. She excelled in her studies both in the public school and within the home, progressing toward high school graduation. Like other residents, Marina continued her private sessions with the home's psychologist and group sessions with the home's social worker to support her (and other mothers') work of establishing emotional and social bonds. Adrián was thriving and had grown into an active toddler, who took his first steps exploring the nursery. But Marina's story does not end here.

When I returned to Palomitáy in 2013, I expected to see Marina, who would have been seventeen years old, and Adrián, who would have been three years old. Adrián was not in the cuna or the preschool classroom, so I asked Katia how both mother and son were doing. She told me that I should ask Rosa. Later that week, as we chatted, Rosa gave a deep sigh. She said, "I think Marina is doing very well now. But Adrián, I don't know." She took a deep drag on her cigarette, then she explained. Marina had seemed to be doing quite well after she had finally made her decision to keep Adrián. She was very smart and progressed very quickly through the public school curriculum. As she neared graduation, another international NGO took note of her academic progress and offered her a scholarship to the university. They would support her if, once she graduated from high school, she wanted to take the entrance exams for the university. The NGO would pay for the costs of the exams and for her postsecondary education.

Over the course of 2012, Marina began talking more and more about going to college. Like Jeni, who expressed disappointment at not being able to continue her education once she left the home, Marina enjoyed studying and viewed attending the university as both key to her more general aspirations to have a better life and as an unexpected opportunity. However, Marina would not be eligible for the scholarship (or be able to attend university) if she were caring for her son. Occasionally, her frustration over the situation emerged in violent outbursts, and the staff and residents of Palomitáy intervened. Palomitáy provided additional counseling for Marina. After a particularly bad incident, when Marina hit Adrián in anger, Rosa consulted with the courts. The judge gave Marina an ultimatum: if Marina used "excessive force" on a subsequent occasion, Adrián would be removed from her care.

Weeks later when Marina—in a rage—pushed Adrián away from her with enough force that he hit the wall, the director returned to the courts. Rosa was concerned about Adrián's well-being, Marina's emotional state, and the future of Palomitáy if Adrián were injured while in their care. The judge removed Adrián from Marina's care and from the custody of Palomitáy. Within days, Marina was moved to an orphanage that accepted older girls. Adrián was placed in another private orphanage as well. He was taken not only from his mother but also from the only home he had ever known, "leaving the entire place flooded in tears."

The director recognized that the decision to permanently relinquish a child was the more difficult path for many young women, but it was Marina's resistance to making the choice that troubled her most. During Marina and Adrián's first year at Palomitáy, while I conducted several months of fieldwork, two other young women had chosen to give their children up for adoption. Treysi spent very little time at Palomitáy, only three months. She arrived while still pregnant after her parents insisted that she leave home. She chafed at the conversations she was required to have with the psychologist, refused to participate during workshops, and dragged her feet when given chores. Just days after she gave birth, her aunt and uncle agreed to adopt her child. Treysi left the next day.

Another young woman, Chaska, also decided to give up her child for adoption. She had no relatives who could take in her daughter. She liked living at Palomitáy, but as she told me in an interview, "To be a mother may be a beautiful thing, but the [other] parents will take better care of her than I can." Chaska had been shuttled between caregivers throughout her childhood. Her mother had sometimes cared for Chaska but would unpredictably leave her with her grandmother, with an older sister, and sometimes on her own. Chaska did not reiterate the director's perspective that giving up one's baby might be an act of love, but instead framed her decision in this way: "Maybe she will have a better life than I did."

From Marina's perspective, being put into the position of having to make that choice was an unfair burden (as was caring for a child without financial support of the biological father). In part, the permanence of the decision caused Marina to hesitate. In Cusco, and in the rural and urban regions of Peru and the Andes more generally, placing a child in an orphanage temporarily or fostering a child with a relative or compadre are not infrequent responses to, or strategies for, caring in situations of insecurity. In fact, the mothers of Jeni, Marina, and Chaska (among many others) followed this course of action. Yet, for a woman to choose to give up her child permanently, so that he or she may be adopted by strangers, resulted in her being labeled as "unnatural" or denigrated as immoral. Although a pregnancy might threaten a young woman's relationships with family members, the suggestion that a young woman might put the child up for adoption could further fray relations. Marina's mother, remember, threatened to cut off ties with her. In the end, as Rosa pointed out to me, Marina "did not choose."

For some in Palomitáy, the moral issue was Marina's desire to pursue an education (instead of caring for her son). For others, the moral issue was her refusal to choose at all. Marina attempted to travel a narrow path—retreating from and approaching the moral dilemma of caring for herself and for another, attempting to maintain those relationships most important to her and

possibilities for a desired future, envisioning and revisiting an understanding of herself as a mother or as not a mother. How young women imagine
themselves as certain types of people with particular moral stances toward
care, thus, requires consideration of the contingencies of events in the lives
of individuals. By contingencies, I mean those things (both mundane and
extraordinary) that *happen* (and may happen to change the course of events).
Additionally, understanding subjectivities requires attention to the shifting
relationships in which people are engaged, the on-the-ground interactions
that are far more tenuous and temporally situated than any representation
written in hindsight. Attending to this aspect of young women's lives—of
"being good" and "doing good" in uncertain circumstances—connects subjectivities to embodied practices, organizational structures, and globally
circulating discourses.

Conclusion

In this chapter I have traced some of the practices and interactions through
which young women develop understandings of themselves as mothers.
Some, like Jeni, develop a sense of self mostly in alignment with the home's
framework of mother and child, taking on particular kinds of labor, modes
of interaction, professional aspirations, and self-presentation. Others, like
Laura and Marina, mobilize ways of caring, or understandings of mothering,
that partially challenge this discourse. For these young women, mothering
may become consequential but not always in the same way or necessarily
through the same routes. Moreover, the cases I have described also illuminate
the ways that forging a self-understanding as a mother requires taking part in
a broader set of dynamic discourses that intertwine morality and inequality
in this transnational context.

By focusing on young women's subjectivities, we gain insight into the ways
relationships of hierarchy are displaced onto moral and affective discourses
of care. Not only do caring practices and talk about caring shape individual
subjectivities, but such embodied social activity may constitute, and even
intensify, unequal social relations, "thereby making those hierarchies feel
morally legitimate" (Buch 2013, 638).[8] As they claim for themselves positions from which to resist negative stereotypes and establish positive ways
of being in the world, young women actively experiment with attributes of
the mother-and-child matrix. For Jeni, Laura, and Marina, internalizing the
emphasis on education and social and economic advancement (circulating
both within Palomitáy and more generally in Peru) creates contradictions
between her own needs and desires (as a daughter, a student, a citizen, and

even as a mother) and those of her child. Determining just whose needs will be met from moment to moment is one aspect of caring for another—of mothering—that these girls take on.

Looking forward to the years that she would be solely responsible for a child, raising him without support from others, Jeni was determined to "be better" than her mother, to "have something," to "enjoy life." Marina was frustrated at the turn her life took when a man—who in ideal terms should have been her protector—caused violence to her, with impunity. She was saddened and angered by the withdrawal of her family's support. Their everyday words and actions illuminate their movements, efforts, and struggles to understand themselves as mothers and establish a sense of self that incorporates care of another. Neither passive victims nor free agents, their stories offer a sense of the complexities and uncertainties of care. Although their abilities to act upon a situation may be constrained, their interpretations and embodied expressions of the possibilities of their lives and their futures are significant, in and of themselves, but also as a window onto social and cultural life more generally.

Whereas I argue for attention to subjectivities, I do not suggest here that the problems faced by Jeni, Laura, or Marina may be ameliorated on an individual basis. As Mikaela Luttrell-Rowland (2012) has argued, the Peruvian state's attempt to protect the rights of children has often conflated the problems faced by women and children, addressing children's issues through their mothers. Moreover, the state has promoted the family as both the primary site of "failure" and the primary site for intervention: children's rights are rights violated *within* the family. Such an orientation obscures the broader structural changes (for example, decreasing violence against girls and women) and the coordinated efforts necessary for the state to enact children's rights. Similarly, the efforts of the staff members at Palomitáy to support individual mother-and-child pairs in order to ameliorate the broader issue of abandoned children direct attention similarly to an individual level. For instance, in the neoliberal and humanitarian arena of the home, the ability to choose (to raise or relinquish a child, for instance) emerges as itself a form of care and a necessary attribute of an adult, citizen, and mother.

Thus, attention to subjectivities allows us to trace the boundaries of what counts as care in particular moments and contexts. When Laura refuses to leave her baby attended only by strangers or when Marina refuses to choose, they challenge or reinterpret a governing matrix that is both about mothering and about less explicit but pervasive schemas of contemporary rationality. As scholars in the social sciences and humanities have pointed out, the liberal state requires and develops the idea of love while obscuring racial and other hierarchies (Ahmed 2004; Eng 2010; Povinelli 2006). Marina's case may trouble us partially because she steps away from a (liberal) notion of mother love and the gendered (and class) obligation to care for the needs of others first. Laura's case challenges the benevolence of the NGO and illuminates the national and transnational racial discourses intertwined with care. Jeni's case reminds us that the hope for a better life may work against one living well (Berlant 2011).

While maintaining a critical perspective on individual subjectivities, then, I also suggest that attributing young women's understandings of themselves (as mothers or not) solely to broad structures of power obscures the complexity of living with and living through insecurity, a constant feature of their lives. Young women encounter and engage with moral, affective, and social risks as they go about daily life—and as they reframe understandings of themselves—at least in part because caring labor is imbricated with systemic structural inequalities. Thus, to understand how individuals might figure themselves as mothers, and as good people, I have considered the dynamics of subjectivities as well as the structuring of desires through broader social discourses. In the following chapters, I focus on a different scale of interaction to trace more closely the ways that individuals collaborate with each other in ongoing situations that no individual alone controls. I explore how people are engaged in variable and uncertain efforts to "live alone" or "move ahead," to hold one's child or to release one's hold, and how their understandings of their own, and each other's, actions emerge through multiple layers of dialogue that cannot be predicted from the outset.

CHAPTER 5

Making Images, (Re)Visioning Mothers
(a Photography Workshop)

DRAWING ON THE WORDS and actions of Jeni, Laura, and Marina, I have argued that within Palomitáy, young women express diverse understandings of "being a mother." Their perspectives, articulated in particular moments, enrich our understandings of social experiences and relationships of motherhood and of care. However, it is not only *that* individuals may have diverse views (or that residents may or may not choose to remain at Palomitáy and raise a child). It is also that individuals engage in a dynamic process of experimenting with and reconfiguring understandings of themselves and their life possibilities, simultaneously pushing against and acquiescing to aspects of broader governing regimes. Just how individuals together might draw on particular discourses and mobilize them to their own ends, negotiate the contingencies of ordinary life, and develop a sense of themselves as "selves" and (only potentially) as "mothers," remains a question. In the remaining chapters, I forefront the dynamic and dialogical character of social life and subjective experience by exploring young women's creative expression.

In this chapter I reflect on young women's efforts to understand themselves, experiment with ways of living, and represent themselves in relation to others through photography. I approach this in two ways. I highlight modes of self-making other than talk by considering the images produced by these young women as expressive texts that are embedded in broader arrays of texts. I also amplify the ongoing, uncertain, and emergent (but not always coherent) process of positioning oneself and coming to see oneself and others in relation by considering photography as an embodied and material practice—of taking photographs and posing for them, of viewing images and curating them for others' eyes. As young women performatively engage with the world to make life better, to become a mother, or to see oneself as a moral and modern person, they encounter moments of clarity and ambiguity embedded in broader relations of power. Although photography may reinforce long-standing hierarchies, producing images may also enable young women to reimagine their position in relation to these structures.

The chapter draws upon my observations of a photography *taller* (workshop) that was run for Palomitáy by another European NGO that I call Sayanchis. The photography teacher, Verónica, who was a staff member for Sayanchis, had already been working with the young mothers of Palomitáy for two months when she announced the final project for the workshop—nude mother and child portraits. I show that interpreting the photographs created in that project, and others, requires attention to the very local history of production that includes young women's use of cameras inside and outside the taller. Visual images—and the practice of visual image-making—may contain traces of the engagements through which young women evoke the world and themselves.

The Final Shoot

All of the young women were seated around two rectangular tables in the classroom on that day when Verónica arrived for the workshop. Some were excited to talk about the fieldtrip of the week before; others were simply sitting, trying to wake up. It was 10 a.m. but most of the young women had been up for several hours already. Verónica smiled warmly at the girls and at me when she came into the room. Her chocolate brown eyes crinkled at the corners when she smiled, and her orange beaded earrings swung back and forth against her neck as she looked around the room, nodding to each girl. Verónica wore purple leggings and a long, flowing blue shirt; a narrow lime green scarf held back her curly black hair. "We have been working together for several weeks now, so let's talk about the final project," Verónica began. "We will be doing portraits of each of you and your child. But these portraits will be a little different; they will be nudes. Maybe the photos will be black and white or maybe they will be in color. Either way, we will choose the best photos and have a show, to display the photographs that you have taken, here in the residence." I saw Jeni's eyes dart toward Faviola. Yaneth looked down at the table. Marina raised her hand and then put it down. "Vale? OK?" Veronica queried, and then moved on to detail what we would be doing that day.

By the next week's class, the girls expressed their confusion. Why would they photograph each other naked? Were both the mothers and their children to undress? Where would they take these photographs? Verónica reassured them that they would only be nude from the waist up and hold their children in such a way that they would not be exposed. To demonstrate what she was envisioning, Verónica suggested we look on the internet.

So we gathered around the ancient computer in the office to search the web. I opened up Firefox and waited for the app to load. I had an idea of what Verónica was imagining. I had seen photographic images in which the subjects—a pregnant woman or a woman with her newborn—were naked but were not highly sexualized (at least in terms of North American aesthetics). I searched Google with the keywords "photography," "mother and child," and "nudes." Then, avoiding the obviously pornographic sites, Verónica and I located the homepage for a studio in the United States that presented black-and-white images of parents and children. "That's it!" said Veronica. She encouraged the girls to gather around the small computer screen to see the photographs: a close-up of a baby's foot held in a woman's hand, a couple facing each other and holding a tiny baby between them, the head and shoulders of a woman whose hair cascaded around her infant. All of the subjects were naked but their bodies were not fully exposed. "Think about how you might take photographs like this," said Verónica.

"Why is there no color in these photos?" asked Marina.

"I think they are really ugly," added Yaneth.

Verónica did not discuss what she saw as interesting, beautiful, or visually appealing in the photos or her rationale for engaging the young women in this particular project as the culmination of their workshop. She let the girls view the images for a few minutes and encouraged them to begin to imagine themselves as subjects and as photographers who might create similar photos. Then she led the girls back to the classroom.

That afternoon Verónica and I shared a taxi back to Cusco's central plaza and I asked her why she planned to do the project. Verónica told me that she envisioned the shoot as the culmination of her work to help the girls develop a higher level of comfort and self-realization about their bodies and their identities as mothers. The skin-to-skin contact between themselves and their children was, she emphasized, an important aspect of the girls bonding with their babies. She talked about creating a moment of affection between mother and child and about making the project meaningful to them *as* mothers. I wondered if the directors of the home knew about the project. When she acknowledged that they did, I asked what they had said when she told them. She shrugged. "Oh, nothing. They said, 'You are the teacher so it is up to you what they do.'" Verónica admitted that she had never done a project like this one, even though she had been doing photography workshops for many years with children. "But, the girls work so well together. They collaborate. I think they can do it."

I could not be present on the afternoon of the final photo shoot. Verónica told me that she received permission from one of the directors to use her apartment (located on the second floor of Palomitáy) for added privacy for the mothers. She hung a sheet as a drape in the main room and positioned as many lamps as she could find for lighting. Verónica wanted the girls to use her DSLR camera rather than the small, digital point-and-shoot cameras. She asked the young women to come in two at a time, each with their baby. One resident acted as photographer, and the other, nude from the waist up, posed with her child. Then the mothers would switch roles. Verónica remained in the room, assisting with the camera, helping the girls find appropriate poses, and keeping an eye on the child of whichever girl was acting as photographer.

In the end, the young women who participated in the final project produced several beautiful portraits in the style of traditional Catholic *retablos,* or sacred images of the Virgin Mary and Jesus, or Madonna and Child.[1] Such images are ubiquitous in the city of Cusco and circulate in wider publics as well, including international humanitarian imagery of suffering mothers and children (for example, Briggs 2003). The retablo project emphasized an intimate mother and child bond more than maternal suffering. Nevertheless, the portraits naturalize the relationship between each young woman and her child, emphasizing love and togetherness without ambivalence. At one level the retablo project might be interpreted as an example of the governance of reproduction, for it extends "familial myths while seeming merely to record actual moments in family history" (Hirsch 1997, 7). I return to this point later in the chapter, but first I elaborate on a somewhat different approach to interpreting the meaning of the photographs.

Drawing on a broadly dialogical approach, anthropologist Kathleen Stewart analyzed the storied lives of people in Appalachia by demonstrating how narrative is always part of broader arrays of relationships; what is told is always a "*version* of the story which has a history and produced effects that can be traced" (1991, 400). I draw inspiration from Stewart and many other scholars who have demonstrated that the meanings of narratives are not solely contained in the referential content of the words spoken but in the relation among various dimensions of communication. Like renderings of stories, images are embedded in ongoing processes of creation, layered upon multiple versions, and interwoven into networks of produced *effects* that may alter, extend, or reinforce the situation at hand.

From this perspective, the meanings of the images created during the final project draw on many other images and texts, not just those that depict a mother and child. The meanings are "contaminated" (Stewart 1991, 400) by moments and uses that include young women's manipulation of cameras inside and outside of Palomitáy. Moreover, the activity of seeing *with a camera* may be as significant as the traces left behind. From this perspective a photograph of a mother and child does not simply resonate symbolically with Madonna images, reflect deep cultural truths that tie together gender, reproduction, and religion, or convey a humanitarian vision of need, imposed from the outside. Meanings may also emerge from the activity of creating images in a particular social context or in terms of a local history of production.

By considering young women's use of cameras in this and other projects in the taller, or workshop, and in less structured activities, I trace strands of ideas momentarily revealed, glimpsed through a viewfinder, and shared with an audience. Whatever the original rhetorical or evidentiary intent of the photographer, photographs are produced and disseminated, viewed and remembered by various publics, in and through broader contexts. Just *how* images mean, how "significance is conveyed in and through objectivated cultural forms or forms that exist transpersonally and in practice" (Stewart 1991, 400) are questions that cannot be answered by focusing solely on the "content" of the image.

This is because, at least in part, images, like talk, circulate in a wider communicative arena, a "language-and-context" matrix (Ochs 2012, 156) through which human beings make meaning.[2] Anthropologists have argued that meanings of words or sentences are inextricably linked to the situation and speakers (see, for example, Ochs 1992; Silverstein 1976). Think, for example, of words such as "I" or "you" that shift in meaning each time a speaker enunciates them. "I" or "you" *points to,* or indexes, a different person depending on the situational context, including who enunciates that word. Even those utterances that seem to primarily be referential in content ("The sky is sure blue today") have the capacity to shift meaning based on context (spoken sarcastically during a week of stormy weather). Moreover, people (including anthropologists) engaging in face-to-face interaction interpret utterances and make sense of events by implicitly or explicitly linking the ongoing talk "to other acts, including the past, the future, the hypothetical, the conspicuously avoided, and so on" (Irvine 1996, 135). In other words, what someone says always has links to the present situation as well as to many other dialogues (Irvine 1996, 140).

I extend this perspective on meaning in language to my analysis of the images that young women created in Palomitáy. I do this to situate the retablo images in a local array of images and to explore how visioning practices are mobilized by young women. Marianne Hirsch (1997) has discussed the ways photos shape people's experience and understandings of family, focusing squarely on a particularly Western array of images, social relationships, and practices.[3] Hirsch (1997, 117) points out that the subjects of family photos may return the photographer's gaze, looking back at the camera. In this chapter, I extend Hirch's reflections on the ways vision structures the day-to-day practices of family life to explore photographs as part of a wider array of texts

Looking back at the camera through a camera. Photo by Palomitáy resident

and as the (by-)product of a social activity that shapes care and subjectivity among young women in Palomitáy.

A Methodological Note

During my initial fieldwork in 2009–2010, young women created photographic images both during a programmed taller that was run by Sayanchis and also while engaged in far more open-ended projects that were linked to my own research. Young women framed themselves with or without their children and in relation to the world outside Palomitáy. They explored body

parts and flowers through close-ups. They captured on video ongoing interactions with each other and scenes from telenovelas or movies. The images
they produced and the embodied and material practices of making, curating,
and interpreting images are tied to wider discourses and contexts.

To analyze the *imaged or pictured* lives of young mothers in Palomitáy
is a task far broader and more complicated than I am able to undertake
here. For one thing, residents were not the only people creating images in
Palomitáy. Volunteers (and anthropologists) snapped photos of the young
mothers as well as of their children, mobilizing digital cameras, iPods, and
iPads. I remember walking to the kitchen with Noelia one afternoon when
she pointed out a volunteer, kneeling on the floor of the bathroom with her
iPad held several inches in front of her. The volunteer was filming one of
the older toddlers, who was taking a bath in a small plastic basin, while his
mother looked on in bemusement. "Who knew we had so many celebrities
living in this residence!" Noelia quipped. At the time, smartphones were
rare, even among European and North American travelers. Though Peruvian
staff sometimes referred to volunteers as "paparazzi," little effort was made
to control the production or circulation of images. A few volunteers would
offer prints to the residents, but most simply displayed the photos and videos on the screen for a brief moment. Some posted images on social media
sites for wider audiences. Those images bolster a much wider assortment of
images of mothers and children, or of children alone, that circulate through
humanitarian media and the popular press (not to mention personal blogs
and social media sites of travelers and volunteers).

Creating and consuming visual and textual representations of selves and
others is saturated by material and social relations of power, and I was cautious of taking photos of children and youth in the residences where I conducted research. However, I began my fieldwork at Palomitáy imagining that
I would use participatory visual methods, especially "photovoice" (Wang
1999; Johnson 2011; Mitchell 2006) in addition to interviews and participant
observation. Urged by the director, I organized a photography workshop that
followed a participatory research framework, acquiring enough relatively
inexpensive equipment to allow ten participants independent use of a camera.
After giving informed consent, the participants and I developed individual
and collaborative activities to learn how to use cameras, document what they
saw as significant issues, events, and relationships in their daily lives, and
use the images as a springboard to further conversations about their lives.
I was entering the second week of the workshop and had only just handed out
the digital point-and-shoot cameras when the directors apologetically told me
that a different taller, run by another independent NGO, would have to take

precedence over my own. Palomitáy had worked with this NGO in the past and wanted to continue their collaboration because Sayanchis offered annual workshops that integrated visual and performing arts into the curriculum. After Sayanchis announced the timing of their workshop and the directors reviewed the residents' schedules, they realized that the two workshops could not proceed simultaneously. I received permission to continue the workshop for another week and to interview participants about their photos during free time. I also asked if I might participate in the new photography taller.

Fortunately, the directors agreed and Verónica, the photography teacher, welcomed my request to observe her workshop and to incorporate it into my research project. Verónica developed and implemented the overall framing of the workshop, curriculum, and projects. My participant observation in Sayanchis's taller included attending the workshop two days per week in the classroom, participating in field trips, and assisting as I was able. The young women who had carried cameras and created images for a week prior to Sayanchis's workshop were joined by others. As I discuss below, the taller participants created a collection of images, some produced through structured taller projects and others produced through relatively unstructured independent use of cameras in the evenings and on weekends.

Verónica had been teaching photography to children in Cusco's orphanages for five years. Each photography program was slightly different and aimed at the specific population of children. Verónica told me later that she had thought a lot about these young women who were already mothers— not only about teaching them the basics of photography but about how to help them *use* photography so they could come to a better understanding of themselves and enhance their self-esteem. She had written up lesson plans that included projects built around the idea of the five senses: taste, touch, hearing, sight, smell. She had met with the directors to review her lesson plans and explained that she hoped the workshop would encourage the residents to access different aspects of themselves, to play, to experience life, and to gain self-confidence. She hoped this workshop would transform them and their relationships with their children.

In hindsight, it was by assisting Verónica and observing the taller that I began thinking about photography in a performative way.[4] I had begun my photovoice project by considering the content of residents' photographs and how residents talked *about* those photographs (to gain a sense of their experiences of a particular place or person). As the Sayanchis taller progressed, I increasingly wondered how *doing* photography was a mode of engagement tied to particular situations and generative of moral and affective stances as well as articulated understandings. Tim Ingold has argued, "Apprehending the world is not a matter of construction but of engagement, not of building but of dwelling, not of making a view of the world but of taking a view in it" (Ingold 2011, 42; see also Anderson and Harrison 2010; Pyyry 2015, 152). From this perspective, photographs may be keys to reflections on or revisionings of the world as much as visual data "of the world."

Learning Skilled Vision in the Taller

Standing at the back of the classroom on the third week of the taller, I was discouraged. The taller had begun well, with Verónica explaining the basics of photography with a PowerPoint presentation. Her slides covered the history of cameras and the structural mechanics of film and digital cameras. "You will not have cameras like these," she said, referring to images of 35mm film cameras and DSLR cameras, "but the fundamentals of framing shots is the same." Verónica illustrated the differences between close-up and wide-angle shots with images from projects that children and youth in other orphanages had created. "Next week, I will bring point-and-shoot cameras that you can use, but the fundamentals are the same." The girls spent the next class period decorating manila folders and answering a questionnaire for Sayanchis. (Those few who could not read and write in Spanish received assistance from Verónica once she realized the situation.) The promised cameras did not appear during the second week or the third. Instead, we spent three class periods watching *Amélie*, gathered around the computer again, because the DVD player was broken. Verónica asked the girls to think about the whimsical film's depiction of experiencing the world through the five senses. She explained to me that she was waiting for her turn to use the NGO's cameras. Immediately, I offered to lend her the ten Lumix I had purchased for my project, but she declined because the cameras were not Canon.

By the fourth week of the workshop, Verónica was frustrated at the difficulty of obtaining the few functioning cameras owned by Sayanchis. As we shared a taxi back to Cusco's main plaza, she explained that all of the photography teachers in her organization shared a handful of cameras. Several cameras had broken and not yet been replaced. "Next week I have the cameras, though," she said. "We have requested more cameras, but the problem is that the cameras just don't hold up very long with so many kids using them." I reminded her that the offer to use my cameras, at least for the workshop at Palomitáy, was still open. "If you want to use them, let me know."

Finally, during the following meeting of the workshop, Verónica announced brightly, "Today you will be painting yourselves and then taking close-up

Choosing colors for the body-painting project

photos of each other!" She had decided to supplement the three Canons from Sayanchis with several Lumix from my project so that the girls could work in pairs, each group sharing one camera.

"But I have a virgin face!" Ana exclaimed. "I have never used makeup at all."

"Let's go outside," replied Verónica. "I have a surprise for you."

Outside, on the retaining wall near the garden, Verónica had lined up several jars of poster paint and paintbrushes. "You are not going to put on makeup. You are going to paint something on your body, whatever you want, wherever you want. Then you can take photos of each other's artwork." She assigned each of the girls a partner and told them to talk with each other about what they wanted to paint.

The sky was sunny, although the air was cool in the shade. The girls initially stalled. Several partners began painting themselves, rather than painting each other. Ana lifted up her shirt and began painting a face on her own stomach: brown eyes under her breasts, a green nose, and a red mouth with blue teeth,

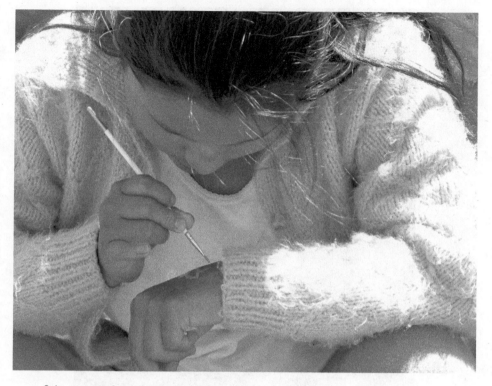

Quiet concentration during the body-painting project

an arrow-pierced heart on the forehead and blue stars on the cheeks. Her partner, Jeni, painted her left hand with her right: eyes and nose along her index finger and mouth along her thumb. Daniela decorated her hand in a series of stars in brilliant blue, moving up her wrist and forearm. Maya took a jar of red paint and began painting flowers on the back of her own hand, but turned to help Marina after several minutes. Marina had begun to paint the image of a girl on her hand, the face near her wrist, the legs her middle and ring fingers. After they had spent several minutes thoroughly focused, the girls began to chat with each other and show each other their efforts, as they continued working.

"All right," said Verónica. "Those of you who have finished can come and get a camera. We'll have to share, so work with your partners to take photos of each other. Remember, when you take close-up shots, you need to move the camera and your whole body close to the subject!" Verónica had explained to them that the zoom on their small point-and-shoot cameras would not do as good a job as simply moving into close proximity with whatever they

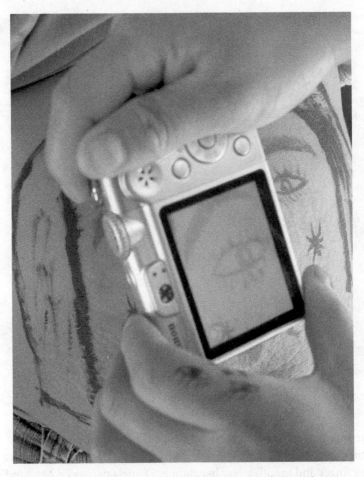

Taking a close-up (of a face on a stomach) during the body-painting project

were trying to photograph. Some became involved immediately with cameras; others leaned against the wall in the sun or sat on the steps in the garden while they waited for a turn with a camera.

The rest of the class period was taken up by the girls practicing with the cameras by framing and shooting (mostly) close-up images of their painted arms, hands, legs, and torsos. Verónica and I shot photos of the girls, framing wider views of the interactions among them.

For Verónica, the day had two objectives: first, to have the girls understand how to produce close-up shots without using the zoom on the camera, and second, to become more aware of their bodies. By painting their bodies, they

Creating multiple images of a resident's hand-person during the body-painting project

could feel the brush, smell the paint, see the colors; they could imagine their hands or stomachs or feet in a different way. Using the cameras to create close-up images of their embodied artwork, eventually the girls drew physically close to each other. One young woman leaned in to photograph the flowers painted on another's neck. Another moved close to photograph the "person" that appeared on her partner's hand. Participants looked through the viewfinder, deliberating about where they wanted to focus the lens with this more limited field of vision. Later, the girls sat together on the ground, leaning their heads close together, in order to see the camera's screen and review each other's images of their creative re-visioning of their bodies.

With technical skills and a great eye developed during her years studying photography in Lima, and her experience teaching workshops to children and youth, Verónica encouraged the young women to imagine and see their bodies in new ways through this project. As Cristina Grasseni points out, visual knowledge is not only culturally constructed but may be "a form of practical, emotional, and sensual knowledge" (2011, 20). She uses the concept of "skilled vision" to analyze various ways of seeing that "employ different kinds of gestural competence, develop within different kinds of apprenticeship, and are differently embodied" (Grasseni 2011, 22; also see Grasseni, ed., 2007). In the photography workshop, participants began learning to see in new ways through explicit instruction, "hands-on" activities, and embodied interaction with people, material objects, and visual media. Other anthropologists have explored methodological and theoretical questions tied to the tacit ways social actors learn how to see or develop "strategies of the eye" (Faeta 2003; cited in Grasseni 2011, 20; Farnell 2011; Ingold 2000) or vision practices.[5] Through the activities of painting the body—seeing two fingers as legs, the navel as nose—and taking close-up photographs, the body-painting project enriched participants' visioning practices.

The photography workshop also allowed young women to engage with a particularly modern skill—photography—in a context that was saturated by affective and moral practices and discourses. Throughout the morning, the girls "played" by painting and photographing themselves and each other. Their children were in the nursery, cared for by volunteers and staff. The participants did not need to concentrate on a lecture or labor over writing anything down or reading movie captions. They focused on the momentary pleasures of creative expression. To some extent the body-painting project opened up an arena in which the young women might experiment with new forms of meaning-making, as they played with their physical, social, and emotional sensibilities. While the written curriculum of the workshop included as an objective "knowing oneself with all of one's senses," Verónica did not make this aim explicit to the participants. Nevertheless, in mobilizing various techniques (painting their hands, moving in close to one another, or taking photos through a sheet of colored cellophane), young women may develop visioning practices that allow them to apprehend "reality" in a new way or reframe one's self from moment to moment.[6]

The photographs created in the photography taller fit into a local history of enskilled visioning, a point to which I return below. Palomitáy residents also engaged with everyday life through photography in other less-structured contexts. Although Verónica made use of the Lumix cameras for a few sessions, eventually her NGO acquired additional Canons. Several girls then

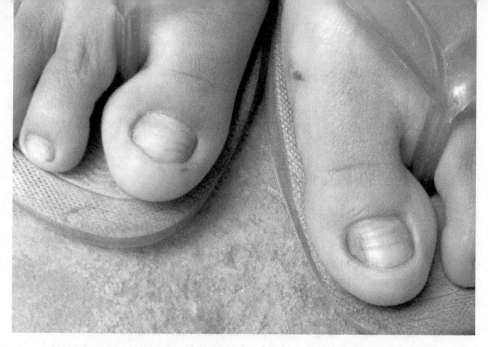

A favorite body part. Photo by Palomitáy resident

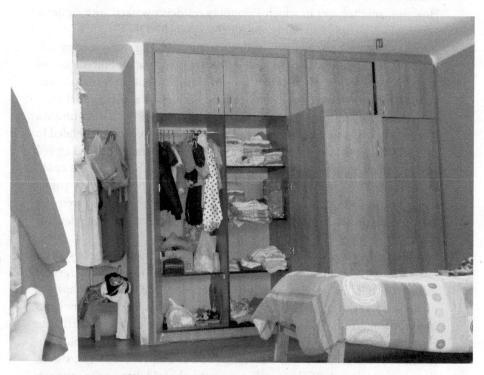

A neatly ordered and well-stocked closet. Photo by Palomitáy resident

asked whether they could keep the Lumix cameras in the evenings and on the weekends. I reassigned the cameras to individual girls and again received permission to use their images in my research. I did not, however, establish any guidelines around what kinds of photos to produce or how to use the cameras "on their own."

Snapshots as Self-Production

Photography is a material and multisensory practice through which "we *sense with the world*," as Noora Pyyry (2015, 150; my emphasis) notes. Distinguishing methodologically between "photowalks" (mobilizing a camera, shooting photos, often in the midst of other communicative interactions, such as hanging out with friends) and "phototalks" (thinking with and talking about images), she notes that both are communicative interactions that take a view "in the world." The body-painting project may be a particularly concentrated moment in which young women "walked with" cameras, mobilizing material objects (cameras, paints, brushes, and so forth) in various ways and as integral aspects of communicative interactions within a particular environment. However, another way in which Palomitáy residents walked with cameras occurred in the days and hours outside the Sayanchis taller.

Young women's engagement in the activity of photography during this period drew upon what they learned in the workshop but mobilized skills of seeing toward various ends. I use the term "independent" to recognize that young women had their own ventures (and no particular assignment from me). Of course, they were not simply free agents snapping photos outside a cultural or organizational framework. Not only were they still embedded in the social framework of the home, and Cusco more generally, they had agreed that any photographs on the chip when they turned in the camera could be integrated into my research. Nevertheless, considering the ways young women walked with the cameras in less-structured engagements forefronts the ongoing production of self through the activities of framing, viewing, and curating images.

Moreover, analyzing the images that the girls created outside the Sayanchis taller allows a "version of the story" about Palomitáy residents to emerge that is distinct from the version produced in the taller. The body of "snapshot" photography created by the young mothers on their own shows patterns strikingly different from the images produced in the retablo project in particular. First, the snapshots serve to position the young women across multiple communities (within and outside Palomitáy) and as mothers, students, sisters, friends, and just girls. If photos tell stories, the photos taken by the residents

Looking out the window during school recess. Photo by Palomitáy resident

of Palomitáy do not tell only a "family" story. Each girl photographed her own child either alone or with other children, but only rarely did an image of a mother with her child appear. From Hirsch's perspective, snapshots of a baby or child may at once normalize the centrality of a child to her mother and produce that centrality. The camera enables a certain kind of gaze. Seeing her child through the camera lens, posing the child amid flowers or with other babies, or occasionally catching a spontaneous moment—as when Ana's daughter crawled rapidly across the bedroom floor and peered through a crack in the doorway after being told not to go out—may reinforce an affective and social relationship.

Though they did not pose with their own children, several young women posed on their own or with a friend. In these photos young women do not present a self that is immediately open to a reading as mother. For instance, one series of images, taken by a Palomitáy resident in the courtyard of the public school, depicts two young women who gaze back in challenge at the camera. The image situates these girls, also both Palomitáy residents, in a place more typically inhabited by Cusco's youth. Standing side by side, one subject wears jeans and a leather jacket, a turquoise belt peeks out from hands held loosely on her hips, and the other wears jeans and platform shoes, her dark hair framing her unsmiling face. Girls posed in other photos as well, in their rooms or in common areas of the residence, on the street, in the market, alone and with companions.

In contrast to the style of photos emphasized in the taller, young women frame entire bodies, as much as possible, and most of their snapshots also carry within the frame some attention to the margins or boundaries of the subject's location. The young women rarely took close-ups on their own.[7] Moreover, many residents carefully considered how they and their children (and other subjects) were dressed when they took a photo. Even casually captured photos demonstrate an awareness of self-presentation, and many young women commented on this aspect of appearance when they evaluated their own and others' images. Their everyday material realities also figured in the images—the toys or medical equipment used by a particular baby, the recognizable traces of a school or marketplace, the mural and garden of the home, and the nterior spaces with wall decorations, books, and computers of the common rooms. Several young women also photographed their bedrooms, creating images of beds neatly made with spreads and pillows, of closets hung with clothes precisely arranged, without adults or children present.

Occasionally, young women framed photos that depicted spontaneous interactions, everyday events, and people inside Palomitáy and also in public school classrooms and nearby buildings, streets, and markets. For instance, in one image taken on a Sunday afternoon when the caregivers for the nursery have a day off, three mothers and two toddlers curl sideways on a bench in the television lounge, while a fourth mother sits on a chair, her hand on the stroller where two infants sleep. Too dark to reproduce, the image has the quality of a painting. "I was just walking past," said Felicia, when I asked her about the photo in which the hegemonic family story of heterosexual couple and children, as well as the romanticized image of Madonna and Child, are disrupted. Felicia documents a stolen moment of rest. "But we are always so tired," she pointed out. Others took photographs of volunteers or staff members at work. They filmed videos of each other while engaged in workshops or tutoring sessions, cooking meals, or enjoying a fieldtrip. They video-recorded television and computer screens to capture scenes of favorite programs or movies to view again later.

Thus, the girls' independent use of cameras index a layering of identifications, their subjectivities not limited to motherhood or to Palomitáy. Having the exclusive use of a camera for an extended period of time meant that individuals could walk with cameras during unscripted moments, photographing

"Where do you think they're going?" Photo by Palomitáy resident

mundane interactions as well as momentous events. Their personal control of a camera allowed for idiosyncratic uses, as tools of humor and joking, as icons of inclusion and exclusion. Not only did young mothers create representations of their worlds in framing photos, but they also enacted and produced themselves, carrying cameras with them.

In recent years, scholars have explored the ways youth envision themselves and engage with the world not only by framing and shooting a digital image but also through curating images: deleting, saving, sharing, posting and reposting to online networking communities. Jon Wargo (2017, 575) has called this constellation of practices "lifestreaming" and has described the ways that LGBTQ youth "negotiate relationships to index identities across temporal

Street views on a Saturday. Photo by Palomitáy resident

and geographic scales." Focusing primarily on Tumblr, Wargo argues that we
need to think about the "materiality and visual embodiment of photo" (2017,
563) at least in part because individuals may photograph, post, and comment
upon material objects as a way to constitute stories about themselves. They
may compose "multiple vignettes of self" or "curated versions of self" that
circulate across multiple and heterogeneous publics by taking and reposting
images of themselves and artifacts, referring to previous versions of themselves and others, and by commenting on posts in various digital venues.

    Although the residents of Palomitáy did not have access to smartphones or
online arenas to create a visual presence, they did engage in less-structured
"projects" to create and curate versions of self. They not only took photos

and videos of particular subjects and localities, but they also captured a scene from a movie to view again immediately or save to watch again later with others. Girls photographed the display screen of a friend's camera or a printed photograph to recapture an image. They removed images permanently from their devices—their efforts appearing as numbered gaps in the images downloaded to my computer—but they also asked that I develop photos, so that they might have a way of keeping a different sort of material trace to view again. Individuals may create representations of their worlds through photographing what they see in the world, and in these images personal memories become intertwined with social myths and modern sensibilities. Indeed, young women seemed to use the cameras as much for viewing their own and each other's images as for shooting them. Young women in these ways engaged in modes of seeing and made claims to belonging in wider publics—families, urban schools, modern nations, and global publics.

In fact, because the very practice of taking photographs in this particular context is tied to a modern and foreign sensibility, walking with a camera may be part of an array of material practices, including caring in particular ways or desiring certain things or relationships, that produce modernity. The temporal and geographical scales along which residents in Palomitáy positioned themselves frequently were more limited than youth who had access to online networks. Nevertheless, the notion that individuals index identities across time and place helps illuminate the ways that photography at least for a time became an extension of how some young women navigated hierarchical relationships. Young women presented themselves with their cameras, interacting with each other and with others. Some became very involved with photography, carrying their cameras everywhere, and creating hundreds of still images and digital video. Just as images of artifacts, such as clothing in a closet, might position a young woman in a wider array of class relationships (to fill a wardrobe with clothing may indicate that someone cares for them and that they care for their child), walking with a camera might position an individual differently in class, racial, and gender hierarchies. "Reading artifacts as sedimented identity texts help tie the material dimensions of youth lives in digital environments to both the real and perceived inequality they face in their day-to-day navigation of school and society" (Wargo 2017, 567). Although Palomitáy residents had no intent to post their images on Tumblr or Instagram, they viewed, shared, and re-viewed these images of everyday objects, spaces, media, and people. Such practices indicate that selves are multiply inflected, even as they are tied to a particular place and to a set of relationships. How one thinks of oneself is also in process and available to interpretation by multiple communities.

Retablo Reprise

Whereas Hirsch (1997, 7) notes that a photograph "gives the illusion of being a simple transcription of the real" and thus has the effect of "naturalizing cultural practices and . . . disguising their stereotyped and coded characteristics," the experience of doing photography promotes a different sensibility. Walking with a camera, framing a shot, viewing images, and curating images may simultaneously freeze ongoing relationships into place and bring attention to the particularities of engaging with the world *through* a camera. Taking pictures is laminated onto other communicative practices. This means that the photographer's gaze always intersects with subjects who look back, but in slightly different ways. Returning to the final project of the photography taller, I ask how situating the retablo project in the wider context of the workshop and in a local history of production might shift potential meanings of images as versions of stories or revised representations of young mothers. When Verónica informed the girls about the retablo project, she had instructed them already for two months, incorporating hands-on use of cameras with other tactile and visual exercises and film viewings into the biweekly meetings. The participants shot the images for the retablo project a full month later, in the final weeks of the taller.

The young women said little about their experiences during the photo shoot. A few girls noted that they "liked" the project and others said that they did not. While most of the resulting portraits frame the head and shoulders of each mother and child, the faces of each subject express a range of sentiments, from joyful to anxious. Several of the young mothers smile or laugh directly into the camera, seeming to enjoy the experience. Babies look at their mothers or at the camera, smiling or solemn or peering calmly out from behind their mother's body. In a few images, the mother looks anxiously down or away from the camera while the baby appears to squirm, fuss, or cry.

A few of the girls modified their participation in the project, so that the retablo is not recognizable as such. Two participants chose not to remove any clothing and used poses that disguised this choice. As Yaneth said to me later, "When I saw the photos on the computer, there was one of someone kissing a baby's foot. I liked that one but not the others." Her partner in the project framed a close-up of Yaneth kissing her baby's foot, her face in profile. Another image depicts a baby's hand and arm held in the larger hands of her mother.

Two of the girls refused to participate in the final project at all. Andrea said simply, "Why would I take off my clothes?" Jeni had kitchen duty that day and told me that she had been relieved. "I like the photography taller, and I usually don't like kitchen duty. But I was not sure about doing that project."

In spite of the variability in young women's participation, Verónica viewed the retablo project as a success for the ways the girls managed the camera, interacted with their children and their partner, and for the actual images they created. Verónica pointed out that although Andrea refused to be photographed, she nevertheless took a series of beautiful images of Laura laughing with her baby.

In a follow-up interview in 2013, I suggested (more directly than I had in earlier conversations with Verónica) that nudity in the shoot might have been particularly difficult for some of the young mothers who had survived traumas of sexual violence. I wondered if some of the young mothers might have perceived posing naked as lacking in dignity or as suggesting sexual availability. "No, I did not think of that," she admitted. "But it is true that some were more nervous. That nervousness came through to their babies, and then the babies were fussing." Verónica reminded me of Marina's image, in which she looked down unhappily while holding a crying baby in her arms, "Maybe . . . I think . . . some were less sure about being mothers. Like Marina. You can look at that photograph and see how unhappy she was then." (I had not heard yet about Marina leaving the home. "Ask Rosa," was all Verónica would say.)

In some ways, Verónica obscures the very real structural and interpersonal hierarchies that these young women navigate within and outside Palomitáy's walls. Verónica viewed Marina's tension as tied more to her ambivalence over caring for a child than to removing her clothing to participate in the photography project. She does not acknowledge that these might be mutually entangled and reinforcing. Instead, Verónica pointed out the importance of the girls making choices for themselves, noting, "I did not force anyone; I gave them the opportunity." From her perspective, each girl made a decision about whether or not to participate (as a subject and as a photographer).

Yet, for some individuals, choosing to create a nude photograph may be a decision fraught with tensions because of the moralizing discourses about sexual availability and single motherhood that are intertwined with racial, gendered, class, and sexual hierarchies. To delve into the ways their decisions might be tied to broader moralizing discourses regarding women's sexual and reproductive practices, then, would disrupt the ways that the retablo project also relies on assumptions of universal mother-and-child bonds that are tied to Christian ideology, global humanitarianism, and state governance.

Jo Spence and Patricia Holland (1991) point out that reading family photographs operates at a "junction between personal memory and social history, between public myth and personal unconscious. Our memory is never fully 'ours,' nor are the pictures ever unmediated representations of our past. Looking at them we both construct a fantastic past and set out on a detective trail to find other versions of a 'real' one" (cited in Hirsch 1997, 13). As I noted in the beginning of the chapter, the photos mimic the Catholic Madonna and Child that appear in images throughout the city of Cusco. In some ways, the photographs of the young mothers might reinforce religious ideologies of gender and family (and especially of women's roles within a heterosexual and stable nuclear family) even as they are refracted through a more secular lens of self-transformation. The retablos are at once conventional and rebellious, drawing upon romanticized or mythical relationships and created in an arena that re-signifies young mothers as like the Virgin Mary.

In this case, young women are visually presented as mothers who are "blessed" and even "redeemed" by their love and care for a child. The retablos side-step questions about the structuring of women's roles, the normalization of particular family configurations, the precarity of economic relations, and the state's reliance on individuals and international NGOs. The images—as retablos—are key to myths, stories, or as in Petchetsky's (1987) discussion of fetal ultrasounds, to a fetish, or "the investment of erotic feeling in a fantasy," of motherhood (Petchetsky 1987, 277; also see Oaks 2000). In her analysis, Petchetsky considers ultrasounds to be a "manifestation of masculine desire to *reproduce* not only babies but also *motherhood*" (1987, 278, cited in Hirsch 1997, 174; my emphasis) and wonders how seeing rather than feeling the baby might make a woman into a "spectator of what goes on in her own body" (Hirsch 1997, 174). The retablos offer a fantasy of motherhood in which love overcomes all, including the violence of conception and the structural violence of poverty.

Moreover, it is by feeling (skin-to-skin) an embodied closeness, and viewing that intimacy again and again in a photograph, that a young woman may develop (or deepen) an affective bond. From Verónica's perspective, the project had a positive and transformational effect: although Marina could not be helped, Verónica maintained that the majority of the mothers benefited from the project. Several, like Nilda, really changed. "You remember Nilda, right? The beautiful girl from the Amazon with that long, long hair? She was thinking of giving up her son, but after the photo shoot, she decided to keep him. It changed her whole mentality. You know, it reprogrammed her (*se cambia su chip*). She really began to connect with him after that." In her discussion of the culminating project for the photography workshop, Verónica emphasizes that a key fulcrum in fostering a "better life" for young women (and their children) is cementing (and stabilizing) the conventionally valued relationship of mother and child. The images link the mundane practices and affective relationship of caring to the sacred figure of the Virgin Mary and Jesus, in Catholic doctrine. Yet, creating and viewing these photos also established an openness for an individual to reframe one's sense of self and one's relationships—to see oneself as "blessed" as a mother.

Hirsch argues (1997, 13) that in the postmodern moment, families are "fractured and subject to conflicting historical and ideological scripts." The photos created for the final project convey physical and emotional well-being more than suffering, yet reinforce both a moral rhetoric of universal mother love and a sense of optimism regarding humanitarian intervention. One script that intersects the retablo project circulates through humanitarian publications as well as newspapers and magazines and depicts, as I have mentioned already, mother and child suffering. Briggs argues that as much as the images have drawn attention to " 'Third World' poverty, hunger or need," especially since World War II, the ubiquity of these representations also "directs attention away from structural explanations for poverty, famine and other disasters, including international, political, military and economic causes" (Briggs 2003, 180). In their book *Humanitarian Photography: A History*, Heide Fehrenbach and Davide Rodogno (2015, 6) offer the reminder that "humanitarian photographs" are produced and disseminated and circulated by diverse individuals and organizations "concerned with aid, relief, rescue, reform, rehabilitation, and development," yet humanitarian imagery "focuses viewer attention on suffering, framing it as unjust yet amenable to remedy. It erases distracting political or social detail that would complicate the duty to act."

The point that humanitarian imagery "is *moral rhetoric* masquerading as visual evidence" (Fehrenbach and Rodogno 2015, 6) calls attention to the overlap between retablos and another set of ideological scripts keyed to a long-standing discourse of maternal love and suffering in Peru. As I noted in chapter 2, state representatives applauded women for "maternal expressions of unconditional and selfless love" and positioned women as suffering and self-sacrificing during the CVR hearings (Bueno-Hansen 2015, 94). Commissioners, who had heard testimonies from several women about being brutally raped by military personnel, responded to one individual in the courtroom by saying, "The love between you and your daughter goes beyond all the terror that happened" (Bueno-Hansen 2015, 95). Pascha Bueno-Hansen (2015, 94–95) argues that while the state recognizes these women's children "in a symbolic reconciliation of the national family . . . the possibility of reconciliation with raped women depends on the extent to which they fulfill their motherhood role" (Bueno-Hansen 2015, 94–95).[8] Framings such as this obscure potential relationships (such as paternity) and responsibilities (criminal investigation of sexual violence, protecting the human rights of citizens) that reinforce race, class, gender, and heterosexual privileges.

Residents looking back at the camera during school recess. (Their cameras are resting on the bench.) Photo by Palomitáy resident

Whether we consider their poses as part of habitual patterning outside an individual's awareness or "highly deliberate choreographies" (Farnell 2011, 151), this, like other human action, is "dynamically embodied discursive practice" (Farnell 2011, 151). In the context of a home for unmarried mothers, of girls who are often positioned as failed or unworthy, the retablo project might also be understood as reasserting morality, value, self-love, or pride. A young woman might reorient herself, enhance a sense of bonding, reject a mode of engagement, further develop her self-confidence through the activity or experience of creating a retablo. It is through their children that young women are able to claim value both in terms of the image itself and in practical material terms as well. It is only by remaining at the home that they have this particular array of experiences and opportunities. Perhaps these photos would become "the means by which family memory would be continued and perpetuated, by which the family's story would henceforth be told" (Hirsch 1997, 6–7). Yet the photos themselves and the process of creating photos throughout the workshop also point to the relational, decentered, and transactional dimensions of subjectivity and the constructed character of what appears transparent and natural.

In this chapter, I have integrated the representational aspects of photographic *expression* and nonrepresentational aspects of photographic *practice*. While some analyses paint a clear divide between the rhetorical and evidential aspects of photography (Fehrenbach and Rodogno 2015, 6), I have drawn on the idea that words are not simply referential and stories are not isolated from the context in which they emerge to reflect on the multiple aspects of meaning-making in image-making. Photographs do not reference a reality "out there," caught at a moment of time, in a straightforward way. Like utterances, images also have meanings tied to the context in which they emerged and the publics through which they circulate. Moreover, like "humanitarian photographs," the photographs I discuss were also produced by diverse social actors in various collective relations. A focus on the activity of photography and the process of self-expression may illuminate variations on what it may mean to be a good (enough) mother or a moral person.

Clearly, individuals may create and deploy a moral rhetoric through their embodied and skilled imaging practices.[9] The residents of Palomitáy produce and circulate images in terms of various aims and concerns. Indeed, attention to their dynamic and contingent visioning practices complicates understanding of the retablo project and, more generally, challenges us to recognize the small ways and unexpected pathways by which individuals reimagine themselves in relation to hierarchies of power. Hirsch (1997, 102) suggests that "we all function as subjects and as objects in a complex visual field not entirely determined by the gaze, but also the product of a series of more individual, local, and contingent looks, which are mutually constitutive, reversible, and reciprocal." The camera records but also structures the relationships of exchange in the family, in the home, and in the community over time. The final project of the workshop keys to more broadly circulating images of mother and child, both in Peru and more generally within humanitarian circulations. However, young women also gaze back, and engage in a variety of efforts to envision themselves within the situation. Their use of the camera produces subjectivities more complicated and dynamic than the retablo images would suggest.

CHAPTER 6

Moral Dialogues, Caring Dilemmas (a Theater Workshop)

Introducing *Natasia's Story*

Onstage, Maya falls to the floor, her arm outstretched, her eyes closed. The play has been running about ten minutes, with Maya performing the lead role of Natasia, and Natasia has just fainted. The plastic cups and plates, which she had been carrying to the table, clatter to the concrete floor. Natasia's father, played by Sandra, and her siblings, played by Faviola and Nilda, erupt in recriminations from the other side of the stage.

"*Burro!* You are so clumsy!"

"What have you done to our dinner? You've ruined it."

"Why does she have to be so careless, Papa?"

Moments later, realizing that she has not risen, Natasia's family members leave their seats at the kitchen table and one by one approach her prone form. "Natasia! Natasia!" yells her brother.

Offstage, the gasps of audience members reflect the shock visible on the faces of Natasia's onstage family. From the front row four-year-old Beto, who has been swinging his legs rhythmically against the rungs of a wooden chair, suddenly (and loudly) asks, "What *happened* to her?" Giggles erupt among audience members and performers alike, but they become quiet as Marina, dressed in a white lab coat for her role as the nurse, bends down to examine Natasia.

The nurse checks her pulse and heart rate; Natasia slowly opens her eyes and groans.

"You have a *novio* (boyfriend), don't you? What have you been up to while your father is out of the house?" the nurse accuses. Not waiting for an answer, the nurse turns to Natasia's father and states, "Did you know that your daughter has a novio? She is pregnant."

• • •

In this chapter, I analyze a story that was created, produced, and performed by twelve of Palomitáy's residents, a story "about a young mother like themselves." The *Historia de Natasia*, or *Natasia's Story*, recounts the life of a young woman who leaves her rural community and travels to the city after her family discovers her pregnancy. Created in the context of a workshop run by two interns, the play was performed publicly only once, to an audience of staff, volunteers, directors, teachers, residents, a handful of their children, and me. The interns initiated the theater workshop and gave the residents the project of collaboratively creating a drama about a young mother. However, multiple meanings emerge in the process of young women cooperating onstage as characters and as performers (and interacting with each other offstage in rehearsals and other arenas of daily life). The girls' creative rendering of the daily experiences and ethical dilemmas of Natasia provide a window onto the contingent and dynamic production of self, social hierarchy, and moral experience in "moment-to-moment thinking, feeling, and being in the world" (Ochs 2012, 144).

Children's "voices" and participation have been increasingly valorized in academia and advocacy arenas. Yet, Allison James (200, 265) argues, adults mostly maintain control of the research process (including how, when, and if children's voices are given prominence). Rather than "adding children's voices" (as an earlier generation added women's voices) to the anthropological record, she advances the idea of attending to children's voices as an analytical standpoint rather than a claim to authenticity (James 2007, 269). By incorporating analysis of the situation in which these young women interact to tell a story, and the micro-politics of expression among characters and performers in the drama, I move beyond a metaphorical use of "children's voices."[1]

The stories we tell about our own lives—and the lives of others—enable us to construct interpretations of experiences and express a sense of self. Stories, and storytelling, may reinforce or challenge relationships of domination or transform how we think about the world (Ochs and Capps 2001; Pollock 2005, 1999; Schiffrin 1996). Taking the perspective that narrative—and, in fact, all talk—is inextricably intertwined with social life, scholars have shown that stories are jointly, or dialogically, produced among multiple individuals and shaped by broader social structures, relationships, and events. Similarly, dramas in theater or ritual are tied to lived contexts.

The plot of this drama reflects the experiences and imagined possible futures of (some) Palomitáy residents. The play begins by situating Natasia in relation to her family and, significantly, a boyfriend. Over the course of the first scene, Natasia is kicked out of the house, travels from her rural community to the city, and is taken in by her aunt. In the next scene, she goes to school and perseveres through the derision of her classmates and teacher. Unexpectedly, she finds a letter from her mother while cleaning her aunt's house. In the third scene, Natasia searches for her mother and reunites with her. Fast forwarding to the future, Natasia becomes a successful business owner. I should note that Natasia's pregnancy is a crucial moment in the drama, sending Natasia out of her home, and an important link between the play and the experiences of the young women at Palomitáy, who are all mothers. Yet, in contrast to the majority of the young women at Palomitáy, Natasia navigates life—including her migration to the city, attending school, and finding work—without a child.

Beyond the referential content, multiple layers of meaningful talk and action are intertwined as characters, actors, audience members involve themselves in the collaborative production of the ongoing drama. My analysis juxtaposes "Natasia's world" (especially the talk and action among the characters in various "scenes," who are, of course, portrayed by social actors, the clients of Palomitáy) and the "world of Palomitáy," (especially the social "situations," such as the theater workshop, in which residents and other social actors engage in ongoing interpersonal interactions). Of course, the broader political, economic, and social world in which Palomitáy is situated (and which the characters and the performers assume is obvious to everyone) encompasses both of these worlds and may be conceived of as a third frame.

In the pages that follow, I attend to the interactional boundary between scene and situation by intertwining discussion of the characters' interactions with ethnographic description of the theater workshop and other everyday situations. I forefront three moments in which identity and moral experience converge. First, I consider the implicit construction of gendered (im)morality among characters in scene 1. In particular, the nurse's questioning of Natasia, and the reactions of Natasia's family members, link the characters' moral evaluations in the scene to the broader frame in which these young women live. Second, I analyze the embedded dialogue in scene 2 that racializes Natasia while drawing from and stitching together the words and actions of characters and social actors. Third, I trace the intertextual connections that link Natasia's imagined future in scene 3 with moral dilemmas that figure in ordinary life. Young women mobilize references to the play to navigate social relations and subjectivities in their encounters within Palomitáy.

Planning programming for a workshop

Natasia's Story is a lens through which I reflect on the ways moral experience emerges in the interactions *between* interlocutors (characters and social actors). In chapter 4, I describe the talk and actions of three individuals (Jeni, Laura, and Marina) to highlight the heterogeneity of girls' understandings of themselves as mothers. Here I focus on the ongoing social situation to show how subjectivities and moral hierarchies of care are jointly produced in dynamic and contingent processes of engagement. I illuminate the broad moral discourses and the lived ethical dilemmas and hopes for relationality that shape the contours of the unfolding drama. I also show how the talk and actions of Natasia and other characters seep into the moral and social dilemmas of everyday life in a residence where doing good and being good, living well for oneself and one's child, is not always a straightforward task.

Situating the Theater Workshop

Before I observed the theater workshop for the first time, I met with Nadia and Luz, the interns, so that they could fill me in on what the participants already had done. We sat outside by the retaining wall. The sky was already gray, with darker clouds boiling up over the mountains, a promise of more rain. Luz, who has long black hair, eyes the color of milk chocolate, and high cheekbones, savored a cigarette while Nadia and I chatted on the steps. Nadia groaned. "I haven't had one in five days," she said, indicating the cigarette with a lift of her chin. She had gone hiking to Machu Picchu over the weekend with her boyfriend and had decided not to smoke cigarettes while on the hike. "It was really hard," she said. "I could hardly catch my breath. I didn't realize I was in such terrible shape." (Hence the twenty-one-year-old's decision to quit.) Nadia, who wore her curly brown hair long and sported a small stud in her left nostril, had an open smile, ready laugh, and an animated way of speaking. Her more relaxed attitude paired well with Luz's directive manner. "I really want to get some things done today," said Luz. She is studying to be a teacher.

Luz explained that they planned to do a run-through of scene 1, and she and Nadia quickly pulled together the details of a warm-up exercise. Then Nadia summarized the first four sessions of the workshop for me. They had introduced the workshop as an opportunity for the residents to tell others about the experiences, the life history, of a girl like themselves. They split the girls into two smaller groups and asked each group to come up with a story of a young mother. They told the participants that it was not a competition, but after each group created a scenario and acted it out, they would decide together which aspects of each story to use for the play. In this way, they hoped that all of the residents could participate in creating the play. By the second week, each group improvised the opening scenes of their stories.

Reminiscing about this moment, Luz described the scene as "disturbing." Recalling her own reaction, Nadia smiled briefly and shook her head. "The first time the groups acted out their script. Wow. Five of them piled on top of poor Yesenia, acting out a rape (violación). They were all grabbing and piling on top of her, holding her down while she struggled. They got into it." A small group of girls came out of the courtyard. "We're ready!" We followed them into the classroom just as thunder rolled.

Nadia and Luz structured the workshop as a participatory endeavor; they aimed to create contexts in which the mothers could collaborate with each other, reflect upon their experiences, and come to know themselves better. Both college students from Europe, they initiated the workshop after having worked at Palomitáy for five months. Both spoke fluent Spanish and had made close connections with the residents and staff by leading short enrichment classes for the young mothers and helping in the nursery; they also occasionally assisted in the office and attended staff meetings.

As the workshop proceeded over the course of the next several weeks, the young mothers brainstormed ideas, played trust games, developed the characters, and established the scenes of the drama. Especially in the beginning,

Nadia and Luz gave the girls free rein to explore ideas and develop plot lines. The young women developed most of the dialogue and action in the scenes of the play through improvisation. Except for three brief interludes in which the recorded voice of a narrator speaks, the script was never written down. Nadia and Luz facilitated the meetings, occasionally offering suggestions about dialogue or action, setting boundaries around residents' interactions, and expediting the logistical aspects of production (finding a location, writing out and recording the narrator's script). Eventually, each young woman volunteered to perform one or more roles, and meetings primarily consisted of rehearsals. The residents also created backdrops, scenery, and costumes. By the final performance, the girls voiced their characters' lines (with some variation and some improvisation) with almost no break in the dialogue. What characters said and how they said it emerged through the interaction of performers onstage.

During the workshop, my role was primarily as an observer. However, when the participants and the interns asked if I would video the performance, I agreed. I recorded parts of one rehearsal; the performers reviewed the video with Nadia and Luz to develop dialogue in scene 2 and determine the theme for the final scene. I also recorded the final performance, leaving copies of the digital video with the interns and with Palomitáy. My analysis is based on these recordings as well as on extensive notes taken during rehearsals of the play.

In order to illustrate how the characters' dialogue and interactions in the scene are entangled with this broader social situation, I return to scene 1, where I left off with the nurse's question to Natasia's father. I focus my analysis on the non-referential meanings that emerge in the talk of characters (especially the inferences implicit in dialogue among characters). Participants (characters or performers) may not be aware of, or explicitly agree with, all of the meanings that I detail. By focusing on the social and communicative work that characters and performers do together to maintain particular situations, I reveal the ways social hierarchies and moral experience are intertwined in mundane interactions on- and offstage.

Scene 1: Staging the Sexuality of Natasia

A long silence ensues after the nurse's diagnosis. Natasia's brother and sister at first say nothing but stare in disbelief. Natasia remains silent, sitting at the kitchen table with her family for the first time since the play began. She looks down at the floor. Her family members then speculate about how this could have happened.

FATHER: The nurse says that your sister is pregnant.
SISTER: How can Natasia be pregnant, Papa? What could have happened to her?
FATHER: I don't know what could have happened with her. No one knows what has happened. She doesn't have a boyfriend.
SISTER: Natasia, where is the father of your baby?
BROTHER: Talk! Hurry up! Say something!
FATHER: Natasia, what has happened? Where is the father of your child?
SISTER: She doesn't say anything. Well, I guess maybe we should believe that there is no father?
FATHER: All right, Natasia. You are going to leave this house.
SISTER: You leave here, Natasia.
BROTHER: Leave now and take your things! You can't stay here. We do not want to have anything more to do with you. Get out of here!
FATHER: You will no longer live in this house.

The conversation among Natasia's family begins with the characters refusing to believe that Natasia might have a boyfriend. Only Natasia's sister asks what could have happened *to* her, raising the possibility that Natasia does not carry primary responsibility for her pregnancy. Yet, when Natasia refuses to say anything, her father reacts by telling her that she will have to leave, that she is no longer welcome to live in the house. Her brother erupts in anger, "We do not want to have anything more to do with you. Get out of here!" Crying, Natasia quietly gathers a few of her things and leaves home.

If we focus on the interaction of the characters, for the moment, and consider the inferences that are necessary for the conversation to move forward, we gain insight into some of the broader assumptions about the social world of Natasia. Interlocutors in everyday life, as well as performed dramas, often acquiesce in routinized ways to cultural and linguistic interactional forms and assumptions about the social world (Mannheim 2015b, 47; Grice 1975; Gumperz 1981). Take, for instance, the nurse's question to Natasia, "What have you been doing while your father is away?" and her statement to Natasia's father, "Did you know that your daughter has a boyfriend?" Neither Natasia nor her father responds to the nurse; however, the nurse's utterances do not *require* responses in order to convey meaning. In the former, the nurse implies something other than a literal interpretation of the referential content: that Natasia has behaved inappropriately (that is, by engaging in consensual heterosexual intimate activity). For the characters, the meaning of the nurse's question rests upon broader understandings of the social world.

In other words, the characters go along with an implicit inference that is shaped by normative (and power-laden) assumptions about the way the world works. Natasia's world is inextricably linked to the social world of Palomitáy, and it is worth stating again that this is a world in which discourses of sexuality are fully racialized.[2] In urban hegemonic discourses in Peru, girls and women are expected to abstain from sex before marriage. Attitudes toward young women's sexuality and sexual comportment may be quite differently configured among Quechua speakers. For example, adults assume that youth will engage in sexual relationships before marriage, and pregnancy is tied to notions of fertility (rather than failed abstinence or disrupted virginity) in many rural Andean communities (for example, Van Vleet 2008). However, these individuals and communities are not isolated from hegemonic national discourses. Moreover, normative discourses of sexuality are used to morally evaluate poor and rural (indigenous) people (even when urban middle-class and elite mestizos fail to follow these precepts themselves). Individuals who live in and through both of these discourses may experience their contradictions as ongoing aspects of gendered and racial oppression.

In scene 1, the nurse's pronouncement, "Your daughter is pregnant," and the ensuing conversation among Natasia's family members (which culminates in Natasia being kicked out of her home) fortify the linkages between paternal authority and the moral culpability of women. Within the frame of "Natasia's world," romantic or intimate encounters are marked as improper for young unmarried women at the same time that heterosexual intimacy is normalized. Moreover, the structuring of the nurse's subsequent question to Natasia's father reinforces the idea that Natasia's actions have brought this situation upon herself and her family. The nurse's question furthermore suggests that Natasia's father has failed in the patriarchal mandate to control and protect the sexuality of his daughters. Whether he answers *yes* or *no*, he is trapped within the implication of the nurse's statement: the fact of Natasia's (purportedly improper, secretive but consensual) relationship with a boyfriend. The characters' responses or nonresponses and actions leave imprecise the history of Natasia's relationship with the young man. The possibility that she became pregnant as the result of coercion or sexual violence is unspoken in the drama.

Moral Ambiguities and Participatory Pitfalls

Multiple interpretations of the scene are possible, of course, and the meanings of the play may develop moment by moment, through the interaction of characters, performers, and audience members. For instance, my interpretation of scene 1 is complicated by the talk and action that proceeded Natasia fainting. Although Natasia's father and siblings did not know that she had a boyfriend, the members of the audience already had been apprised of that situation in the opening words of the play. Spoken in a young girl's high-pitched voice, recorded and replayed on a computer, the play began with the following words: "Once there was a girl called Natasia who lived in a small community with her father, brother, and sister. Her mother had gone away a long time before, and Natasia hardly remembered her. Natasia was left with all the responsibilities of the household: cleaning, mopping, cooking, and washing clothes. And she didn't like to do any of this." The action of the play begins with Natasia serving her family a meal while her brother yells at her to hurry up, complains about the food that she has made, and criticizes her for laziness. Natasia does not react to these recriminations but remains silent.

After her father and siblings leave for work, the narrator intervenes once more to note, "In reality, what she really liked to do was listen to music, watch *telenovelas* (soap operas), hang out with her girlfriends, and go out with her boyfriend." At this point, Natasia's novio, portrayed with verve by Mónica, swaggers up to the house, and when Natasia opens the door, he grabs her arm and tries to pull her outside. He tells her that he wants to go strolling around town and asks if she will come with him. She refuses, saying she has to stay home and do her housework; she is afraid that her family will arrive home and discover her absence. The second time we see Natasia's novio, he pushes past her and saunters through the kitchen to take a seat at the table. He announces that he is leaving; he is not sure how long he will be gone but plans to find work in a city. As Natasia begins to cry quietly, he promises to return. Natasia does not hear from the young man again and her days continue much as before.

Then, Natasia faints while bringing food to the table for her family.

For the audience (who witnessed Natasia's boyfriend coming into the house), the nurse's utterance ("You have a novio, don't you? What have you been up to while your father is out of the house?") relies for meaning upon the previous action in the scene as well as the more general understanding of the social world. Although performers enact a young woman's agency in seeking pleasures or possibilities beyond the walls of their homes, they also perform a world in which Natasia's pregnancy is interpreted by others (family members, medical professionals) as resulting from her own inappropriate actions and her parent's failure to control her sexuality. Natasia is presented as acting in ways that position her as morally suspect even as the scene points to the coercive or violent ontology of heterosexual sexual relations and male authority in Peru.

The experiences of the performers serve as unspoken but simultaneously circulating texts through which social actors, offstage, interpret the words and actions of characters onstage. Even though the first scene does not include an explicit presentation of rape or sexual violence, the scene and broader social situation are linked through the experiences and life histories of the performers. Many in the audience knew the performers to varying degrees. Short-term volunteers are briefed about the physical, sexual, and structural violence that many young women experienced before coming to the home. Long-term interns and staff receive more finely detailed background and weekly progress reports about each client, interact with girls in formal and informal situations, and establish caring relationships with them and their children. Residents come to know each other through participating in classes and workshops, sleeping in the same rooms, hanging out with each other, and helping each other with child care. They share pieces of their past histories and current experiences in ongoing social situations.

Additionally, performers, and perhaps some audience members, may have linked this scene to the other version of events that workshop participants developed early in their productive process. As I mentioned, the participants split into two groups and created two different versions of events leading up to Natasia leaving home. They improvised the scenes for each other, and in one group's portrayal, Natasia was gang-raped. Although Nadia and Luz confessed to being "shocked" by the portrayal, they went forward with their plan to have the workshop participants vote to choose which version of events would be used in the play. The majority chose the rape scene.

Nadia and Luz intervened infrequently to shape the plot of the drama, but one of those instances occurred at this moment, in the early days of the workshop. After a long weekend of conversation, Nadia and Luz decided that the group would need to use the scenario in which Natasia's boyfriend abandons her, instead of the rape scene. They told me that the audience for the final performance would include very young children, as well as administrators, teachers, and volunteers. They were concerned about the level of violence in the scene and just how they would explain to the three-, four-, and five-year-olds what was happening. They also explained that the directors believed that all too often the young women were framed as victims of sexual violence. (In a different context, Rosa had expressed frustration to me that volunteers, NGOs, and others focused so much on the trauma of sexual violence that they obscured the complexity of the residents as individuals and the various and structured forms of violence that girls may encounter in stratified contexts.) To what extent the director or other staff members were involved in their decision is unclear. In this case, the interns rationalized their refusal to highlight gang rape in terms of their assumptions about the appropriateness of certain topics for young children and of characterizing the experiences of young mothers with a particularly stigmatizing form of violence, experienced by only a handful of residents.

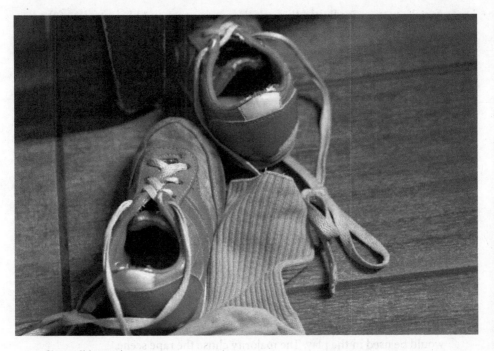

Shoes off for naptime

Palomitáy as an institution, and both residents and interns as individuals, often challenge both legal and political structures and public discourses that denigrate young mothers as sexually promiscuous or sexually available; staff, interns, and volunteers teach residents about reproductive health, human rights, and childcare. By refusing to allow young women to represent what they saw as significant aspects of their experiences, the interns establish their own authority, police the boundaries of what may be spoken about in particular contexts, and reinforce the violence of institutional and transnational hierarchies. Feminist and postcolonialist theorists, including anthropologists, have pointed out that individuals and agencies established to support survivors of violence, or poor children and youth, or indigenous communities may frame them as culpable, thus reproducing structures of inequality, even inadvertently (for example, Luttrell-Roland 2012; Oliart 2007; Vargas 2010). This example serves as a reminder that individuals (including interns and ethnographers) do not exist outside more general context structured by race, class, and gender inequalities and other forms of privilege, including nationality. Just as significant, the representations of self and other are entangled with moral evaluations at the level of interpersonal interactions.

The micro-politics of interaction are a crucial site at which we might explore the pervasive problem of becoming involved in reproducing hierarchies of power, even those that we aim to dismantle.

Scene 2: Positioning Natasia as an "Other"

One way to think about the interactional production of identity and inequality is to draw on insights of scholars such as Raymond McDermott and Henry Tylbor (1995, 219), who have argued persuasively that any communicative interaction requires some degree of "collusion" among participants in order for the interaction to occur at all. From this perspective, the characters in the scene (and audience members watching the action onstage) shape their talk to "fit the contours of the world in which they are embedded" (McDermott and Tylbor 1995, 220). Rather than challenge the underlying implications of the nurse's questions, for example, participants "play into each other's hands, pushing and pulling each other toward a strong sense of what is probable or possible, for a sense of what can be hoped for and/or obscured."[3] Not only characters in a play, but people everywhere are entangled in hierarchies that are extended through mundane interactions. The analytical concept of collusion recognizes that participants may be unaware of the work that they do to maintain a situation; however, the term "collusion" carries negative implications of intentionality. For this reason, I use the phrase "interactional involvement" to refer to the processes through which participants tacitly agree to a version of the story or an understanding of "what's happening" in the midst of a social situation. Reflecting on interactional involvement means making *situations* (rather than words or individuals) the fulcrum of analysis. This perspective advances understanding of how participants may contribute to the maintenance of hierarchical relationships, without explicitly agreeing with the terms of their engagement.

Dramatic performances are shaped by the multiple levels at which characters, performers, and audience members collaborate with each other or become interactionally involved.[4] Writing the play required explicitly collaborative effort—negotiation, cooperation, interpersonal investment—from the girls. Writing, performing—and watching—the drama also requires involvement among social actors. For instance, performers and audience members become involved interactionally in order to maintain the parameters of the event. When Beto shouts out "What happened to her?" performers and audience members alike are reminded of the implicit conventions of theater (for example, that audience members remain mostly silent). They are also made aware of their involvement or engagement with each other (at a previously unremarked upon or unnoticed level) to maintain this particular situation, a theatrical performance.

Social actors rely on (often unspoken) understandings about social and linguistic interaction. Moreover, participants in a conversation are empowered to "use local circumstances to shape their knowledge into mutually perceptible and reflexively consequential chunks" (McDermott and Tylbor 1995, 220). This is true whether they are reflecting on their life experiences through the process of "telling a story" of a mother "like themselves" or participating in ordinary life. In scene 2 the dialogue among characters reinforces structures of power built around race, ethnicity, and class even as performers critically evaluate those relationships of difference.[5] Natasia is racialized as a serrana and positioned as an "other." Participants in *Natasia's Story* work to maintain some understanding of the world that the characters inhabit and that the social actors (the performers and audience members) inhabit and help to create. By considering the micro-politics of interactions, especially the ways performers are tied to characters through embedded dialogue, I unpack what may be "mutually perceptible" for characters and acknowledge, simultaneously, the gaps or disjunctures in "chunks" of comprehension among characters, performers, and audience members.

At the beginning of scene 2, Natasia arrives at her aunt's home, distraught and in search of her mother. Natasia's mother had left to work in the city at some point in the distant past. Natasia's aunt insists that she does not know the whereabouts of Natasia's mother, but she comforts Natasia and offers her a place to live. The next day, she takes Natasia to enroll in school. Throughout the scene, Natasia's otherness as a serrana is performatively established through the interaction of characters in a public-school classroom, a social setting fraught with class, racial, and gender hierarchies. Natasia is teased by students and criticized by the teacher.

As the students begin entering the classroom, one student, played by Ana, notices Natasia. "This cholita, who is she? Ay, how scared she looks!" she exclaims to the general laughter of the other students, who have now seated themselves in chairs.[6]

The teacher, played by Marina (who also played the nurse) says, "Good morning," and the students respond, "Good morning, Teacher."

Continuing her criticism of Natasia, the student exclaims, "Why is this cholita here, my God!"

The teacher says to Natasia, "All right! Introduce yourself to the class, please! Introduce yourself!"

Natasia walks around to the front of the classroom.

"Ay, wasn't it better when you were with your sheep?" says the student in an undertone, causing laughter among the other students in the scene as well as the audience.

Barely audible, Natasia says, "My name is Natasia, and I am from the countryside, near here."

"What did she say? What did she say, Teacher? I couldn't hear anything she said. That's not the way to introduce yourself!"

"That's it then. Teach her how to introduce herself."

The student moves to the front of the room; speaking very rapidly and loudly, she says, "My friends and my esteemed teacher, I wish you all a good morning. I will now introduce myself. My name is Elizabeth. I am from the city of Cusco. I am fifteen years old." After a brief pause, she adds, "And that's how the other young lady (*señorita*) should have presented herself!"

Elizabeth sits down and the class continues. Natasia does not answer any of the questions the teacher asks her. At the end of the class, once the other students have left, the teacher scolds Natasia. "I don't know why your aunt brought you here. You don't know how to introduce yourself. You don't know how to sit properly. After everything that we have covered in class, you still haven't learned anything. You are dirty; all of your clothes are full of dust! Don't you even know how to bathe yourself? Don't even bother coming back here tomorrow. Goodbye!"

In scene 1, Natasia's brother laces his critical commentary of Natasia with terms like, "lazy" and "burro," and Natasia does work (like cooking and cleaning) that would be accomplished by an empleada (or domestic worker) in most mestizo (middle-class or elite) households in Peru. Nonetheless, throughout most of the play's first scene, Natasia's racial positioning is ambiguous. However, for the characters in scene 2, Natasia's subordinated racial and gender positionality is enacted through direct labeling (as when one student explicitly refers to Natasia as a cholita or sarcastically as "señorita"), salient symbolic distinctions between rural and urban, and marked and embodied enactments (such as speaking quietly and looking down). Later the teacher reiterates a litany of failings that range from deficiencies of knowledge to lack of cleanliness, all of which are keyed to racial stereotypes. Performers draw on mutually comprehensible arrays of knowledge about the social world to render this scene. Moreover, as social actors they make sense of events, like this play or a remembered conversation, by implicitly or explicitly linking the ongoing talk "to other acts, including the past, the future, the hypothetical, the conspicuously avoided, and so on" (Irvine 1996, 135; also see Hanks 1990, 254).

If meanings are produced along the borderline of the drama and the social situation, one approach to revealing the connections between characters and performers is to trace the layering of dialogue in reported speech. In the play, the performers animate, or actually give voice to, talk that is attributed to the character (not necessarily the performer). Narrative scholars point out that reported speech, including the citation of another's words through direct quotation or stylistic features such as pauses, repetitions, or onomatopoeia, may radically alter the surface meaning of a story (Tedlock 1983, 54, 58–60). Even very simple conversations exhibit complexly organized layerings of relationships (for example Hanks 1990; Irvine 1996). Erving Goffman (1981, 1976) has argued that reported speech requires attention to the various roles that participants play—and that these participant roles are neither static nor neatly aligned with individual speakers.[7] In this scene, Marina, performing in the role of the teacher, says, "After everything that we have covered in class, you still haven't learned anything. You are dirty; all of your clothes are full of dust!" Marina is the individual who physically utters the words, but it is the teacher, a character in the play, who stands behind those words. At the same time, neither Marina nor the teacher (a character in a drama) composed the words; instead, authorship is dispersed among the participants of the workshop.

The characters and performers are closely intertwined with each other in other ways as well. Several of the performers, of course, have had experiences similar to Natasia's. They are painfully aware of the ways people position each other along a social hierarchy using implicit and explicit references to and evaluations of stereotypical activities (herding sheep), locations (the countryside), and characteristics (ignorance, dirtiness) and overtly racialized labels. For instance, Marina (who performs as the teacher and the nurse) was born and raised in a small Quechua-speaking community several hours from the city of Cusco. Like the young woman who plays Natasia, she draws on her own experiences in acting out this scene. These young women both mobilize racialized discourses and performances and also implicitly critique the oppressing moves of the students and teacher by evoking them explicitly. Neither the teacher nor the urban student is presented in a positive light. Nevertheless, to be positioned as dirty or uneducated, as a cholita or serrana, is also problematic for Palomitáy residents, as I make clear below.

Maya Refuses Her Role

By illuminating the unspoken connections between scene and situational contexts, we may better understand how characters and actors become entangled with, or involved in, broader discourses even as they offer implicit (or even explicit) critiques. Conversely, attention to various moments in the theater workshop (or in everyday life in the residence) illustrates how the politics of interaction among characters may seep into the politics of interaction among performers. An incident that illustrates the mutual implication of scene and situation occurred just two weeks before the final performance.

By that time, the girls mostly rehearsed scenes, attempting to move through the entire production over the course of the two meetings. One afternoon, I walked through the front entryway later than usual to find that only a few of the girls were already in the living room, lying on the couches. Graciela, Faviola, Mónica, and Ana were all sitting with Nadia and waiting for the rest of the girls. After a few minutes, Maya came in. As soon as she sat down, Maya started crying. Graciela and Ana went over and hugged her. Nadia asked if she wanted to talk. "No," said Maya. But she could not stop the tears from spilling over and running down her cheeks. No one spoke while we waited for Marina and Nilda. Finally, Nadia decided to begin. "Let's all get up and dance. You can dance in character!" The girls didn't move. Nadia said, "Let's get some energy moving!" Still, the girls remained sitting and leaning against each other.

Eventually Nadia gave up on the warmup and the girls agreed that they would do a run-through of the play. Maya asked to be excused from performing. Nadia agreed. "Would someone volunteer to take Maya's place? Who wants to perform as Natasia?" When no one volunteered, even for the afternoon, she assigned Yaneth to the role.

Yaneth tipped her head to the side and obediently got up and stood in the center of the room. Sandra, Faviola, and Nilda, who had the roles of Natasia's family members, moved to the front of the room as well, but simply sat. They did not shout or talk among themselves as they usually did when in character. Nadia gave stage directions. Yaneth smiled and shifted her weight to the other foot. Maya watched from the benches.

Finally, Nadia concluded the workshop half an hour early. Maya stayed behind as the other girls left.

"I don't want to perform as Natasia anymore. I quit," she said.

"What's wrong? What happened?" Nadia asked again.

"Nothing. I just don't want to do it anymore."

"Please, tell us, Maya, what's going on?" we encouraged, and after some hesitation, Maya began telling a story filled with a recounting of other interactions from conversations that had occurred from a few hours before to a few months before. Later that day, I wrote in my fieldnotes that what struck me most was Maya's anxiety, her fearfulness expanding to fill the room. On the surface, Maya faced a dilemma about how to deal with a dispute with another resident. Nadia and I soon realized that from Maya's perspective, much more was at stake.

Maya reported this: sometime over the Christmas holidays, while the director was away, someone borrowed the DVD player from her apartment and broke it. Because no one confessed to knowing anything about the DVD player, Noelia said that each girl would have to contribute money toward replacing it. A few of the girls earn money in a studio making purses for the tourist market and others receive small gifts of money from relatives. One or two receive monthly allowances for their children because of court-ordered settlements. Several have no money at all. Laura had no money at all and could only pay her share of the DVD player if she could borrow the money.

Under some duress from the social worker, Maya had lent money (sixteen *soles,* or about four U.S. dollars) to Laura. Three months later Maya asked Laura for the money back. "It was not for me," Maya pointed out. Maya wanted the money to buy yarn for an embroidery project for Vaso de Leche, an organization that provides milk and food for poor mothers. Several young mothers at Palomitáy decided to participate in the project (embroidering plastic woven bags with the word "Mamitáy" and then filling the bags with clothes and food to give them to mothers who were worse off than themselves). Noelia and the social worker Elizabeth suggested that the girls pay for the embroidery project themselves, "to make it more meaningful."

Unfortunately, Laura still had no money, so she could not return what Maya had lent her. Then Maya learned that Laura's uncle had visited and given Laura two pairs of shoes. So, Maya confronted Laura, demanding a pair of shoes to settle the debt. Laura refused because the shoes were not hers; her uncle had simply asked if Laura could pass the shoes on to her aunt. Besides, Laura pointed out, each pair was worth forty soles. "I don't owe you that much!"

Meanwhile, the argument between Maya and Laura came to the attention of Noelia, the educational coordinator who remained at Palomitáy after-hours. Noelia intervened, scolding Maya for asking Laura to return the money. "Why are you asking Laura for money? Her family has no money! They don't give her any money! And she is not able to earn anything because she can't work yet. Her baby is too young!" said Noelia (according to Maya).

Maya also overheard Noelia telling the director about the incident. According to Maya, Noelia exaggerated what Maya had said. By the time Maya got to this point in her story, she was weeping again.

"But what are you afraid of?" asked Nadia. "None of this seems that serious. Why are you so worried?"

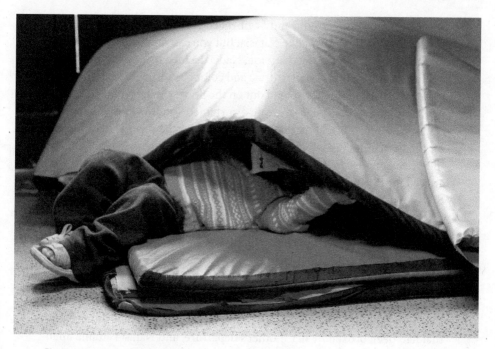

Playing peek-a-boo in the nursery

"I don't know if I can stand it to live here!"

"Maya, I don't understand," said Nadia.

"Noelia is trying to make me so mad that I will have to leave. I will have to put my child up for adoption and they will put me in a different place."

"What do you mean?"

Maya replied. "I keep thinking that I'll have to put my baby up for adoption."

"But this residence is here so that you can keep your child," said Nadia. "Mama Rosa would not want you to feel this way. She is not trying to have you give your child away."

Maya shrugged, unconvinced. "After what Noelia is saying about me, Mama Rosa may not think so."

Eventually Maya calmed down and decided that she wanted to talk with Juan, the psychologist. Nadia promised that she would talk with the director (without referring to Maya) about what had been happening at Palomitáy while Noelia was in charge. But, for the next week, Maya refused the role of Natasia, a role she had performed since the beginning of the taller. No one else would take on the role in a permanent way, and the date of the performance was fast approaching. Nadia and Luz begged Natasia to come back, saying, "We know that you are not like Natasia. But you can do this! No one else can perform her." During the next session, Nadia decided to have the performers take a break from rehearsing to draw and color backdrops for each scene on large pieces of paper. They spread out on the floor with crayons and colored pencils, working in groups to create a curtained window for the kitchen of Natasia's house, a blackboard and books for the school, and a fruit display for the market stall in which Natasia is reunited with her mother. They laid their heads on each other's stomachs and shoulders and chatted. When I arrived for the last rehearsal before our dress rehearsal, Maya was acting in the role of Natasia again.

Scene 3: Natasia Finds Her Mother

In some ways, Natasia is an ambiguously positioned character. Young women may identify with her or position themselves against her. This becomes more evident as the final scene unfolds. In the final scene, performers enact desired future possibilities. Natasia reunites with her mother, reestablishing a bond that had been broken by her mother's departure, and Natasia attains financial success. In previous scenes, the characters navigate the uneven moral terrain of young women's sexual activity and pregnancy and embed Natasia in a hegemonic racial and moral regime by positioning her as a serrana in the classroom. In the final scene, Natasia establishes herself as a daughter in need of (and deserving of) care and as a person who successfully advances to live a better life. In this scene, performers implicitly critique the actions of Natasia's family while presenting Natasia in a more positive light.

Scene 3 occurs almost without dialogue in three brief vignettes set in the kitchen of Natasia's aunt's house, near the fruit vendors' stands at the market, and in an office. The audience watches Natasia return to the stage, turn on a radio, and begin to dance while she dusts her aunt's kitchen. She accidentally knocks a box off a shelf and scatters papers across the floor. When picking up the papers, Natasia discovers a letter to her aunt from her mother. Natasia realizes that her aunt has hidden the knowledge that Natasia's mother works in the nearby market selling fruit. In the next vignette, Natasia searches for her mother in the market. She hands the letter to a vendor, who says, "Where did you get this? This is a letter to my sister! Who are you?" And Natasia replies, "I am Natasia." The mother and daughter embrace. As the two characters walk off the stage, Natasia's mother says, "Come home with me, my daughter." In the third vignette, Natasia is older. She sits behind a desk, where a long line of people wait to request her help. Natasia's former schoolteacher reaches the front of the line and begs her for a job. Natasia sends her out to clean toilets.

Natasia's actions at one level reinforce the promise of class advancement. Succeeding in business after many years, Natasia may treat her former teacher with seeming kindness while offering her a job that only the poor might do. It is not inconsequential that throughout the play, Natasia labors in her family's and her aunt's households. The domestic labor that Natasia performs also resonates with the chores that residents share in Palomitáy. As Jeanine Anderson (2010, 99) notes, based on long-term research with poor, rural-to-urban migrants living in Lima shantytowns, people became "passionately involved in self-improvement, self-expression, and make-over projects that expressed a vision of transcendence and an effort to overcome limitations." Natasia is engaged in such a self-improvement project, as are the performers themselves. When Natasia encounters her teacher in this imagined future, the relational terms of engagement flip. Natasia no longer does the menial labor that she offers to the teacher.

At the same time, an underlying current throughout the play is the moral evaluation of characters' actions and interactions, especially their treatment of Natasia. Her father and siblings berated her, her boyfriend abandoned her, and her aunt misled her. Natasia is treated more like an empleada than a beloved daughter or niece who is cared for by her family. Natasia initially is isolated in her father's house and struggles to attend school in the city. Yet when Natasia finally finds her mother, her mother holds her daughter and invites her home. Natasia expresses hope as well as uncertainty when she nods, agreeing to follow the mother she has not seen for many years. Natasia reestablishes a relationship with her mother, and as a daughter, Natasia becomes financially successful.

This moment of reunion between Natasia and her mother, and its aftermath, may be particularly significant for the residents of Palomitáy. All of these young women are displaced from their families. Some families relinquish their daughters as they attempt to navigate situations of extreme insecurity. Some young women leave their families on their own as they seek opportunities to work, while others leave under duress, rejected by relatives or removed by the state. The ambivalence and ambiguity of characters' actions develop in contexts where precarious life circumstances intersect with long-standing inequalities. Similarly, the individuals who become residents of this home navigate insecurities and uncertainties. They may hope for relationships in which they are cared for by relatives rather than strangers, or for circumstances in which they may position themselves as daughters rather than mothers.

Moreover, the meanings of becoming a successful businesswoman extends beyond what may be hegemonically valued. Natasia may have sent her teacher to clean bathrooms, a small revenge, but she also gave her work. For many native Andean and working-class women in Peru, maintaining self-sufficiency and household viability is a value that extends into other social, economic, and political relations. Microbusinesses and self-employment "are a channel to the Andean ideal for economic independence and self-sufficiency. They are a showcase for skills involving production, planning, budgeting, and abstemiousness. Businesses that accumulate wealth permit their owners to become generous patrons. They select from members of the kin network and invest in the careers of brothers and sisters, children, nieces, nephews and grandchildren they deem most loyal and worthy" (Anderson 2010, 91). From this perspective, Natasia attains a position as a worthy daughter (of her mother) and a generous patron (to her teacher).

Unspoken Insecurities, Moral Uncertainties

By integrating scene and situation, I advance an admittedly imperfect way of glimpsing the unfolding experience of sense-making and self-representation in everyday life. Perhaps most famously among anthropologists, Victor Turner (1986) argued that dramatic events offer opportunities for individuals and collectivities to render and refract social relationships, events, and understandings. For Turner, the social dramas enacted in ritual and in theater bring participants into an experience through the power of aesthetics and have a transformative effect on the performers themselves and on the broader context.

As linguistic anthropologist Elinor Ochs (2012, 152) points out, Turner's (1986, 42) opposition between theater and ordinary life does not align with contemporary understandings of culture. For Turner theater "transpires in 'the subjective mood of culture', i.e. 'the mood of maybe, might be, as if, hypothesis, fantasy, conjecture, desire', while ordinary life transpires in 'the indicative mood, where we expect the invariant operation of cause and effect, of rationality and commonsense.'"[8] Yet, contemporary anthropologists view culture as processual. In ordinary life, as in drama, people enact desires and possibilities; their interpretations unfold in and through their interactions and cannot be predicted from the outset.

Young mothers engage in "temporal bursts of sense-making" and moral involvement in relation to each other but also in relation to the voices and bodies of others, who may be present or absent, remembered or imagined. The script of the drama was not written word for word, but the participants in the performance were not free agents. They worked together so as not to disrupt the conditions of engagement. These include the story of the play itself and the overarching situation of being placed in institutionalized care and able to access the resources of the residence only by engaging in particular actions. As social actors, the girls were "always already" caught up in ongoing social, political, and economic relationships—including raising their children and participating in educational and enrichment opportunities in terms of a racial and gendered discourse of "bettering oneself." Their representations of self and of moral experience were not laid out completely in advance but were not detached from circumstances and contingencies of interaction, either.

Natasia's Story does not explicitly address the young mothers' location in a humanitarian organization or a state structured by a confluence of inequalities. However, in creating and performing the character and life story of Natasia, the young women open the possibilities of reflecting on facets of their own experiences. The perspective I take here insists on recognizing the ways that subjectivities and moral experiences are jointly constructed through talk and actions. Social actors render and refract understandings of themselves, of their own ethical actions and those of others, and of the broader social context. They shape reality through their ongoing social and linguistic interactions in dynamic and creative ways. But they do not do this alone or in ways that they entirely control. By tracing the presuppositions and shifting participant roles that tie scene and situation together, I reveal the ways characters and social actors produce social and moral hierarchies, including those that intertwine gender and racial subordination while obscuring violence in the play and in everyday life. To understand the play requires that we appreciate the context in which it is embedded, including the ways individuals may mobilize the drama to navigate a social situation.

Young women in Palomitáy negotiate social hierarchies even as they present themselves *as* and *to* diversely positioned others. Young women may align with, or distance themselves from, Natasia. The content of *Natasia's Story* offers a fairly straightforward rendering of a young woman as she overcomes obstacles, a reading that incorporates the hegemonic discourse of a shift from one category to another, from "indian" to "mestizo." However, by focusing on non-referential content, and especially the unspoken or implicit meanings that emerge between scene and situation, a more complicated view emerges. The disjunctures between the utterances of characters and the spoken or overheard, past or imagined, utterances of social actors, offer a complicated layering of frames. This allows for multiple interpretations of utterances and events and reveals the complex interactional web of ordinary talk that expands our understanding of young women's "voices."

Just how Natasia identifies herself, or how young mothers identify *themselves*, is ambiguous and negotiated in the ongoing social dynamics of everyday relationships. Of course, several everyday dramas occurred over the months that I conducted fieldwork in the home; some were mundane and others significant. In the example I describe, Maya's attempt to deal with a moral dilemma enveloped her and the other participants in negotiations around relationships and social identities onstage and offstage. At one level the negotiations centered on Maya lending another young mother some money; more broadly, Maya and other residents navigate the relative wealth among them, the limits on their earning power, and the power of the institution that requires them to give to others. At the same time, Maya is worried over her self-presentation in the play—her feelings of shame (*vergüenza*) and ambivalence are partly about the ways in which the main character, Natasia, was interlinked with herself. Maya's uncertainties over the kinds of social relationships and obligations demanded of her (for which she had little precedent) are laminated onto other uncertainties, including being able to keep and raise her daughter. Maya refused to perform the role of Natasia as she attempted to figure out her positioning in relation to other girls at the home and her sense of herself as a moral person.

I also show that performers frame Natasia as a daughter more than as a mother, and in this way I also shed light on the ways that Palomitáy residents envision themselves as daughters. Throughout the play, performers enact Natasia's relationships with kin—her father and brothers, her aunt, and her mother—and her efforts to navigate these and other relationships and events in her life. Natasia's reunion with her mother, who takes her in and cares for her until she achieves success, provides an implicit contrast to (and critique of) the other people in Natasia's life. Ultimately, Natasia is successful. The referential content of the drama presents the possibility of individually overcoming obstacles conditioned by racial, class, and gendered inequalities (becoming a successful entrepreneur). My analysis illuminates a more ambiguous set of relationships and entangled meanings in which young women tacitly consent to stereotypes of women and indigenous people, and to the structural underpinnings of gender and racial hierarchies, even as they challenge the hierarchies upon which narratives of upward mobility rely.

Girls navigate moral dilemmas that cannot be completely controlled by any individual. By reflecting on the interpretive constraints as well as "improvisational possibilities" (Joseph 1998, 8) of this socially and linguistically heterogeneous arena, I enrich understanding of the dynamic and contingent ways people engage in moral life. Any communicative interaction has some degree of creativity; participants may interpret the ongoing talk in variable ways; the outcome of interactions is uncertain. In the third scene, young women convey moral evaluations through their performance even as the characters in the play position themselves vis-á-vis other characters and situations. Throughout the performance of the drama *Natasia's Story*, young women engage in an embodied and interactive practice that produces meanings, including meanings that develop moment by moment, among characters, among actors, and between characters, actors, and audience members. The final scene shifts to a creative and aspirational frame in which young women are daughters as much as mothers.

As Cheryl Mattingly argues, "narrative provides a useful approach for investigating projects of moral becoming riddled by uncertain possibilities and informed by pluralistic moral values, concerns, and communities" (2014, 20). When the young women at Palomitáy "storied" aspects of their own experiences as they developed the play, they shaped the events of their individual lives toward common contours, collaborating with each other to jointly author a singular narrative. When they performed the play, the actors worked with each other as well as with audience members to maintain the situation, leaving unspoken certain assumptions and allowing for multiple interpretations. People participate together, often below their level of awareness, to produce complex activities and reinforce sometimes hegemonic understandings of the world but also to engage in moral experiences of everyday life.

Conclusion

THE LAST TIME I SAW JENI was as she stepped onto a *combi* with her daughter. Ángela was seven and wearing an "Angry Birds" backpack. Jeni was twenty and wearing jeans and a turquoise blouse. We had met at the bus stop that was on her route from home to Ángela's school. We found a kiosk where I bought coffee and sweet rolls for all of us. After we dropped off Ángela, Jeni told me that she had only a short time to run errands before reporting to work. I asked her, "How's it been? How are you doing?"

In the three years since I had been to Cusco, Jeni and Ángela had moved out of Palomitáy. At first she was happy about the freedom, she said. She had found a job as a housekeeper in a hotel, which had good hours, but she was fired from that job after she told her boss that she was afraid to clean the room of a patron who had forced himself on her. Although she found another job, in a restaurant, the hours were very long, and because she had no one to help her pick up Ángela from school, she had to quit. Earning enough money to pay for their room was difficult until she met a young man. She liked him, and they decided to move in together. They lived together for five months and shared the cost of some furniture and household items. One day when she came home from work, he—and everything in the apartment—was gone. It was in that crisis that she went to Palomitáy and asked for help. Rosa suggested that Jeni find a room to rent near Palomitáy so that Ángela could go to the nearby school and then come to the residence after school each day. She had recommended this to Jeni previously, but Jeni had refused. Now Jeni agreed to accept this offer of support in the form of childcare.

When I went to Cusco for follow-up research in 2013, I knew that many of the residents whom I had come to know in 2009–2010 would no longer be living at Palomitáy. I had hoped to find a few of them at the residence or in the city. Nilda gave me a huge smile and embraced me when I came over to her to say hello as she was working on a history project. She was now attending school on Saturdays; she was close to finishing high school but would not graduate before she turned eighteen and had to leave. Her son was in the local public school. A few days later, Faviola and I sat down to chat. She had graduated and was attending a training program for nursing. "I don't attend most of the workshops now because my classes are in the city center," she noted proudly. She had been close friends with Yaneth, so I asked if she knew how she was doing. Faviola sighed, "I don't know," she admitted. "Maybe she went back to her community."

Katia and Teresa, the nursery room staff, told me of their growing families. I played with the young toddlers, balancing plastic blocks on my head and walking across the room and then having them follow me with blocks on their heads. I asked about Laura. Katia told me that the last they had heard about her was when Faviola had bumped into her in a Cusco market. Laura had been transferred back to her family. "They had never mistreated her," noted Katia. "It's just that they could not afford to feed another mouth. But Laura could never adjust to life here [in Palomitáy.]" Faviola had asked Laura how she and her daughter were doing, but Laura refused to enter into conversation. "Faviola said that she had another baby on her back and her daughter was there with her too. And they all looked ok, so maybe they are fine." Marina, as I have already noted, was studying at the university. Mónica had planned to return to her family in a small community in the sierra. Her father visited her regularly while she was at Palomitáy, sometimes bringing food or clothing. No one at Palomitáy knew how she was faring.

Palomitáy does not maintain contact with young women once they leave, and I was unable to locate the other young women who had participated in my research. In spite of Rosa knowing of Jeni's whereabouts, it was several days before I actually saw her. Jeni started her day early in the morning, getting Ángela ready for school and dropping her off; she worked in a small restaurant, a *pollería*, but rarely could leave before 9 p.m. After a few days of missing each other at Palomitáy, I got directions and stopped into the pollería, a tiny, dim place situated between car garages and furniture factories. It was decidedly not a restaurant aimed at tourists, but I bought a chicken dinner and drank an Inca Cola, as Jeni ran between customers. We were not able to talk that night, but as I left, we agreed on a plan to meet that Monday morning. "Ideally, young women become independent," Rosa pointed out. "Some do not want to remember this time in their lives. But sometimes, a former resident will show up at the door just to thank us for helping them."

On another evening, I talked with Noelia, who had been the educational coordinator during my fieldwork period but was herself back in school. I had asked her whether many young women returned to their communities after leaving Palomitáy. Noelia shrugged and said, "It's not easy for the mothers who have been here to return to their communities. They learn things. They see things differently. They don't want to be treated the same way because they know their rights." Noelia had been one of Palomitáy's first residents. Her son was born when Noelia was just twelve years old. From Rosa's perspective, Noelia had grown up *with* her son in Palomitáy. Like many of the young women who pass through Palomitáy's doors, she attended school, participated in workshops, learned about human rights and family planning; later, she began to teach these things to other young women. As Noelia pointed out to me, living at Palomitáy shapes a person, and not just by learning to care for children in particular ways but also by being cared for by others.

In this book, I trace the ways individuals come to see themselves—as urban, as modern, as youth, as students, as daughters, and especially, as mothers. I have argued that identifying as a mother is a dynamic and processual aspect of subjectivity. Moreover, attending to the ways that young women at Palomitáy navigate the contingencies of relationships illuminates not only motherhood but their agentive action within structured hierarchies. Of course, these young women are uniquely positioned. They live in a group home for young mothers rather than in a community in the rural sierra or an urban neighborhood; they do not live with relatives, partners, or on their own. In many ways they navigate within a context that overdetermines their identification as mothers. Broad public discourses, state policies, moral regimes, and humanitarian efforts govern the reproductive lives of these and other young women. Thus, in their efforts to imagine and enact themselves as mothers, these young women navigate various moralizing and affective discourses that reinforce particular ways of being a mother, a worker, a citizen in neoliberal Peru.

Even as young women are framed *as mothers*, their lives and subjectivities are neither unidimensional nor static. To illuminate the hopes and uncertainties, moral dilemmas, and mundane experiences of young women at Palomitáy, I highlight individuals' involvement with each other through specific moments of interaction and in various *situations*. I consider individuals' explicitly stated understandings as well as their creative expression to trace the temporal and dynamic processes of coming to understand oneself, of maintaining social relationships, and of "making life better" even in uncertain circumstances. To understand young women's caring practices, and their developing senses of self, requires attending to individuals' dialogical engagements with others and their mobilization of resources (materials, relationships, commodities) that are thoroughly embedded in a global arena.

From this perspective, young women's self-understanding, or subjectivity, as mothers is partially shaped by the humanitarian organization's emphasis on a unitary mother and child. Moreover, mothering becomes a significant facet through which girls counter moralizing discourses and challenge the constraints on their everyday relationships. Women—and more specifically, mothers—are often expected or obligated to do the labor of care, often with little or no remuneration for or acknowledgment of the significance of that labor (Folbre 2002). Residents are separated from relatives or community and encouraged to be themselves and their children, and affectively bonded to their children. Emphasis on the mother's responsibility—whether she received support from an institution like Palomitáy or not—sets out a clearly defined locus of labor, resources, and sociality from which children are expected to be supported. Moreover, the majority of the staff and volunteers who help to care for these young mothers and their children are also mostly girls and women, which further reinforces the feminization of this intimate labor. Thus, the practices aimed at establishing these bonds of tenderness enable girls to deal with potentially difficult circumstances but also do important ideological work.

This moral and affective orientation may empower young women to challenge their circumstances within a situational and national context that is highly constrained. Mobilizing this affective discourse may also reinforce, even intensify, certain forms of systematic structural inequality. Palomitáy's residents, and women and youth in Peru more generally, are embedded in contexts of hierarchy that are shaped by broad social, political, and economic relationships. Racial and (hetero)sexual oppression, everyday violence, and global capitalism are intertwined realities, not easily separated in everyday life. These relationships are crucial to understanding not only contemporary global politics but also intimacies and hierarchies of social and affective ties. The broad structures and historical circumstances that shape these young women's paths to Palomitáy do not disappear while they attend classes and workshops and care for their children. By pursuing educational aspirations and modern sensibilities within Palomitáy, young women may challenge their circumstances. Once they leave the home, the lack of affordable and secure housing, unequal access to education, dearth of jobs paying a living wage, civil codes that control women's sexual and reproductive choices, and structural and interpersonal violence of multiple kinds continue to impact their lives and the lives of their children.

Understanding moral experience and intimate involvement in Palomitáy is important—not only to the individuals who pass through the front gate. Reflecting on Palomitáy enables a deeper understanding of how affective relationships, morality, and entrenched social, political, and economic inequalities are entangled with and lived by individuals. I have focused on the contingent and dynamic ways in which individuals identify themselves and make sense of their lives while living at Palomitáy. Of course, their senses of self and of moral personhood are tied to past experiences, present interactions, and future imaginings. In the following pages, I reflect on the implications of my analysis of young women's mundane talk and creative expression for anthropological approaches to gender and family in the Andes, care in the context of global capitalism, and uncertainty and creativity in our interpretations of moral experience.

Rethinking Relatedness

Attending to the lives and relationships of young women at Palomitáy challenges anthropologists to develop flexible and incisive analytical frames to interpret gender and relatedness in the contemporary Andes. Jeni's emphasis that "just me and my child are enough" unearths the assumption of compulsory heterosexuality embedded in Andean notions of duality, state and church gender ideologies, and anthropological analyses. Jeni's statement also has to be understood alongside the complex and divergent perspectives of other young women and Jeni's own shifting understandings of self over time. Some girls imagine a boyfriend or husband in their futures; others do not conceive of marriage as possible or even desirable. Some girls have encountered ideologies of gender and kinship in schools and churches, print and visual media, households and courtrooms, and among the national and foreign staff and volunteers at the home. Individuals may try out certain ideas, position themselves in certain circumstances but not others, or reassess their aims. How they build their lives and establish social connections, then, requires attention to both the mobility of bodies and of ideas and to the contemporaneity of discourses. Their experiences and desires cannot be explained by or contained within the concept but challenge us to consider the limitations and extensions of complementary opposition as a locus of gender and kinship relations in the Andes.

For decades now, feminist scholars and activists have incorporated attention to intersectionality, to the mutual shaping of experience through gendered, racial, class, and sexual hierarchies. The young mothers at Palomitáy do not simply follow the ideologies of gender and family promoted by the home or model themselves on the people around them, but they engage with them in ambiguous and creative ways. They also develop empathetic relationships with people in the home. This analysis challenges us to recognize and take seriously the relationships among women and the ways that affective and supportive relationships of apprenticeship enable girls to express subjectivities, to reframe or envision themselves (as modern girls or virtuous mothers), and to see the world in different ways.

Individuals in the highland Andes engage in processes to make people into kin—to establish and/or dissolve "relatedness" through everyday practices and ritualized events. Yet the presumption that mothers are defined by birth of a child is at once pervasive and contested in Palomitáy. Whereas individuals do not solely rely upon notions of genetic or biological reproduction, this case suggests that we direct attention to specific contexts in which "biological" relationships are differentially significant. Structurally, the obligation of a mother to care for a biological child is entrenched by the state and naturalized within the NGO in ways that the obligation of a father to care for a biological child is not. Young women live in the home because of a pregnancy, and although pregnancy is an insufficient condition, it is a necessary one. Palomitáy offers young women the possibility of relinquishing a child for adoption, and staff members may talk with young mothers about the ways that giving up a child may be an act of love. However, the home works within the broader parameters of the state and reinforces the unity and salience of mother and child.

Whether a young woman keeps her child or puts her child up for adoption, she must engage with hegemonic understandings of family and gender that assume mother and child as the predominant relationship. This case raises theoretical and ethnographic questions that seep into the cracks of monolithic orientations. To develop a contemporary and complex, sensitive and robust analysis of gender and kinship, we need to recognize the multiple, sometimes contradictory, yet mutually reinforcing discourses that circulate in the region. We also need to enrich understandings of affective and social bonds with attention to racial and class oppressions as well as gendered hierarchies. Race and affect are mutually implicated as young women produce a sense of themselves as mothers and navigate the opportunities and constraints of the institution in which they live. Removed from families and from extended frameworks of sociality in communities, native Andean practices and conceptions of relatedness are obscured. Yet mundane practices and moral discourses of mothering, and of care more generally, are cross-cut by class and racialized hierarchies.

Caring (for) Youth

My discussion also encourages further reflection on the circulations of care globally, and in particular the articulation of discourses of youth and hierarchies of care in local contexts. Focusing on care enriches understanding of these relationships by drawing into a singular frame the practices and discourses around young women as mothers and as vulnerable youth, the transnational circulation of people, ideas, and commodities that ground humanitarianism, and the activities and understandings of living better that emerge in contemporary Peru, where the state has consistently withdrawn support from women and children.

As Mendoza-Denton and Boum (2015) point out, we can learn a great deal about how the state positions its citizens and the norms around youth in any particular society based upon discussion of those who are exceptional or "breach" cases. "For actors to participate in the body politic, they must be ratified to do so, and the erection of barriers to their participation in society takes place in the heated boundaries between actors that are considered competent versus those considered incompetent to make their own decisions" (Mendoza-Denton and Boum 2015, 296). Anthropologists have shown that children and youth are taken up as symbols of the nation. Young mothers, such as those who live at Palomitáy, challenge us to recognize the ways that institutions and individuals, religious and state authorities, adults and youth, shape the boundaries of the very category of "youth" or "child." Just who is competent and capable, who gains access to which resources, who establishes relationships, who is cared for by others, and who does the unpaid labor of care extends into the everyday negotiation of relationships among individuals.

My analysis suggests that attending to the various situations in which an individual is framed as, or claims belonging to, the categories of youth or adult may illuminate relations of power. The young women live in Palomitáy because they are minors, younger than eighteen years old. Removed from their families by the state, they are placed in the custody of an NGO-run orphanage. Yet many of these young women originally went to the state for assistance when they found themselves pregnant. The majority were framed as sexual agents and adults. The staff and volunteers in Palomitáy consistently frame these young women as mothers, reinforcing their responsibilities and obligations as adults in the mother-child relationship. At the same time, within Palomitáy, young mothers are also viewed as youth, in need of educational and enrichment opportunities, play and emotional support, structure and material help. Young women themselves actively navigate these relationships and boundaries. They take responsibility for their children and exhibit and take pride in their caretaking skills. They also position themselves as youth—not adults—who enjoy attending school and hanging out with friends, and they chafe at the strictures that constrain their relationships. Sometimes they express jealousy for the care their infants and toddlers receive, and they express sadness at their isolation from their own mothers and from the other people who may care for them.

My analysis suggests that the actions, creative interventions, and everyday practices of youth are both shaped by wider cultural relationships and are transforming or shaping them. By mobilizing the discourse of mother and child, young women may challenge the constraints of personal circumstances and navigate broader structural inequalities in contemporary Peru. Some young women strengthen their sense of self, forge intimate connections with their children, and garner some of the social and cultural capital necessary for supporting themselves and their children in the future while living in Palomitáy. At the same time, for a young woman to become a (modern) mother requires that she reconfigure, reframe, and at times undermine particular practices and ideals while reinforcing others.

Children and youth in the Andes actively engage in determining their life courses: they migrate from rural communities at early ages, pursue educational goals, labor in their family's agricultural plots or in the households of strangers, spend their earnings and pursue romance, and care for themselves and for others. By acknowledging that young parents are active social agents and by asking how their capacity to act (and their political and social status) may be constrained differently than that of adults, this book also contributes to recent theoretical approaches that forefront children and youth as social actors who are engaged in producing cultural meanings and relationships.

In the process of exploring how young women come to see themselves as mothers, I also have touched on the ways subjectivities of care intertwine racial and class discourses with affective and moral orientations. Young mothers, not young fathers, live in the home and care for children. Primarily young women volunteer in the home and participate in the work of care. The presence of a set of caregivers for children, all of whom identify as girls and women, reinforces the gendered aspect of parenting regardless of class or nationality. The labor of care also racializes young Peruvian women, even as they practice more "modern" forms of care. I have argued that this case illuminates the transnational class and racial privileges that separate some caregivers from others. The young mothers know the exhaustion of waking up in the middle of the night, night after night, to care for a child. They experience the stress of finding work to support a child in an economy where very little well-paid work is available. They express the sorrow and anger of not being able to afford medical care for a sick child and the frustration of giving up educational opportunities and relationships with friends. Some take on the care for another that extends over the course of many years. Some allow themselves to love or become attached to a child in a way that generates an ongoing material, psychological, and affective relationship. Reflecting on Palomitáy shows how caring for another, or being cared for, may be tied to the stratification of privileges and constraints, shaping moral experience under neoliberal capitalism.

Moral Entanglements, Embodied Involvement

The young women I describe in these pages face moral and ethical dilemmas, not the least of which is how to best care for a child. Of course, we all encounter dilemmas in our own lives. We all engage in moral thinking—sometimes in quite habitual ways—as we navigate our relationships among loved ones and neighbors, coworkers and classmates, acquaintances and strangers. We present ourselves as good people at the same time that the contingencies and ambiguities of events and interactions mean that this is a presentation that must constantly be negotiated. Sometimes fleeting moments of ambiguity or moral deliberation are arenas in which individuals interactively produce a sense of self and sensibilities of sociality in ordinary life.

I focus on young women who enter the home as residents in order to trace the governance of care and the everyday contours of moral experience. I take a dialogical perspective to demonstrate that moral experience requires attention to individuals' involvement with each other. As Agamben (1993, 19; cited in Ochs 2012, 152) notes, "we understand little about how embodied, situated enactments of language *in situ* articulate with thinking, feeling, consciousness, and the 'incessant emergence' of existence." I show that young women enact self and other in situated and embodied interactions, such as performing a play or taking photographs or chatting with each other. I argue for attention to both the micro-politics of interaction and the macro-politics of social and historical relationships to explore ways of being good and having a good life.

This ethnographic case also contributes to a broader exploration of moral discourse and hierarchy in everyday life. Publicly circulating moral discourses and entangled hierarchies of power may shape individual practices and understandings. Yet just how social actors engage with each other in the world is not clear at the outset of an interaction. What people say to each other, how they interpret a situation, come to love another, access support, or reject a relationship are fundamentally based in interactions that require joint effort. To focus simply on what people *say* without also acknowledging the temporal and ongoing and uncertain character of linguistic interaction is to miss a fundamental character of human life. The words spoken do not have meaning on their own. People interpret their spatial and temporal relations to the world, access unequally shared material and symbolic resources, and involve themselves with other people and with objects in various situations.

This creates challenges and opportunities for ethnographic research. A researcher (or some other individual) might lift a conversation or an utterance from the context, transcribe and translate it, and then freeze it into place in a written text. However, in living ongoing interactions, we as humans make sense of the world in complicated ways, mobilizing visual, aural, tactile, and kinesthetic resources that cannot be conveyed easily on the page. Individuals may interact with each other without knowing what their interlocutors know or think. Miscommunication and ambiguity as well as creativity and flexibility abound in our communicative interactions. Moreover, individuals may align themselves with or distance themselves from each other, and negotiate relationships of belonging and alterity in tacit and overt ways. These are crucial aspects of participation that link interactional practices to broader political and economic contexts.

To make sense of intertwined moral discourses and entrenched social, political, and economic hierarchies, anthropologists might attend to the micropolitics of situations as well as broader historical relationships or arrays of semiotic meanings. A play, or a photograph, or a conversation emerges in a specific context—not in a vacuum. To take seriously the heterogeneity of social contexts and participants means that we recognize the uncertainty and the possibilities of interaction. People have unequal access to material and ideational resources, to forms of knowledge and experience. This requires that anthropologists trace the ways that participants are tied to each other, to institutions, to places, and to layered dialogues in diverse ways. By exploring the relationships and interactions among these young mothers, we may gain a more nuanced perspective on care and on moral engagement as imagined and enacted. People become involved with each other in social relationships and within institutions, even when they may not completely consent to them. Bringing attention to intimate involvement, we might understand the ways individuals experience the world as moral persons and navigate global relationships of power in embodied and affective relationships.

Ethnographic Engagement

Unlike many travelers, anthropologists are trained to consider the presumptions, schemas, and unmarked background against which we assess others. This does not mean that we are always aware of biases and habitual understandings. For instance, "third world feminists argue that development interventions are largely—if contradictorily and incompletely—premised on North-South postcolonial relations and that white/Western feminist do not speak from a position of neutrality or innocence in these debates" (Radcliffe et al. 2004, 389; see also Escobar 1995; Mohanty 1984; Mignolo and Schiwy 2003). While anthropologists aim for openness to different standards and categories, we also recognize the ways these standards of morality and "proper" behavior are developed and keyed to political, economic, and social inequalities, to relations of power that are personal, local, national, and global in scope. In an institution like Palomitáy, people presume hegemonic understandings of time and place, of family and gender, that insert poor or indigenous people into the present in ways that normalize non-native histories, geographies, and expectations (Dhillon 2017; Povinelli 2006; Rifkin 2017).

In writing about girls as young as twelve who have given birth and are in the process of learning the responsibilities and rewards of parenting, I have had to reflect on the embodied protections and cherished privileges of security that class and race, if not gender, have afforded me and my own daughters. Hearing, reading, and remembering young women's stories, I have felt stymied by the enormity and long-standing intractability of the problem of intimate violence. I have been humbled by the efforts that individuals working in organizations such as Palomitáy have made to ameliorate the suffering of children and youth, to create contexts in which young people might access support, and to provide foundation for future well-being. At the same time, I have attempted to convey the ways racial and class inequalities are consistently reproduced inside and outside these homes.

In addition to writing about mothering as keyed to social and political relationships and precarities, Scheper-Hughes (1992) acknowledges that women in Bom de Jesus demanded that she act as a companion, not just a researcher. She offers a vision of how anthropologists might respond to, as well as record, the lives and deaths of marginalized people. My research subjects voiced few such demands. Perhaps this was because of the differences in our ages and structural positions. (I had not previously known them in the ways that Scheper-Hughes had known some of her interlocutors from previous years as a Peace Corps volunteer and community organizer.) Perhaps the residents of

Palomitáy had become accustomed to the constant movement of individuals from the United States and the Netherlands, Spain and Great Britain, France and Canada in and out of their lives and were cautious (for this and other reasons) of making attachments. Nevertheless, to write with both respect and compassion requires some attempt to address even unspoken requests.

Ethical standards in anthropology include the principle to enhance rather than detract from the well-being and dignity of those with whom we interact. Doing ethnographic research with young women in this particular organization, I am mindful that anthropological efforts to respect the rights of others, avoid harm, and enhance the lives of those with whom we interact is always an ambivalent endeavor. We encounter individuals who are differently positioned and who might have very different understandings of what obligations or potential harms might mean. Attempts to do no harm, like attempts to care (for example, Stevenson 2014), may have unintended consequences. To recognize the humanity of individuals requires that I simultaneously acknowledge that my presence also supports an institution that is saturated by inequalities. Jeni and other young women are embedded in arrays of relationships, shaped by circulating ideologies of care or moral comportment and by broad structures of racial, class, and gendered inequality. The young women in the book who are residents—and, of course, the directors and staff, interns and volunteers, and me—all at various moments speak against power and support it. Tracing the dialogical interactions among people, including the ways that we become tied up in producing power, is one pathway toward conveying the humanity of the people with whom we interact and the complexity of the social, political, and economic relationships in which all of us live.

Glossary

All terms are Spanish unless indicated otherwise.

almuerzo	lunch, main meal of the day
campesino	someone who lives in the rural regions of Peru, peasant, often of a lower socioeconomic class or indigenous heritage
chicas	girls, usually older girls and young women
ch'uñu (Quechua)	freeze-dried potatoes, a staple food produced and consumed throughout the Andes
comadre	the godmother of one's child
combi	shared minibus that travels set routes
compadrazgo	spiritual or ritual kin
compadres	godparent of one's child, co-parents, spiritual kin
cumbia	music and dance style of Colombia, popular throughout Latin America
cuna	used to refer to the nursery, also cradle or crib
de modo	in style, stylish, modern
empleada	maid, often a girl or young woman working in a non-relative's household
gente decente	"decent people," often elites of Spanish descent, of a higher socioeconomic class
llik'lla (Quechua)	traditional carrying cloth, may be handwoven or machine-made
madrina	godmother
mamás	mothers

mazamorra morada	traditional Peruvian pudding
mestizo	the normative racial category, often in symbolic opposition to serrano; someone of mixed Spanish and indigenous descent
novio	boyfriend or fiancé
Pachamama (Quechua)	Mother Earth, an animate, gendered, sacred space-time in Andean cosmology
padrinos	godparents
papas fritas	french fries
patrones	employers, bosses
platos típicos	traditional Peruvian dishes
pollera	traditional full skirt worn by indigenous women in the sierra
pollería	restaurant specializing in broiled chicken
retablo	tableau, or traditional Catholic portraits depicting Madonna and Child
sapalla (Quechua)	alone, or "just by myself"
serrana/o(s)	a person from the sierra, indigenous woman or man, sometimes derogatory
superarse	to improve oneself, to exceed or go above and beyond
taller(es)	workshop(s), may indicate a program or a space
vergüenza	shame or embarrassment
violación	rape, or sexual violence more generally

Notes

Chapter 1. Young Mothers, Moral Experience, and the Politics of Care

1. All of the names of organizations and individuals (except government bodies or officials) are pseudonyms.

2. I interchange the terms "girls," "young women," "residents," and "young mothers" in reference to the clients of Palomitáy to indicate the dynamic aspect of their self-identification. Young mothers typically referred to themselves as "girls" (*chicas*); staff most often referred to them as "mothers" (*mamás*). I use the term "children" to refer to the sons and daughters of Palomitáy's primary clients.

3. Lauren Berlant develops the notion of "cruel optimism" to describe a relation "when something you desire is actually an obstacle to your flourishing" (2011:1) or "the condition of maintaining an attachment to a significantly problematic object" (2011:24). In particular she considers people's affective attachment to what we call "the good life," which is "for so many a bad life that wears out the subjects who nonetheless, and at the same time, find their conditions of possibility within it" (2011:27).

4. On everyday material and affective practices and interactions of relatedness in the Andes, see among many Allen 2002, 2011; Anderson 2009; Babb 2018; Bastia 2009; Leinaweaver 2007, 2008a; Rae-Espinoza 2010; Roberts 2012a; Tapias 2006, 2016; Van Vleet 2002, 2006, 2008; Walmsley 2008; Weismantel 1995.

5. On complementary opposition see among others Allen 2002, 2011; Babb 2018; Burman 2011; de la Cadena 1995; Forstner 2013; Harris 1978; Paulson and Bailey 2003; Van Vleet 2008.

6. See Alcalde 1995, 2010; Boesten 2010; Campoamor 2016; Cáceres et al. 2008; Crain 1994; Francke 1990; Fuller 2003; Lind 2003; Lutrell-Rowland 2012; Roberts 2012a, 2012b. I discuss this further in chapter 2. See also Fonseca 2003, 1986 and Seligmann 2009 on sex, gender, and the state and Tapias 2016, 2006 on motherhood.

7. See http://www.npr.org/sections/parallels/2015/12/14/459098779/all-across-latin
-america-unwed-mothers-are-now-the-norm, accessed March 29, 2016. Single mothers are increasing worldwide; however, the broader social, political, and economic
relationships that shape the contours of this demographic shift may be differently
configured in specific places.

8. I use the concept of a "good life" in a general sense, drawing from anthropology
of morality and ordinary ethics. See especially Mattingly 2014. Also see Das 2012;
Fischer 2014; Lambeck 2010; Zigon and Throop 2014. A more specific but extensive
literature on "living well" (or "*sumaq kawsay*" in Quechua, or "*buen vivir*" in Spanish) has developed around indigenous social movements and development in the
Andes. See, for instance, Bastian 2012; Colloredo-Mansfeld 2009; Huanacuni 2010;
Postero and Zamosc 2004; Pribilsky 2016; Radcliffe et al. 2004; Villaba 2013; Viola
2014; Whitten and Whitten 2015.

9. Anthropologists have argued for more ethnographic accounts of individuals
engaged in ethical or moral endeavors in a variety of circumstances. See among many
Das 2010, 2012; Fassin 2011, 2013; Fassin and Das 2012; Fassin et al. 2008; Fiske and
Mason 1990; Gooldin 2008; Lambek 2010; Ochs and Kremer-Sadlik 2007; Robbins
2007; Throop 2003, 2010; Willen 2014; Zigon 2007, 2013; Zigon and Throop 2014.

10. Kimberlé Crenshaw 1991 coined the term "intersectionality"; several texts fore-
shadowed use of this term, including Anzaldúa 1987; Combahee River Collective
1983; Mohanty 1984; Moraga and Anzaldúa 1981. On methodological complexities
of intersectional analysis, see Khandelwal 2009; McCall 2005.

11. The passage from which this is drawn reads: "The understanding of agency that
I propose, which I call 'active subjectivity' and which I contrast with the influential
understanding of agency of late modernity, is highly attenuated. It does not presuppose the individual subject and it does not presuppose collective intentionality of
collectivities of the same. It is adumbrated to consciousness by a moving with people,
by the difficulties as well as the concrete possibilities of such movings. It is a sense of
intentionality that we can reinforce and sense as lively in paying attention to people
and to the enormously variegated ways of connection among people without privileg-
ing the word or a monological understanding of sense. We can reinforce and influence
the direction of intention in small ways by sensing/understanding the movement of
desires, beliefs, and signs among people" (Lugones 2003:6). For feminist decolonial
perspectives, also see Alexander 1994; Álvarez et al. 2003; Babb 2018; Duarte Bastian
2012; Franke 1990; Grewal and Kaplan 1994; Khandelwal 2009; Lugones 2007, 2014.

12. Several linguistic anthropologists have expanded on the classic formulations
of dialogism in Bakhtin 1981 and Vološinov 1986. See Irvine 1996, 1995; Mannheim
and Tedlock 1995; Mannheim and Van Vleet 1998; Tomlinson 2017.

13. For influential approaches to language as social action or ethnography of speaking, see Ahearn 2001; Basso 1985; Bauman 1977; Bauman and Briggs 1990; Duranti
and Goodwin 1992; Gal 1991; Goodwin and Goodwin 2000; Goodwin 2006; Hanks
1990; Irvine 1996; Mannheim 2015a; McElhinney 2007; Ochs 1992; Ochs and Capps
2001; Tedlock and Mannheim, eds. 1995; Urban 1991.

14. In "everyday" assumptions about language in the United States, talk consists of the "utterances" (words, phrases) that speakers and hearers exchange as if they were throwing a ball back and forth. Many cultural anthropologists and other scholars rely on this "everyday" concept of language and only consider the symbolic meaning of language. Ochs (2012:143–44) points out that linguistic anthropologists, in contrast, "look deeply into the manifold ways in which the temporal unfolding of language in and across situations—not just words but phonology, morphology, syntax, and discourse—is implicated in moment-to-moment thinking, feeling, and being in the world." Linguistic anthropologists analyze the complex ways talk and experience are intertwined.

15. See Goffman 1981, 1974; Goodwin 2006; Goodwin and Goodwin 2000; Irvine 1996 for further discussion of participation.

16. The Inca civilization, the largest in pre-Columbian America, developed from highland populations sometime in the early thirteenth century and probably reached its height between 1438 and 1533, when the Incas controlled a territory stretching from southern parts of Columbian to northern Argentina and Chile.

17. Much of the tourism industry is in foreign hands, and revenues from tourism mostly return to other countries. See Babb 2010, 2012; Ypeij and Zoomers 2006; Steel 2008.

18. This description is based on Palomitáy's intake documents, 2000–2012. For further discussion of sexual violence, see chapter 2.

19. See especially Luttrell-Rowland 2012 on Demunas in Peru.

20. In the United States, sexual reproduction, and genetic or biological ties, are typically presumed to be the "natural" grounding of those affective and economic relationships that we call family (Yanagisako and Delaney 1995; Franklin and McKinnon 2002). People in other cultural contexts may rely upon different ontological grounds. Additionally, economic, gendered, and racial inequalities and national and global processes (including the movements of ideas, technologies, and of children themselves) shape the reproduction and kinship in various contexts. See Adams and Pigg 2005; Anderson 2009; Briggs 2012; Browner and Sargent 2011; Carsten, ed. 2000; Cole and Durham 2008; Curtis 2009; Fonseca 2003, 1986; Ginsburg and Rapp 1991, 1995; Ragoné and Twine, eds. 2000; Roberts 2012a, 2012b; Scheper-Hughes 1992; Seligmann 2009; Volkman 2005.

21. On mothering, see, for instance, Barlow 2010; Barlow and Chapin 2010; Bejarano 2002; Briggs 2012; Campoamor 2016; Fuentes 2013; Mattingly 2014; Rae-Espinoza 2010; Scheper-Hughes 1992; Tapias 2016, 2006.

22. McElhinney (2010:317) notes that analyses of paid caring labor draw attention to "the interaction of the negative impact of structural adjustment policies in the Global South with the privatization of health, elder care, and child care in the Global North and the tragic irony of Third World women supporting their own families by leaving them to care for First World families." On caring, intimate, or affective labor, see Adams and Dickey, eds. 2000; Barker and Susan Feiner 2009; Blofiled 2012; Boris and Salazar 2010; Colen 1995; Folbre 2002; Glenn 2010; Han

2011; Hennessy and Ingraham 1997; Himmelweit 2013; Nouvet 2014; Pande 2014; Stevenson 2014.

23. On children as caregivers, see Cheney 2017; Cox 2015; Hunleth 2017; Leinaweaver 2008.

24. Many orphanages make contractual agreements with language institutes or local tourism companies. As an "independent" volunteer and researcher, I was asked to assist in some fashion (by teaching English, photography, or yoga classes, helping in the kitchen or garden, or supporting children with their homework). Service tourism and the experiences of foreign youth in Cusco is a fascinating topic for further analysis, but it is not one I pursue here. Nor do I explore foreign volunteers' conceptions of care, gender, motherhood, family, race, or nationality.

Chapter 2. Dimensions of Precarity and Possibility in Peru

1. On youth and children, generally, see for instance, Bucholtz 2002; Caputo 1995; Cole and Durham 2008; Curtis 2009; Durham 2004; James 2007; Korbin 2003; Mendoza-Denton and Boum 2015; Stephens 1995.

2. Approximately 15 percent of Peru's population is over the age of fifty-five. In comparison, in the United States the percentage of the population under twenty-five years old is just over 32 percent, and that over age fifty-five is approximately 28 percent. The twenty-five- to fifty-four-year-old population is the most similar, with 39.6 percent in the United States and 36.86 percent of people in Peru.

3. See Hunefeldt 2000, Premo 2005, Silverblatt 1987 on gender and family in colonial Peru. The concept of settler colonialism mostly has been used to analyze the continuing oppression and extraction of resources from Native and First Peoples in North American and Oceania. Speed (2017) argues that bringing attention to settler coloniality in conjunction with neoliberal capitalism deepens analysis of oppression in Latin American contexts. See Castellanos 2017; Castellanos et al. 2012; Wolfe 1999; Dhillon 2017; Quijano 2000.

4. Freeman 2014, Harvey 1989, 2005; Ong 2006, Tsing 2005.

5. On performativity theory, see Bucholtz and Hall 2005; Butler 1990, 1993; Kulick 2003; Hall 2001.

6. For further discussion of the ways patriarchalism intersects with race and class in the Andes, see for example Boesten 2010, 2014; Bueno-Hansen 2015; Burman 2011; Miles 2000; Oliart 2007; Roberts 2012a; Robillard 2010; Stephenson 1999; Weismantel 2001.

7. Patria potestad derives from canon law and persisted into the late twentieth century based on Peru's civil code (Htun 2003). Many laws in the civil code are related to family (including divorce, abortion, marriage) and understood to guide moral as well as social behavior (Htun 2003, 10–11). Stern (1995, 16) argues that patria potestad supported racial and gender distinctions in Mexico; in fact "gendered codes of honor and the social control of women and sexuality proved fundamental to the construction, perpetuation, and self-legitimation of the color-class order."

8. On the articulation of sexuality, reproduction, and religion in the region, see Anderson 2013; Cáceres et al. 2008; Guy 2000; Morgan 1997, 2014; Radliffe and Westwood 1993, 15–16; Yon 2014.

9. See Yon (2014, 109) on girls' notion that "being sexy was . . . a consubstantial dimension of beauty and modernity" in Ayacucho, Peru, incorporating fashion, among other aspects. Also see Feminias 2005.

10. Anthropologists of the Andean region have long acknowledged the intense discrimination faced by Quechua speakers in rural and urban contexts but have not always incorporated analytical attention to racism (Weismantel and Eisenman 1998, 121). See Berg 2015; Canessa 2005, 2012; de la Cadena 1991, 1995, 2000, 2005; Franco 2006; García 2005, 2013; Greene 2006, 2007; Haynes 2013; Oliart 2007; Rahier 2014; Seligmann 1993; Vasquez de Aguila 2014; Wade 1997; Weber 2013; Weismantel 2001; Whitten 2003, 2007. Also see Boesten 2014; Comisión de la Verdad y la Reconciliación 2003; Degregori 1991, 2002, 2015; de la Cadena 2003; Manrique 1995; 2002; Mantilla Falcón 2005a, 2005b, 2007; Portocarrero 2012; Theidon 2012 on race in relation to Peru's internal conflict.

11. On racial formation I draw on Omi and Winant 2015 [1986]; Martinez HoSang et al. 2012.

12. Huayhua (2014) notes that scholarly discussions of race often rely on the everyday conceptual categories (e.g. "indio," "mestizo," "criollo") developed in national urban contexts. Quechua and Aymara speakers do not use these categories but talk about themselves in terms of their national identity, language group, or ethnic or ayllu name, tying themselves to a specific location, or a relational and highly contextual belonging.

13. Also see Perez and Bendezú 2008; Mannheim 1991. Most North Americans and Europeans, who are operating within a different racial system and with little or no exposure to Quechua phonology or to variations in Spanish in the Andean region, are mostly unaware of these distinctions.

14. See for instance Canessa 2012; Leinaweaver 2008; Miles 2000; Van Vleet 2008 on discourses of "getting ahead." Berg (2014, 45–46) notes that notions of "improving oneself" or "advancing" are grounded in a broader history of migration and exchange as well as "moral and cultural imperatives about class mobility." Also see Alcalde 2018 on class in Peru.

15. See Anderson 2010; Degregori 1991; García 2005; Leinaweaver 2008a, 111–15, 117; Portocarrero and Oliart 1989 on education as a way out of poverty.

16. UN (2011) Population Statistics. Department of Social and Economic Affairs, Population Division. Per http://esa.un.org/unpd/wpp/unpp/panel_population.htm (accessed June 9, 2017), 56 percent of the population lives on the coast, 30 percent in the Andes, and 14 percent in the Amazon.

17. https://www.cia.gov/library/publications/the-world-factbook/geos/pe.html, accessed June 9, 2017.

18. Peru's second most populated city, Arequipa (840,000), is located in the southern sierra; its population is dwarfed by that of Lima (almost ten million).

19. The coastal region is ideologically associated with Peru's social, political, and economic elite, with Lima as the center of governance, industrialization, and modernity. The tropical lowland jungle of the sparsely populated Amazon Basin encompasses the traditional territories of diverse indigenous groups. Rich in natural resources, it is also the location of intense national and transnational commercial exploitation including agribusinesses, oil and natural gas extraction, and mining.

20. On migration see Alcalde 2018; Berg 2015; Mayer 2002; Ødegaard 2010; Parregard 2015.

21. The revolutionary efforts of Sendero Luminoso (Shining Path) officially began with an attack on a polling station in the Department of Ayacucho in 1980. The violence spread from the southern highlands to parts of the Amazonian region. The government imposed a state of emergency in 1982. As time wore on "a difficult-to-distinguish mix of conflicts: the 'popular war,' as Shining Path called its actions; the counterinsurgency battle; and internal settling of scores, common crimes, cattle rustling; and emerging conflicts as a result of displacements and refugees in existing settlements" (Boesten 2014, 3) engulfed the region. By the late 1980s, the internal conflict reached the city of Lima with Sendero Luminoso claiming responsibility for car bombs, coordinated power outages, and assassinations. The violence sharply declined after the detainment of Abimael Guzmán and other key leaders in 1992. No national peace accord or formalized end to hostilities or disarmament was enacted.

22. Of the more than sixty-nine thousand dead and disappeared, 75 percent were native speakers of Quechua or another indigenous language. Explaining how the insurgency developed and the conflict gained such force, scholars point to the entrenched social, political, and economic inequalities (especially cultural and racial discrimination against native populations and women), a centralized government, and a military response that failed to distinguish between civilians and insurgents and engaged in abuses of power. See Barrig, ed. 2007; Comisión de la Verdad y la Reconciliación 2003; Coral-Cordero 2005; Degregori 1991, 2015; de la Cadena 2003; Faverón-Patriau 2006; Henríquez-Ayín 2006; Manrique 1995; 2002; Mantilla Falcón 2005a, 2005b, 2007; Portocarrero 2012.

23. Available at: https://data.worldbank.org/indicator/SP.HOU.FEMA.ZS?end=2012 &locations=PE&start=1992&view=chart, accessed August 13, 2018.

24. Leinaweaver (2008a) argues that the circulation of children between households is tied to efforts to enhance familial survival and individual advancement as well as Andean kinship ideologies. Also see Anderson 2010; Van Vleet 2008; Walmsley 2008; Weismantel 1995.

25. On intimate violence in the Andean region see, among others, Alcalde 2010, 1995; Boesten 2010, 2015; Bunt 2008; Canessa 2005, 2012; Estremadoyro 2001; Gezmes et al. 2002; Mujica 2013; Van Vleet 2002. MIMDES is now the Ministry of Women and Vulnerable Populations (MIMP).

26. On sexual violence, especially related to Peru's internal conflict, see among others Boesten 2014, Bueno-Hansen 2015; CVR 2003; Getgen 2009; Mantilla Falcón 2005a, 2005b, 2007; Theidon 2012, 2015; Villanueva Flores 2007. Of the 538 reported

cases of rape, 527 were committed against women (and eleven against men); 83 percent were attributable to armed agents of the state (Theidon 2012, 106–7). Under patria potestad, women received protection from sexual violence only if she was "decent" and if the perpetrator was not her husband or father. "The delineation between decency and immorality was a matter of life and death for women, as a husband was allowed to kill an adulterous wife; no woman had parallel right to take the life of an unfaithful husband" (Dore 1997, 109).

27. The Peruvian Truth and Reconciliation Commission (Comisión de la Verdad y la Reconciliación, CVR) worked from 2001 to 2003, investigating the internal armed conflict, with a focus on human rights violations (torture, extrajudicial execution, kidnapping, assassination, and disappearance). Pascha Bueno-Hansen (2015, 53) shows that only international pressure, funding sources that required a gender component, and the advocacy of Peruvian women's and feminist movements compelled commissioners to integrate gender into their investigation at all. The CVR used a broad definition of sexual violence: "a type of human rights violation, [including] forced prostitution, forced unions, sexual slavery, forced abortions, and forced nudity" (Theidon 2012, 106). The CVR made a distinction between "extraordinary violence" and "ordinary violence" (Bueno-Hansen 2015, 62) with massacres framed as extraordinary (occurring only during the conflict) and sexual violence as ordinary (occurring in everyday circumstances). Ordinary violence might be "criminal" but not "political" (Bueno-Hansen 2015, 63). As Boesten (2014, 53) points out, sexual violence (and the gender, racial, and class inequalities in which such violence is embedded) are made to seem natural in part because of the "embodied, intimate, and reproductive experience it imposes on both perpetrator and victim."

28. See Boesten 2014; Theidon 2012 on the *pichana*, or gang rape, that nevertheless treated women differentially by perceived race and class. More generally, acts of sexualized violence may inscribe "racial and sexual identities . . . on bodies through rituals of domination and submission" (Weismantel 2001, 134). On the simultaneous production of masculinity, sexuality, and race in the military see Canessa 2005; Gill 1995; Theidon 2012. In a different postcolonial context, see Meiu 2016.

29. Bueno-Hansen (2015, 94) explains that in sexual violence testimonies, children "embody the physical evidence of rape" and "the failure of the state to take responsibility, in that state actors, national police, and armed forces father children and neglect their paternal obligations." I return to this point in chapter 5.

30. For a landmark case brought before United Nations Human Rights Committee, see https://www.reproductiverights.org/press-room/peruvian-government-publicly -recognizes-human-rights-violations-against-rape-survivor, accessed July 7, 2017.

31. Recently some of these services, including emergency contraception, have been restored. See https://www.reproductiverights.org/press-room/new-human-rights -case-filed-on-behalf-of-peruvian-rape-survivor-denied-emergency-contraception, accessed July 7, 2017. On reproductive politics in Latin America, see among others Chavez and Coe 2007; Coe 2004; Ewig 2006, 2010; Gribble et al. 2007; Jelin and Diaz 2003; Leifsen 2006; Raguz 2001; Taylor 2004; Unnithan and Pigg 2014; Yon 2014.

Chapter 3. Shaping (Modern) Mothers in Palomitáy

1. Many of these analyses have drawn on Michel Foucault's (1990) distinction between "governance through sovereign power (or explicit force) and governance through biopower, in which subjects come to govern themselves on intimate bodily levels" (Morgan and Roberts 2012, 243). For example, McElhinney (2005, 183) shows that U.S. concerns over child-rearing practices of Philippine natives in the early twentieth century were about "transforming people into modern citizens as much as safeguarding an 'at risk' population." Additional examples linking motherhood, children, and citizenship include Anagnost 2000; Browner and Sargent 1998; Jolly 1998a; Smith-Oka 2013; Stoler 2002, 2006; Tabbush and Gentile 2013; Stoler 1989, 2001, 2002; Tapias 2016, 2006; Taylor 2006.

2. Scholarship on both development and humanitarianism is extensive. Among those incorporating analyses of gender in Latin America, see Barrig 2007; Bernal and Grewal 2014; Escobar 1995; Guilhot 2012; Murdock 2003; Radcliffe et al. 2004; Ypeij and Zoomers 2006. More generally, see Bornstein 2012, 2009; Bornstein and Redfield, eds., 2010; Fehrenbach and Rodogno 2015; Redfield and Bornstein 2010; Tickten 2011. Recent analyses of humanitarianism may focus on missionary groups, international organizations, NGOs, and development organizations and show that liberalism, Christianity, and capitalism intertwine in colonial and postcolonial contexts.

3. Young women are also responsible for their own well-being. Especially, enrichment workshops emphasize that a young mother cares for herself as well as her child. Space does not permit a discussion of wellness here, but thanks to Isabel Kovacs for pointing out the salience of this topic and discussing the ways "wellness" may also be linked to undeclared but deep-seated expectations of neoliberal self-sufficiency. For additional perspectives on the intersection of affect and neoliberal capitalism, see Ameeriar 2015; Curtis 2009; Fabricant and Postero 2013; Freeman 2014; Martin 2013; Ramos-Zayas 2011; Richard and Rudnyckyj 2009; Rutherford 2009.

4. Palomitáy may be understood as a "white social space" (Hill 1998; Urcioli 1996). For another recent usage in Peru, see Berg 2015.

5. For further discussion of phenomenological approaches to embodiment and affect that extend understandings of governance, see Berg and Ramos-Zayas 2015; Csordas 2015; Desjarlais 2015; Gieser 2008; Hoenes del Pinal 2011; Ram and Houston 2015; Richard and Rudnyckyj 2009; Rudnyckyj 2015; Van Wolputte 2004.

6. As Margaret Jolly (1998b, 181) explains, maternal and infant welfare campaigns in colonial Southeast Asia implicitly and explicitly condemned indigenous modes of birthing, nurturing, and kinship. These campaigns also eroded traditional sources of knowledge and power (especially perhaps the knowledge and power of women) within communities. McElhinney (2005, 186) shows that infant mortality was blamed on "ignorant and negligent mothers, especially working class women" in the Philippenes under U.S. imperial governments. In certain circumstances, women's overly affectionate treatment of babies (kissing, rocking, and holding) was singled out as the cause of sickness and, more importantly, of spoiling a child so that he (especially he) will not grow up to be efficient, amenable to discipline (McElhinney 2005, 188).

Women's caring practices came to represent a society's inability to modernize. Also see Smith-Oka 2013.

7. An unintended consequence of this is that fathers have greater ability to pursue opportunities elsewhere, and Andean networks of care may further deteriorate.

8. For instance, see Strong 2001, 2005 on Native American children in the United States and Canada who were removed from families and placed in boarding schools (or adoptive families) that aimed to assimilate and "civilize" them, and often convert them to Christianity. The impulse of government officials and church authorities "to help" articulated with deep-seated racialized policies and imperialist world views; these practices have had long-term deleterious effects on families and communities. Although I cannot address the question fully within the page limits of this book, we might keep in mind the strong possibility that international humanitarian institutions—often unknowingly—contribute to the fragmentation of indigenous communities or poor families or align themselves with long-standing hierarchies of power through these notions of the civilized, modern, and educated. Additionally, how communities and families are impacted by removal of children over long periods of time is a question that deserves further empirical research. I am grateful to the participants in Brown University's 2015 "Indigenous Performance" symposium for helping me develop this point.

9. Asad (1973, 17) notes, "The colonial power structure made the object of anthropological study accessible and safe—because of it sustained physical proximity between the observing European the living non-European became a practical possibility." Similar structures of power in postcolonial states enable the movement of tourists, humanitarian workers, and anthropologists into arenas of care like Palomitáy.

10. Meena Khandelwal (2009, 583) points out: "Most people in the United States, including students, the general public, and some feminists, consistently overestimate their own agency in the face of discursive and institutional structures and underestimate that of women elsewhere—and this occurs in a contemporary U.S. context where agency defines personhood."

Chapter 4. Dynamic Selves, Uncertain Desires

1. On subjectivity, see Ahmed 2004; Boellstorf 2003; Curtis 2004; Das 2000, 2008; Edwards and Williams 2000; Gammeltoft 2007; Good et al. 2008; Holland et al. 1998; Hoestetler and Herdt 1998; Mageo 2002; Mahmoud 2005; Mahoney and Yngvesson 1992; Mattingly 2014; Ortner 2005; Patosalmi 2009; Villalobos 2014.

2. See, on young mothers, Cosgrove 2016; Cox 2015, Edin and Kefalas 2005; Edwards and Williams 2000; Hing 1998; Jacobs and Mollborn 2012; Kirkman et al. 2001; Luker 1996; Rios-Salas and Meyer 2014; Solinger 1992; Tabbush and Gentile 2013; Underberg 2013; Villalobos 2014.

3. When she discovered her pregnancy, Jeni requested assistance from the Demuna and was questioned about her sexual history. When she told officials that she had sexual intercourse with another restaurant employee, they barred her from submitting a formal complaint against her stepfather because the identity of the biological

father was unclear. The last incident of violence had occurred several weeks prior (before she arrived in Cusco), and she could not show evidence of physical harm.

4. Feminist philosopher Maria Lugones (2003, 7) writes, "One way of imagining my concern with intentionality and active subjectivity is to focus on the 'traveling' of our own against the grain, resistant, oppositional thoughts, movements, gestures among variegated, heterogeneous aggregates of subjects negotiating a life in the tensions of various oppressing/resisting relations." She also understands movement as epistemic: "I am providing ways of witnessing faithfully and of conveying meaning against the oppressive grain. To witness faithfully is difficult, given the manyness of worlds of sense related through power so that oppressive and fragmenting meanings saturate many worlds of sense in hard to detect ways" (Lugones 2003, 7).

5. Thanks to Natasha Soto (personal communication, September 5, 2012), whose undergraduate independent study noted this 2011 change in policy and prompted me to include this in follow-up interviews in 2013. The change was instituted after a North American psychologist visiting the home emphasized the dangers of sudden infant crib death. Rosa noted that having the children sleep in cribs was one of the most difficult changes in day-to-day procedures that they had instituted.

6. As Jacobs and Mollborn (2012, 929) note in their research on early motherhood in the United States, many young women indicate experiencing a "break with their emotional and social support system" in response to their pregnancy. Although autonomy, in this narrower sense, is also an aspect of young women's lives, I aim to develop a broader conception in order to illuminate young women's resistances to various relations of power.

7. The notion that boys would support parents in their old age is common in the region (Van Vleet 2008). Many of the young mothers at Palomitáy also said they preferred boys, but their reasoning was that "girls suffer too much."

8. Buch (2013, 638) discusses home health-care workers in Chicago to explore "the ways that the reproduction of particular forms of social personhood might be intimately tied to the intensification of inequality through embodied care practices."

Chapter 5. Making Images, (Re)Visioning Mothers

1. On Madonna and Child images in Latin America and elsewhere, see for instance Briggs 2003; Calderón Muñoz 2014; Crandon-Malamude 1993; de la Cruz 2009; Derks and Heessels 2011; Hermkens 2008; Taylor 2006.

2. The extended quote reads: "This essay petitions anthropologists addressing culture and experience to infuse sensibilities about existential doubt, suffering, desire, morality, empathy, mind-reading, healing, temporality, transformation, sense of self, and the making of persons with complementary sensibilities about the indexical formation of language-and-context as a primal unit of meaning-making and perfectly ordinary utterances in everyday life as themselves experiential moments that have everything to do with the psychic management of life's contingencies" (Ochs 2012, 156).

3. For instance, Hirsch argued that with the invention of the Kodak camera by George Eastman in 1888, photography became "the family's primary instrument of self-knowledge and representation—the means by which family memory would be

continued and perpetuated, by which the family's story would henceforth be told" (Hirsch 1997, 6–7). Clearly this presumes access to cameras. See Figueroa 2016; Poole 1997; Sinervo and Hill 2011; Ulfe and Malaga Sabogal 2016; Underberg and Zorn 2013 on photography in Peru. Also see Banks, Marcus, and Jay Ruby 2011; Brown and Phu, eds. 2014.

4. Those class periods that passed without any hands-on photography and those in which young women did photography may contribute to developing particular ways of seeing. During the first day that the girls had cameras, they took photographs of the favorite parts of their bodies. The next class period, when they did not have cameras, Verónica reviewed the photos with them, commenting on composition and lighting. Then she taught the young women how to make wallets out of rectangular one-liter juice and milk boxes during the remainder of the class. Overtly the craft project encouraged the young women to use their hands, follow directions, and express themselves creatively by decorating the wallets. As the young women transformed trash into functional personal items, they may have acquired practice in skilled visioning in a covert way as well. To look at an empty juice box and see a (potential) wallet, to look at one's feet and see a (potential) photograph require embodied practical skills of vision.

5. See also Goodwin (2003) for a linguistic anthropologist's analysis of the embodied production of knowledge among archaeologists. See Conklin 1980 for discussion of using visual and material artifacts to translate "local constellations of knowledge (performative, bodily, corporeal, even visceral)" (Grasseni 2011, 30) into shareable forms. See Brown and Phu 2014; Pauwels 2015.

6. This project and others left material and digital traces. Not only did participants view images during the project itself but they also received prints of selected images. The digital files circulated between between the photography professor and myself and the two NGOs. Though I did not interview participants about these images, Pyyry (2015, 158) notes that photography may give a "push" to new ways of thinking and talking.

7. Young women also took many photos of their infants and children. I do not include examples of these in order to protect the identities of individuals.

8. Rocío Silva Santiesteban points out that this response invokes the "original bastard" icon of the colonial encounter in which the "rape of indigenous women by Spanish men does not lead to fathers recognizing filiation" but instead to the retrenchment of race, class, gender, and heterosexual privilege (cited in Bueno-Hansen 2015, 94).

9. Methodological discussions of visual research with children and youth also point to the moral rhetoric that seeps into analyses. See Clark 2004; Johnson 2011; Mitchell 2006.

Chapter 6. Moral Dialogues, Caring Dilemmas

1. On voice as a metaphor, see Gal 1991; Van Vleet 2017.

2. See Allen 2008; 2011; Bunt 2008; Mujica 2013; Robillard 2010; Santiesteban 2009; Theidon 2015; Yon 2014.

3. In their now classic analysis of a reading lesson in an elementary school, they

show how the children and teacher use words, eye contact, gesture, and timing to uphold the idea that "we are all learning to read" while at the same time determining that *some* kids really do *not* know how to read and are not going to get a turn to read (McDermott and Tylbor 1995, 219). Significantly, students and teacher are mostly unaware of achieving this.

4. Victor Turner (1986) famously argued that dramatic events offer opportunities for individuals and collectivities to render and transform social relationships and understandings. More recently, linguistic anthropologists have analyzed the specific mechanisms by which language and social contexts are linked within performances. See Coupland 2007; Divita 2014; Ochs 2010; Wirtz 2011; Wozniak and Allen 2012.

5. I use "indigeneity" provisionally to indicate a subject position tied to relations of domination by colonial and postcolonial states and also linked to identification with, and reclamation of, language, place, and ethnicity. On indigeneity in Peru, see Degregori 2002; de la Cadena 2008; Femenías 2008; García 2008; García and Lucero 2004, 2008; Muratorio 1998; Ødegaard 2010; Oliart 2007; Seligmann 2004. On indigeniety in the Andes, also see Albó 1991; Berg and Ramos-Zayas 2015; Colloredo-Mansfeld 1998; Fischer 2007; Lazar 2010; Postero and Zamosc, eds. 2004; Weismantel 2001. Also see chapter 2 and the sources cited in chapter 2, note 10 for a discussion of race and racial discourses in Peru. I analyze the micro-politics of race and gender in this particular performance in Van Vleet (2019).

6. The audience's laughter is keyed to a disjuncture between frames, especially the audience's perception of the performer, Ana, as social actor and her performance as a character (Elizabeth) in the play. On humor, also see Sue and Golash Bok 2013.

7. A "speaker" may be divided into four roles, from Erving Goffman's (1974, 517ff) perspective: 1. The "animator" physically speaks the words, whether they are her own or not; 2. The "author" composes or scripts the words; 3. The "principal" is the person who stands behind the words, whose opinion is expressed or ideas are put forth; and 4. The "figure" is "the character, persona, or entity projected into the audience's imagination" by the utterance (Irvine 1996,132). These constantly shift from utterance to utterance. Extending Goffman's (1976, 1981) elaboration of the inadequacies of the speaker-hearer dichotomy, Judith Irvine (1996) has argued that we imagine multiple utterance events—each with their array of speakers performing participant roles—as laminated upon each other.

8. As Ochs (2012, 153–54) puts it, ordinary life also has the subjunctive mood very much in evidence: doubt is endemic, and causal relations are "pieced together contingently, situationally, and non-linearly as much as they are drawn from a bank of a priori knowledge, beliefs, dispositions, and expectations." If we consider informal everyday experience as living experience, anthropologists must develop ways of analyzing and representing people experiencing meaning as it unfolds.

References

Adams, Kathleen, and Sara Dickey, eds. 2000. *Home and Hegemony: Domestic Service and Identity Politics in South and Southeast Asia*. Ann Arbor: University of Michigan Press.

Adams, Vicanne, and Stacey Leigh Pigg. 2005. *Sex in Development: Science, Sexuality, and Morality in Global Perspective*. Durham, NC: Duke University Press.

Agamben, Giorgio. 1993. *The Coming Community*. Minneapolis: University of Minnesota Press.

Ahmed, Sara. 2004. *The Cultural Politics of Emotion*. New York: Routledge.

Albó, Xavier. 2011. "Suma quamaña = convivir bien. ¿Cómo medirlo?" In *Vivir bien: ¿Paradigma no capitalista?*, edited by Ivonne Farah H. and L. Vasapollo, 133–44. La Paz, Bolivia: CIDES-UMSA.

———. 1991. "El retorno del indio." *Revista andina* 9(2): 299–366.

Alcalde, Cristina M. 2010. *The Woman in the Violence: Gender, Poverty, and Resistance in Peru*. Nashville, TN: Vanderbilt University Press.

Alexander, M. Jacqui. 1994. "Not Just (Any) Body Can Be a Citizen: The Politics of Law, Sexuality, and Postcoloniality in Trinidad and Tobago and the Bahamas." *Feminist Review* 48: 5–23.

Alfonso, Mariana. 2008. "Girls Just Want to Have Fun? Sexuality, Pregnancy, and Motherhood among Bolivian Teenagers." *Research Department Working Paper 615*. Washington, DC: Inter-American Development Bank.

Allen, Catherine. 2002 [1987]. *The Hold Life Has: Coca and Cultural Identity in an Andean Community*. Washington, DC: Smithsonian Institution.

———. 2011. *Foxboy: Intimacy and Aesthetics in the Andes*. Austin: University of Texas Press.

Altamirano, Teófilo. 2003. "From Country to City: Internal Migration." *ReVista: Harvard Review of Latin America*. https://revista.drclas.harvard.edu/book/country-city-english-version, accessed August 13, 2018.

Álvarez, Sonia E., Elisabeth Jay Friedman, Ericka Beckman, Maylei Blackwell, Norma Stoltz Chinchilla, Nathalie Lebon, Marysa Navarro, and Marcela Ríos Tobar. 2003. "Encountering Latin American and Caribbean Feminisms." *Signs* 28(2): 537–79.

Ameeriar, Lalaie. 2015. "Pedagogies of Affect: Docility and Deference in the Making of Immigrant Women Subjects." *Signs* 40(2): 467–86.

Anagnost, Ann. 2000. "Scenes of Misrecognition: Maternal Citizenship in the Age of Transnational Adoption." *Positions: East Asia Cultures Critique* 8(2): 390–421.

Anderson, Ben, and Paul Harrison. 2010. *Taking-Place: Non-Representational Theories and Geography*. Farnham, UK: Ashgate.

Anderson, Jeanine. 2013. *Religión, sexualidad y política: Explorando saberes y actitudes, Ayacucho, Lima, y Pucallpa*. Lima: Católicas por el Derecho a Decidir–Perú, Urbana Edición y Diseño SAC.

———. 2010. "Incommensurable Worlds of Practice and Value: A View from the Shantytowns of Lima." In *Indelible Inequalities in Latin America: Insights from History, Politics, and Culture*, edited by Paul Gootenberg and Luis Reygadas, 81–105. Durham, NC: Duke University Press.

———. 2009. "Assembling and Disassembling Families." *Journal of Latin American and Caribbean Anthropology* 14(1): 185–98.

Andolina, Robert, Nina Laurie, and Sarah A. Radcliffe. 2009. *Indigenous Development in the Andes: Culture, Power, and Transnationalism*. Durham, NC: Duke University Press.

Anzaldúa, Gloria. 1987. *Borderlands/La Frontera*. San Francisco: Aunt Lute Books.

Anzaldúa, Gloria, and Cherríe Moraga. 1981. *This Bridge Called My Back: Writings by Radical Women of Color*. New York: Kitchen Table Press.

Asad, Talal. 1973. *Anthropology and the Colonial Encounter*. New York: Humanities Press.

Babb, Florence E. 2018. *Women's Place in the Andes: Engaging Decolonial Feminist Anthropology*. Berkeley: University of California Press.

———. 2012. "Theorizing Gender, Race, and Cultural Tourism in Latin America: A View from Peru and Mexico." *Latin American Perspectives* 39(6): 36–50.

———. 2010. *The Tourism Encounter: Fashioning Latin American Nations and Histories*. Stanford, CA: Stanford University Press.

Bakhtin, M. M. 1981. *The Dialogic Imagination: Four Essays by M. M. Bakhtin*. Edited by Michael Holquist; translated by Caryl Emerson and Michael Holquist. Austin: University of Texas Press.

Banks, Marcus, and Jay Ruby. 2011. *Made to Be Seen: Perspectives on the History of Visual Anthropology*. Chicago: University of Chicago Press.

Bant, Astrid, and Françoise Girard. 2008. "Sexuality, Health, and Human Rights: Self-Identified Priorities of Indigenous Women in Peru." *Gender and Development* 16(2): 247–56.

Barker, Drucilla K., and Susan F. Feiner. 2009. "Affect, Race, and Class: An Interpretive Reading of Caring Labor." *Frontiers: A Journal of Women Studies* 30(1): 41–54.

Barlow, Kathleen. 2010. "Sharing Food, Sharing Values: Mothering and Empathy in Murik Society." *Ethos* 38(4): 339–53.

Barlow, Kathleen, and Bambi L. Chapin. 2010. "The Practice of Mothering: An Introduction." *Ethos* 38(4): 324–38.

Barrig, Maruja, ed. 2007. *Fronteras interiores: Identidad, diferencia y protagonismo de las mujeres*. Lima: Instituto de Estudios Peruanos.

Basso, Ellen B. 1985. *A Musical View of the Universe: Kalapalo Myth and Ritual Performances*. Philadelphia: University of Pennsylvania Press.

Bastia, Tanja. 2009. "Women's Migration and the Crisis of Care: Grandmothers Caring for Grandchildren in Urban Bolivia." *Gender and Development* 17(3): 389–401.

Bastian Duarte, Ángela Ixkic. 2012. "From the Margins of Latin American Feminism: Indigenous and Lesbian Feminisms." *Signs* 38(1): 153–78.

Bauman, Richard. 1977. *Verbal Art as Performance*. Prospect Heights, IL: Waveland Press.

Bauman, Richard, and Charles Briggs. 1990. "Poetics and Performance as Critical Perspectives on Language and Social Life." *Annual Review of Anthropology* 19: 59–88.

Bejarano, Cynthia. 2002. "Las Supermadres de Latino America: Transforming Motherhood by Challenging Violence in Mexico, Argentina, and El Salvador." *Frontiers* 23(1): 126–50.

Berg, Ulla D. 2015. *Mobile Selves: Race, Migration, and Belonging in Peru and the U.S.* New York: New York University Press.

Berg, Ulla D., and Ana Y. Ramos-Zayas. 2015. "Racializing Affect: A Theoretical Proposition." *Current Anthropology* 56(5): 654–77.

Berlant, Lauren. 2011. *Cruel Optimism*. Durham, NC: Duke University Press.

Bernal, Victoria, and Inderpal Grewal, eds. 2014. *Theorizing NGOs: States, Feminisms, and Neoliberalism*. Durham, NC: Duke University Press.

Berry, Maya, Claudia Chávez Arguelles, Shanya Cordis, Sarah Ihmoud, and Elizabeth Velásquez Estrada. 2017. "Toward a Fugitive Anthropology: Gender, Race, and Violence in the Field." *Cultural Anthropology* 32(4): 537–65.

Blofield, Merike. 2012. *Care Work and Class: Domestic Workers' Struggle for Equal Rights in Latin America*. University Park: Penn State University Press.

Boellstorff, Tom. 2003. "Dubbing Culture: Indonesian Gay and Lesbi Subjectivities in an Already Globalized World." *American Ethnologist* 30(2): 225–42.

Boesten, Jelke. 2014. *Sexual Violence during War and Peace: Gender, Power, and Post-Conflict Justice in Peru*. New York: Palgrave.

———. 2010. *Intersecting Inequalities: Women and Social Policy in Peru, 1990–2000*. University Park: Penn State University Press.

———. 2006. "Pushing Back the Boundaries: Social Policy, Domestic Violence, and Women's Organizations in Peru." *Journal of Latin American Studies* 38: 355–78.

Boris, Eileen, and Rhacel Salazar Parreñas. 2010. *Intimate Labors: Cultures, Technologies, and the Politics of Care*. Stanford, CA: Stanford University Press.

Bornstein, Erica. 2012. *Disquieting Gifts: Humanitarianism in New Delhi*. Stanford, CA: Stanford University Press.

———. 2009. "The Impulse of Philanthropy." *Cultural Anthropology* 24(4): 622–51.

Bornstein, Erica, and Peter Redfield, eds. 2010. *Forces of Compassion: Humanitarianism between Ethics and Politics*. Santa Fe, NM: School for Advanced Research Press.

Bourdieu, Pierre. 1986. "Forms of Capital." In *Handbook of Theory and Research for the Sociology of Education*, edited by John G. Richardson, 241–58. Westport, CT: Greenwood.

Briggs, Laura. 2012. *Somebody's Children: The Politics of Transracial and Transnational Adoption*. Durham, NC: Duke University Press.

———. 2003. "Mother, Child, Race, Nation: The Visual Iconography of Rescue and the Politics of Transnational and Transracial Adoption." *Gender and History* 15(2): 179–200.

Brown, Elspeth H., and Thy Phu, eds. 2014. *Feeling Photography*. Durham, NC: Duke University Press.

Brown, Wendy. 2006. "Neoliberalism, Neoconservatism, and De-Democratization." *Political Theory* 24(5): 690–714.

Browner, Carole, and Carolyn Sargent, eds. 2011. *Reproduction, Globalization and the State: New Theoretical and Ethnographic Perspectives*. Durham, NC: Duke University Press.

Buch, Elana D. 2013. "Senses of Care: Embodying Inequality and Sustaining Personhood in the Home Care of Older Adults in Chicago." *American Ethnologist* 40(4): 637–50.

Bucholtz, Mary. 2002. "Youth and Cultural Practice." *Annual Review of Anthropology* 31(1): 525–52.

Bucholtz, Mary, and Kira Hall. 2005. "Identity and Interaction: A Sociocultural Linguistic Approach." *Discourse Studies* 7(4–5): 585–614.

Bueno-Hansen, Pascha. 2015. *Feminist and Human Rights Struggles in Peru: Decolonizing Transitional Justice*. Urbana: University of Illinois Press.

Bunt, Laura A. 2008. "A Quest for Justice in Cuzco, Peru: Race and Evidence in the Case of Mercedes Ccorimanya Lavilla." *PoLAR* 31(2): 286–302.

Burman, Anders. 2011. "*Chachawarmi*: Silence and Rival Voices in Decolonisation and Gender Politics in Andean Bolivia." *Journal of Latin American Studies* 43(1): 65–91.

Butler, Judith. 1993. *Bodies That Matter: On the Discursive Limits of "Sex."* New York: Routledge.

———. 1990. *Gender Trouble: Feminism and the Subversion of Identity*. New York: Routledge.

Cáceres, Carlos, Marcos Cueto, and Nancy Palomino. 2008. "Policies around Sexual and Reproductive Health and Rights in Peru." *Global Public Health* 3(S2): 39–57.

Caggiano, Sergio. 2007. "Madres en la frontera: género, nación, y los peligros de la reproducción." *Íconos: Revista de ciencias sociales* 28: 93–106.

Calderón Muñoz, María. 2014. "From Religious Icon to 'Our Mother from Heaven': The Appropriation of the Virgin Mary by Catholic Women in Quito." *Culture and Religion* 15(1): 58–71.

Campoamor, Leigh. 2016. "'Who Are You Calling Exploitative?': Defensive Motherhood, Child Labor, and Urban Poverty in Lima, Peru." *Journal of Latin American and Caribbean Anthropology* 21(1): 151–72.

Canessa, Andrew. 2012. *Intimate Indigeneities: Race, Sex, and History in the Small Spaces of Andean Life, Narrating Native Histories*. Durham, NC: Duke University Press.

———, ed. 2005. *Natives Making Nation: Gender, Indigeneity, and the State in the Andes*. Tucson: University of Arizona Press.

Caputo, Virginia. 1995. "Anthropology's Silent 'Others.'" In *Youth Cultures*, edited by Vered Amit-Talai and Helena Wulff, 19–42. New York: Routledge.

Carsten, Janet, ed. 2000. *Cultures of Relatedness: New Approaches to the Study of Kinship*. Cambridge, UK: Cambridge University Press.

Castellanos, M. Bianet. 2017. "Introduction: Settler Colonialism in Latin America." *American Quarterly* 69(4): 777–81.

Castellanos, M. Bianet, Lourdes Gutiérrez Nájera, and Arturo Adama, eds. 2012. *Comparative Indigeneities of the Américas: Toward a Hemispheric Approach*. Tucson: University of Arizona Press.

Central Intelligence Agency (CIA). 2019. "The World Factbook." https://www.cia.gov/library/publications/the-world-factbook/geos/pe.html, accessed March 9, 2019.

Chavez, Susana, and Anna-Britt Coe. 2007. "Emergency Contraception in Peru: Shifting Government and Donor Policies and Influences." *Reproductive Health Matters* 15(29): 139–48.

Cheney, Kristen. 2017. *Crying for Our Elders: African Orphanhood in the Age of HIV and AIDS*. Chicago: University of Chicago Press.

Cho, Sumi, Kimberlé Williams Crenshaw, and Leslie McCall. 2013. "Toward a Field of Intersectionality Studies: Theory, Applications, and Praxis." *Signs* 38(4): 785–810.

Clark, Cindy Dell. 2004. "Visual Metaphor as Method in Interviews with Children." *Journal of Linguistic Anthropology* 14(2): 171–85.

Coe, Anna-Britt. 2004. "From Anti-Natalist to Ultra-Conservative: Restricting Reproductive Choice in Peru." *Reproductive Health Matters* 12(24): 56–69.

Cole, Jenifer, and Deborah Durham, eds. 2008. *Figuring the Future: Globalization and the Temporalities of Children and Youth*. Santa Fe, NM: School for Advanced Research.

Colen, Shellee. 1995. "'Like a Mother to Them': Stratified Reproduction and West Indian Childcare Workers and Employers in New York." In *Conceiving the New World Order: The Global Politics of Reproduction*, edited by Faye Ginsburg and Rayna Rapp, 78–102. Berkeley: University of California Press.

Colloredo-Mansfeld, Rudi. 2009. *Fighting Like a Community: Andean Civil Society in an Era of Indian Uprisings*. Chicago: University of Chicago Press.

———. 1998. "'Dirty Indians,' Radical *Indígenas*, and the Political Economy of Social Difference in Modern Ecuador." *Bulletin of Latin American Research* 17(2): 185–205.

Combahee River Collective. 1983 [1978]. "The Combahee River Collective Statement." In *Home Girls: A Black Feminist Anthology*, edited by Barbara Smith. New York: Kitchen Table Press.

Comisión de la Verdad y la Reconciliación. 2003. *Información final de la Comisión de la Verdad y la Reconciliación*. Lima: Comisión de la Verdad y la Reconciliación.

Conklin, Harold. 1980. *Ethnographic Atlas of Ifuagao: A Study of Environment, Culture, and Society in Northern Luzon*. New Haven, CT: Yale University Press.

Coral-Cordero, Isabel. 2005. "Women in War: Impact and Responses." In *Shining and*

Other Paths: War and Society in Peru, 1980–1995, edited by Steve J. Stern, 345–74. Durham, NC: Duke University Press.

Cosgrove, Serena. 2016. "The Absent State: Teen Mothers and New Patriarchal Forms of Gender Subordination." In *Gender Violence in Peace and War*. New Brunswick, NJ: Rutgers University Press.

Coupland, Nikolas. 2007. *Style: Language Variation and Identity*. Cambridge, UK: Cambridge University Press.

Cox, Aimee Meredith. 2015. *Shapeshifters: Black Girls and the Choreography of Citizenship*. Durham, NC: Duke University Press.

Crain, Mary M. 1994. "Unruly Mothers: Gender Identities, Peasant Political Discourses, and Struggles for Social Space in the Ecuadorean Andes." *PoLAR* 17(2): 85–98.

Crandon-Malamud, Libbet. 1993. "Blessings of the Virgin in Capitalist Society: The Transformation of a Rural Bolivian Fiesta." *American Anthropologist* 95(3): 574–96.

Crenshaw, Kimberlé. 1991. "Mapping the Margins: Intersectionality, Identity Politics, and Violence against Women of Color." *Stanford Law Review* 43 (6): 1241–99.

Csordas, Thomas J. 2015. "Toward a Cultural Phenomenology of Body-World Relations." In *Phenomenology in Anthropology: A Sense of Perspective*, edited by Kalpana Ram and Christopher Houston, 50–67. Bloomington: Indiana University Press.

Curtis, Debra. 2009. *Pleasures and Perils: Girls' Sexuality in a Caribbean Consumer Culture*. New Brunswick, NJ: Rutgers University Press.

———. 2004. "Commodities and Sexual Subjectivities: A Look at Capitalism and Its Desires." *Cultural Anthropology* 19(1): 95–121.

Das, Veena. 2012. "Ordinary Ethics." In *A Companion to Ordinary Ethics*, edited by Didier Fassin and Veena Das, 133–149. Malden, MA: Wiley Blackwell.

———. 2010. "Engaging the Life of the Other: Love and Everyday Life." In *Ordinary Ethics: Anthropology, Language, and Action*, edited by Michael Lambek, 376–99. New York: Fordham University Press.

———. 2008. "Violence, Gender, and Subjectivity." *Annual Review of Anthropology* 37: 283–99.

———. 2000. "The Act of Witnessing: Violence, Poisonous Knowledge, and Subjectivity." In *Violence and Subjectivity*, edited by Veena Das, Arthur Kleinman, Mamphela Ramphele, and Pamela Reynolds, 205–25. Berkeley: University of California Press.

Degregori, Carlos Iván. 2002. "Identidád étnica, movimientos sociales y participación en el Perú." In *Estados nacionales, etnicidád y democracia en América Latina*, edited by Y. Mutsuo and C. I. Degregori, 161–78. Osaka, Japan: JCAS, National Museum of Ethnology.

———. 2015. *Jamás tan cerca arremetió lo lejos: Sendero Luminoso y la violencia política. Obras Escogidas X*. Lima: IEP.

———. 1991. "How Difficult It Is to Be God: Ideology and Political Violence in Sendero Luminoso." *Critique of Anthropology* 11(3): 233–50.

De la Cadena, Marisol. 2008. "Alternative Indigeneities: Conceptual Proposals." *Latin American and Caribbean Ethnic Studies* 3(3): 341–49.

———. 2005. "Are Mestizos Hybrids? The Conceptual Politics of Andean Identities." *Journal of Latin American Studies* 37: 259–84.

———. 2003. "Discriminación etnica." *Cuestión del estado* 32: 1–9.

———. 2000. *Indigenous Mestizos: The Politics of Race and Culture in Cuzco, Peru, 1919–1991.* Durham, NC: Duke University Press.

———. 1991. "'Las mujeres son más indias': Etnicidad y género en una comunidad del Cusco." *Revista andina* 9(1): 7–29.

De la Cruz, Deirdre. 2009. "Coincidence and Consequence: Marianism and the Mass Media in the Global Philippines." *Cultural Anthropology* 24(3): 455–88.

Delaney, Carol, and Sylvia Yanagisako, eds. 1995. *Naturalizing Power: Essays in Feminist Cultural Analysis.* New York: Routledge Press.

Derks, Sanne, and Meike Heessels. 2011. "Battered Women Venerating a Vicious Virgin: Reconsidering Marianismo at a Bolivian Pilgrimage Shrine." *Culture and Religion* 12: 303–16.

Desjarlais, Robert. 2015. "Seared with Reality: Phenomenology through Photography, in Nepal." In *Phenomenology in Anthropology: A Sense of Perspective*, edited by Kalpana Ram and Christopher Houston, 197–223. Bloomington: Indiana University Press.

De Soto, H. 1987. *El otro sendero: La revolución informal.* Lima: Instituto Libertad y Democracia.

Dhillon, Jaskiran. 2017. *Prairie Rising: Indigenous Youth, Decolonization, and the Politics of Intervention.* Toronto: University of Toronto Press.

Dickey, Sara. 2012. "The Pleasures and Anxieties of Being in the Middle: Emerging Middle-Class Identities in Urban South India." *Modern Asian Studies* 46(3): 559–99.

Divita, David. 2014. "From Paris to Pueblo and Back: (Re-)Emigration and the Modernist Chronotope in Cultural Performance." *Journal of Linguistic Anthropology* 24(1): 1–18.

Dore, Elizabeth. 1997. "The Holy Family: Imagined Households in Latin American History." In *Gender Politics in Latin America: Debates in Theory and Practice*, edited by Elizabeth Dore, 101–17. New York: Monthly Review Press.

Duarte Bastian, Ángela Ixkic. 2012. "From the Margins of Latin American Feminism: Indigenous and Lesbian Feminisms." *Signs* 38(1): 153–78.

Duranti, Alessandro, and Charles Goodwin. 1992. *Rethinking Context.* Cambridge, UK: Cambridge University Press.

Durham, Deborah. 2004. "Disappearing Youth: Youth as a Social Shifter in Botswana." *American Ethnologist* 31(4):589–605.

Eckert, Penelope, and McConnell-Ginet. 1995. "Constructing Meaning, Constructing Selves: Snapshots of Language, Gender, and Class from Belten High." In *Gender Articulated: Language and the Socially Constructed Self*, edited by Kira Hall and Mary Bucholtz, 469–507. New York: Routledge.

Edin, Kathryn, and Maria Kefalas. 2005. *Promises I Can Keep: Why Poor Women Put Motherhood before Marriage.* Berkeley: University of California Press.

Edwards, Christine E., and Christine L. Williams. 2000. "Adopting Change: Birth Mothers in Maternity Homes Today." *Gender and Society* 14(1): 160–83.

Eng, David L. 2010. *The Feeling of Kinship: Queer Liberalism and the Racialization of Intimacy*. Durham, NC: Duke University Press.

Escobar, Arturo. 1995. *Encountering Development: The Making and Unmaking of the Third World*. Princeton, NJ: Princeton University Press.

Estremadoyro, Julieta. 2001. "Domestic Violence in Andean Communities of Peru." *Law, Social Justice, and Global Development* 1(2). www.lgdjournal.org.

Ewig, Christina. 2010. *Second-Wave Neoliberalism: Gender, Race, and Health Sector Reform in Peru*. University Park: Penn State University Press.

———. 2006. "Hijacking Global Feminism: Feminists, the Catholic Church, and the Family Planning Debacle in Peru." *Feminist Studies* 32(3): 633–59.

Fabricant, Nicole, and Nancy Postero. 2013. "Contested Bodies, Contested States: Performance, Emotions, and New Forms of Regional Governance in Santa Cruz, Bolivia." *Journal of Latin American and Caribbean Anthropology* 18(2): 187–211.

Faeta, Francesco. 2003. *Strategie dell'occhio: Saggi di antropologia visiva*. Milan, Italy: Franco Angeli.

Farmer, Paul. 1996. "On Suffering and Structural Violence: A View from Below." *Daedalus* 125(1): 261–83.

Farnell, Brenda. 2011. "Theorizing 'the Body' in Visual Culture." In *Made to Be Seen: Perspectives on the History of Visual Anthropolog*, edited by Marcus Banks and Jay Ruby, 136–58. Chicago: University of Chicago Press.

Fassin, Didier. 2013. "On Resentment and *Ressentiment*: The Politics and Ethics of Moral Emotions." *Current Anthropology* 54(3): 249–67.

———. 2011. *Humanitarian Reason: A Moral History of the Present*. Berkeley: University of California Press.

Fassin, Didier, and Veena Das, eds. 2012. *A Companion to Moral Anthropology*. Malden, MA: Wiley-Blackwell.

Fassin, Didier, Frédéric Le Marcis, and Todd Lethata. 2008. "Life and Times of Magda A: Telling a Story of Violence in South Africa." *Current Anthropology* 49(2): 225–46.

Faverón-Patriau, Gustavo, ed. 2006. *Toda la sangre: Antología de cuentos peruanos sobre la violencia política*. Lima: Grupo Editorial Matalamanga.

Fehrenbach, Heide, and Davide Rodogno. 2015. "Introduction: The Morality of Sight: Humanitarian Photography in History." In *Humanitarian Photography: A History*, edited by Heide Fehrenbach and Davide Rodogno, 1–21. New York: Cambridge University Press.

Femenías, Blenda. 2005. *Gender and the Boundaries of Dress in Contemporary Peru*. Austin: University of Texas Press.

Figueroa, Mercedes. 2016. "Gazing at the Face of Absence: Signification and Re-Signification of Family Photographs of Disappeared University Students in Peru." In *Photography in Latin America: Images and Identities across Time and Space*, edited by Gisela Cánepa Koch and Ingrid Kummels, 195–217. Bielefeld, Germany: Verlag.

Fischer, Edward F. 2014. *The Good Life: Aspiration, Dignity, and the Anthropology of Wellbeing*. Stanford, CA: Stanford University Press.

———. 2007. "Introduction: Indigenous Peoples, Neo-liberal Regimes, and Varieties of Civil Society in Latin America." *Social Analysis: The International Journal of Social and Cultural Practice* 51(2): 1–18.

Fiske, Alan Page, and Kathryn F. Mason. 1990. "Introduction: Moral Relativism." *Ethos* 18(2): 131–39.

Folbre, Nancy. 2002. *The Invisible Heart: Economics and Family Values*. New York: New Press.

Fonseca, Claudia. 2003. "Patterns of Shared Parenthood among the Brazilian Poor." *Social Text* 21(1): 111–27.

———. 1986. "Orphanages, Foundlings, and Foster Mothers: The System of Child Circulation in a Brazilian Squatter Settlement." *Anthropological Quarterly* 59(1): 15–27.

Forstner, Kathrin. 2013. "Women's Group-Based Work and Rural Gender Relations in the Southern Peruvian Andes." *Bulletin of Latin American Research* 32(1): 46–60.

Foucault, Michel. 1990. *The History of Sexuality, Volume 1*. New York: Vintage.

Francke, Marfil. 1990. "Género, clase y etnia: La trenza de la dominación." In *Tiempos de ira y amor: Nuevos actores para viejos problemas*, edited by Carlos Iván Degregori et al., 79–103. Lima: DESCO.

Franco, Jean. 2006. "Alien to Modernity: The Rationalization of Discrimination." *A contracorriente* 3(3): 1–16.

Franklin, Sarah, and Susan McKinnon, eds. 2002. *Relative Values: Reconfiguring Kinship Studies*. Durham, NC: Duke University Press.

Frederic, Karin. 2014. "Violence against Women and the Contradictions of Rights-in-Practice in Rural Ecuador." *Latin American Perspectives* 41(1): 19–38.

Freeman, Carla. 2014. *Entrepreneurial Selves: Neoliberal Respectability and the Making of a Caribbean Middle Class*. Durham, NC: Duke University Press.

Fuentes, Emma. 2013. "Political Mothering: Latina and African American Mothers in the Struggle for Educational Justice." *Anthropology and Education Quarterly* 44(3): 304–19.

Fuller, Norma. 2003. "The Social Constitution of Gender among Peruvian Males." In *Changing Men and Masculinities in Latin America*, edited by Matthew Gutmann, 134–52. Durham, NC: Duke University Press.

Gal, Susan. 1991. "Between Speech and Silence: The Problematics of Research on Language and Gender." In *Gender at the Crossroads of Knowledge: Feminist Anthropology in the Postmodern Era*, edited by Micaela di Leonardo, 175–203. Berkeley: University of California Press.

Gammeltoft, Tine M. 2007. "Prenatal Diagnosis in Postwar Vietnam: Power, Subjectivity, and Citizenship." *American Anthropologist* 109(1): 153–63.

García, María Elena. 2013. "The Taste of Conquest: Colonialism, Cosmopolitics, and the Dark Side of Peru's Gastronomic Boom." *Journal of Latin American and Caribbean Anthropology* 18(3): 505–24.

———. 2008. "Introduction: Indigenous Encounters in Contemporary Peru." *Journal of Latin American and Caribbean Ethnic Studies* 3(3): 217–26.

———. 2005. *Making Indigenous Citizens: Identities, Development, and Multicultural Development in Peru*. Stanford, CA: Stanford University Press.

García, María Elena, and José Antonio Lucero. 2004. "Un país sin indígenas? Rethinking Indigenous Politics in Peru." In *The Struggle for Indigenous Rights in Latin America*, edited by Nancy Postero and L. Zamosc, 157–88. Brighton, UK: Sussex Academic Press.

———. 2008. "Exceptional Others: Politicians, Rottweilers, and Alterity in the 2006 Presidential Elections." *Latin American and Caribbean Ethnic Studies* 3(3): 253–70.

Getgen, Jocelyn E. 2009. "Untold Truths: The Exclusion of Enforced Sterilizations from the Peruvian Truth Commission's Final Report." *Boston College Third World Law Journal* 29(1): 1–34.

Gezmes, Ana, Nancy Palomino, and Miguel Ramos. 2002. *Violencia sexual y física contra las mujeres en el Perú*. Lima: Flora Tristán.

Gieser, Thorsten. 2008. "Embodiment, Emotion, and Empathy: A Phenomenological Approach to Apprenticeship Learning." *Anthropological Theory* 8: 299–318.

Ginsburg, Faye, and Rayna Rapp, eds. 1995. *Conceiving the New World Order: The Global Politics of Reproduction*. Berkeley: University of California Press.

———. 1991. "The Politics of Reproduction." *Annual Review of Anthropology* 20: 311–43.

Glenn, Evelyn Nagano. 2010. *Forced to Care: Coercion and Caregiving in America*. Cambridge, MA: Harvard University Press.

———. 1992. "From Servitude to Service Work: Historical continuities in the Racial Division of Paid Reproductive Labor." *Signs* 18(1): 1–43.

Goffman, Erving. 1981. *Forms of Talk*. Philadelphia: University of Pennsylvania Press.

———. 1976. "Replies and Responses." *Language in Society* 5(3): 257–313.

———. 1974. *Frame Analysis: An Essay on the Organization of Experience*. New York: Harper.

Goldstein, Donna M. 2009. "Perils of Witnessing and Ambivalence of Writing: Whiteness, Sexuality, and Violence in Rio de Janeiro Shantytowns." In *Women Fielding Danger: Negotiating Ethnographic Identities in Field Research*, edited by Martha K. Huggins and Marie-Louise Glebbeek, 227–49. Lanham, MD: Rowman and Littlefield.

Good, Byron J., Mary-Jo DelVecchio Good, Sandra Theresa Hyde, and Sarah Pinto. 2008. "Postcolonial Disorders: Reflections on Subjectivity in the Contemporary World." In *Postcolonial Disorders*, edited by Mary-Jo DelVecchio Good, Sandra Theresa Hyde, Sarah Pinto, and Byron J. Good, 1–40. Berkeley: University of California Press.

Goodale, Mark. 2008. *Dilemmas of Modernity: Bolivian Encounters with Law and Liberalism*. Stanford, CA: Stanford University Press.

Goodale, Mark, and Nancy Postero. 2013. *Neoliberalism, Interrupted: Social Change and Contested Governance in Contemporary Latin America*. Stanford, CA: Stanford University Press.

Goodwin, Charles. 2003. "The Body in Action." In *Discourse, the Body, and Identity*, edited by Justine Coupland and Richard Gwyn, 19–42. New York: Palgrave.

Goodwin, Charles, and Marjorie Harness Goodwin. 2000. "Emotion within Situated

Activity." In *Linguistic Anthropology: A Reader*, edited by Alessandro Duranti, 239–57. Oxford, UK: Blackwell.

Goodwin, Marjorie Harness. 2006. *The Hidden Life of Girls: Games of Stance, Status and Exclusion*. Oxford, UK: Blackwell.

Gooldin, Sigal. 2008. "Being Anorexic: Hunger, Subjectivity, and Embodied Morality." *Medical Anthropology Quarterly* 22 (3): 274–96.

Grasseni, Cristina. 2011. "Skilled Visions: Toward and Ecology of Visual Inscriptions." In *Made to Be Seen: Perspectives on the History of Visual Anthropology*, edited by Marcus Banks and Jay Ruby, 19–44. Chicago: University of Chicago Press.

———, ed. 2007. *Skilled Visions: Between Apprenticeship and Standards*. Oxford, UK: Berghahn.

Greene, Shane. 2007. *"Entre lo indio, lo negro, y lo incaico:* The spatial hierarchies of difference in multicultural Peru." *Journal of Latin American and Caribbean Anthropology* 12(2): 441–74.

———. 2006. "Getting over the Andes: The Geo-Eco-Politics of Indigenous Movements in Peru's 21st Century Inca Empire." *Journal of Latin American Studies* 38(2): 327–54.

Grewal, Inderpal, and Caren Kaplan. 1994. *Scattered Hegemonies: Postmodernity and Transnational Feminist Practices*. Minneapolis: University of Minnesota Press.

Gribble, James N., Suneeta Sharma, and Elaine P. Menotti. 2007. "Family Planning Policies and Their Impacts on the Poor: Peru's Experience." *International Family Planning Perspectives* 33(4): 176–81.

Grice, H. P. 1975. "Logic and Conversation." In *Syntax and Semantics*, Volume 3: *Speech Acts*, edited by Peter Cole and J. L. Morgan, 41–58. New York: Academic.

Guilhot, Nicolas. 2012. "The Anthropologist as Witness: Humanitarianism between Ethnography and Critique." *Humanity* 3(1): 81–101.

Gumperz, John Joseph. 1981. "The Retrieval of Sociocultural Knowledge in Conversation." *Poetics Today* 1: 273–86.

Guy, Donna. 2000. *White Slavery and Mothers Alive and Dead: The Troubled Meeting of Sex, Gender, Public Health, and Progress in Latin America*. Lincoln: University of Nebraska Press.

Hall, Kira. 2001. "Performativity." In *Key Terms in Language and Culture*, edited by Alessandro Duranti, 180–83. Malden, MA: Blackwell.

Han, Clara. 2011. "Symptoms of Another Life: Time, Possibility, and Domestic Relations in Chile's Credit Economy." *Cultural Anthropology* 26(1): 7–32.

Hanks, William. 1995. *Language and Communicative Practices*. Boulder, CO: Westview.

———. 1990. *Referential Practice: Language and Lived Space among the Maya*. Chicago: University of Chicago Press.

Harris, Olivia. 1978. "Complementarity and Conflict: An Andean View of Women and Men." In *Sex and Age as Principles of Social Differentiation*, edited by J. S. LaFontaine, 21–40. New York: Academic Press.

Haynes, Nell. 2013. "Global Cholas: Reworking Tradition and Modernity in Bolivian Lucha Libre." *Journal of Latin American and Caribbean Anthropology* 18(3): 432–46.

Hennesy, R., and C. Ingraham, eds. 1997. *Materialist Feminism: A Reader in Class, Difference, and Women's Lives*. New York: Routledge.

Henríquez-Ayín, Narda. 2006. *Cuestiones de género y poder en el conflicto armado en el Perú*. Lima: CONYTE (Consejo Nacional de Ciencia, Tecnología e Innovación).

Hermkens, Anna-Karina. 2008. "Josephine's Journey: Gender-Based Violence and Marian Devotion in Urban Papua New Guinea." *Oceania* 78(2): 151–67.

Hiatt, Willie. 2007. "Flying 'Cholo': Incas, Airplanes, and the Construction of Andean Modernity in 1920s Cuzco, Peru." *The Americas* 63(3): 327–58.

Hill, Jane H. 1998. "Language, Race, and White Public Space." *American Anthropologist* 100(3): 680–89.

Himley, M. 2012. "Regularizing Extraction in Andean Peru: Mining and Social Mobilization in an Age of Corporate Social Responsibility." *Antipode* 45(2): 394–416.

Himmelweit, Susan. 2013. "Care: Feminist Economic Theory and Policy Challenges." *Journal of Gender Studies Ochanomizu University* 16: 1–18.

Hing, Ai Yun. 1998. "Delinquent Daughters' Struggle for Autonomy, Morality, Pleasure . . . and Motherhood." *Sojourn* 13(2): 263–84.

Hirsch, Marianne. 1997. *Family Frames: Photography, Narrative, and Postmemory*. Cambridge, MA: Harvard University Press.

Hoenes del Pinal, Eric. 2011. "Towards an Ideology of Gesture: Gesture, Body Movement, and Language Ideology among Q'eqchi'-Maya Catholics." *Anthropological Quarterly* 84(3): 595–630.

Hoffman, Diane M. 2012. "Saving Children, Saving Haiti? Child Vulnerability and Narratives of the Nation." *Childhood* 19 (2): 155–68.

Holland, Dorothy, William Lachicotte Jr., Debra Skinner, and Carole Cain. 1998. *Identity and Agency in Cultural Worlds*. Cambridge, MA: Harvard University Press.

Hollman, Laurie. 2010. "The Impact of Observation on the Evolution of a Relationship between an At-Risk Mother and Infant." *Infant Observation* 13(3): 325–38.

Hostetler, Andrew, and Gilbert Herdt. 1998. "Culture, Sexual Lifeways, and Developmental Subjectivities: Rethinking Sexual Taxonomies." *Social Research* 65(2): 249–90.

Htun, Mala. 2003. *Sex and the State: Abortion, Divorce, and the Family under Latin American Dictatorships and Democracies*. New York: Cambridge University Press.

Huanacuni Mamani, Fernando. 2010. *Buen vivir / vivir bien: Filosofía, políticas, estrategias y experiencias regionales andinas*. Lima: Coordinadora Andina de Organizaciones Indígenas (CAOI).

Huayhua, Margarita. 2014. "Racism and Social Interaction in a Southern Peruvian Combi." *Ethnic and Racial Studies* 37(13): 2399–417.

———. 2010. *Runama Kani icha Alquchu? Everyday Discrimination in the Southern Andes*. PhD diss., University of Michigan.

Hünefeldt, Christine. 2000. *Liberalism in the Bedroom: Quarreling Spouses in Nineteenth-Century Lima*. University Park: Penn State University Press.

Hunleth, Jean. 2017. *Children as Caregivers: The Global Fight against Tuberculosis and HIV in Zambia*. New Brunswick, NJ: Rutgers University Press.

INEI (Instituto Nacional de Estadística e Informática del Perú). 2014. "Producción y empleo informal en el Perú." Lima: INEI. Available at http://www.inei.gob.pe /media/MenuRecursivo/publicaciones_digitales/Est/Lib1154/index.html, accessed July 23, 2014.

———. 2008. *Peru: Migraciones internas 1993–2007*. Lima: INEI.

Ingold, Timothy. 2011. *Being Alive: Essays on Movement, Knowledge, and Description*. London: Routledge.

———. 2000. *The Perception of the Environment: Essays on Livelihood, Dwelling, and Skill*. London: Routledge.

Irvine, Judith. 1996. "Shadow Conversations: The Indeterminacy of Participant Roles." In *Natural Histories of Discourse*, edited by Michael Silverstein and Greg Urban, 131–59. Chicago: University of Chicago Press.

———. 1995. "Waiting for the Mouse: Constructed Dialogue in Conversation." In *The Dialogic Emergence of Culture*, edited by Dennis Tedlock and Bruce Mannheim, 198–217. Urbana: University of Illinois Press.

Jacobs, Janet, and Stefanie Mollborn. 2012. "Early Motherhood and the Disruption in Significant Attachments: Autonomy and Reconnection as a Response to Separation and Loss among African American and Latina Teen Mothers." *Gender and Society* 26(6): 922–44.

James, Allison 2007. "Giving Voice to Children's Voices: Practices and Problems, Pitfalls and Potentials." *American Anthropologist* 109(2): 261–72.

Jelin, Elizabeth, and Ana Rita Diaz-Muñoz. 2003. *Major Trends Affecting Families: South America in Perspective*. Report prepared for United Nations Department of Economic and Social Affairs, Division for Social Policy and Development, Programme on the Family, New York.

Johnson, Ginger A. 2011. "A Child's Right to Participation: Photovoice as Methodology for Documenting the Experiences of Children Living in Kenyan Orphanages." *Visual Anthropology Review* 27(2): 141–61.

Jolly, Margaret. 1998a. "Introduction: Colonial and Postcolonial Plots in Histories of Maternities and Modernities." In *Maternities and Modernities: Colonial and Postcolonial Experiences in Asia and the Pacific*, edited by Kalpana Ram and Margaret Jolly, 177–212. Cambridge, UK: Cambridge University Press.

———. 1998b. "Other Mothers: Maternal 'Insouciance' and the Depopulation Debate in Fiji and Vanuatu, 1890–1930." In *Maternities and Modernities: Colonial and Postcolonial Experiences in Asia and the Pacific*, edited by Kalpana Ram and Margaret Jolly, 1–25. Cambridge, UK: Cambridge University Press.

Joseph, Gilbert. 1998. "Close Encounters: Toward a New Cultural History of U.S.–Latin American Relations." In *Close Encounters of Empire: Writing the Cultural History of U.S.-Latin American Relations*, edited by Gilbert Joseph, Catherine Legrand, and Ricardo Donato Salvatore, 3–46. Durham, NC: Duke University Press.

Khandelwal, Meena. 2009. "Arranging Love: Interrogating the Vantage Point in Cross-Border Feminism." *Signs* 34 (3): 583–609.

Kirkman, Maggie, Lyn Harrison, Lynn Hiller, and Priscilla Pyett. 2001. "'I know I'm doing a good job': Canonical and Autobiographical Narratives of Teenage Mothers." *Culture, Health, and Sexuality* 3(3): 279–94.

Korbin, Jill E. 2003. "Children, Childhoods, and Violence." *Annual Review of Anthropology* 32(1): 431–46.

Kovats-Bernat, J. Christopher. 2002. "Negotiating Dangerous Fields: Pragmatic Strategies for Fieldwork amid Violence and Terror." *American Anthropologist* 104(1): 208–22.

Kulick, Don. 2003. "NO." In *The Language and Sexuality Reader*, edited by Deborah Cameron and Don Kulick, 285–93. New York: Routledge.

———. 1998. *Travestí: Sex, Gender, and Culture among Brazilian Transgendered Prostitutes*. Chicago: University of Chicago Press.

Lambek, Michael, ed. 2010. *Ordinary Ethics: Anthropology, Language, and Action*. New York: Fordham University Press.

Larson, Brooke, Olivia Harris, and Enrique Tandeter, eds. 1995. *Ethnicity, Markets, and Migration in the Andes: At the Crossroads of History and Anthropology*. Durham, NC: Duke University Press.

Lazar, Sian. 2010. "Schooling and Critical Citizenship: Pedagogies of Political Agency in El Alto, Bolivia." *Anthropology and Education Quarterly* 41(2): 181–205.

Leifsen, Esben. 2006. *Moralities and Politics of Belonging: Governing Female Reproduction in 20th Century Quito*. Oslo: UNIPUB.

Leinaweaver, Jessaca. 2008a. *The Circulation of Children: Kinship, Adoption, and Morality in Andean Peru*. Durham, NC: Duke University Press.

———. 2008b. "Improving Oneself: Young People Getting Ahead in the Peruvian Andes." *Latin American Perspectives* 35(4): 65–78.

———. 2007. "On Moving Children: The Social Implications of Andean Child Circulation." *American Ethnologist* 34(1): 163–80.

Lind, Amy. 2003. "Gender and Neoliberal States: Feminists Remake the Nation in Ecuador." *Latin American Perspectives* 30(1): 181–207.

Lugones, María. 2014. "Musing: Reading the Non-diasporic from within Diasporas." *Hypatia* 29(1): 18–22.

———. 2007. "Heterosexualism and the Colonial/Modern Gender System." *Hypatia* 22(1): 186–209.

———. 2003. *Pilgrimages/Peregrinajes: Theorizing Coalition against Multiple Oppressions*. Lanham, MD: Rowman and Littlefield.

Luker, Kristin. 1996. *Dubious Conceptions: The Politics of Teenage Pregnancy*. Cambridge, MA: Harvard University Press.

Luttrell-Rowland, Mikaela. 2012. "Ambivalence, Conflation, and Invisibility: A Feminist Analysis of State Enactment of Children's Rights in Peru." *Signs* 38(1): 179–202.

Mageo, Jeannette Marie. 2002. "Toward a Multidimensional Model of the Self." *Journal of Anthropological Research* 58(3): 339–65.

Mahmoud, Saba. 2005. *Politics of Piety: The Islamic Revival and the Feminist Subject*. Princeton, NJ: Princeton University Press.

Mahoney, Maureen A., and Barbara Yngvesson. 1992. "The Construction of Subjectivity and the Paradox of Resistance: Reintegrating Feminist Anthropology and Psychology." *Signs* 18(1): 44–73.

Mannheim, Bruce. 2015a. "All Translation Is Radical Translation." In *Translating Worlds: The Epistemological Space of Translation*, edited by Carlo Severi and William Hanks, 199–219. Chicago: Hau.

———. 2015b. "The Social Imaginary Unspoken in Verbal Art." In *The Routledge Handbook of Linguistic Anthropology*, edited by Nancy Bonvillain, 44–61. New York: Routledge.

———. 1991. *The Language of the Inka since the European Invasion*. Austin: University of Texas Press.

Mannheim, Bruce, and Dennis Tedlock. 1995. "Introduction." In *The Dialogic Emergence of Culture*, edited by Denis Tedlock and Bruce Mannheim, 1–32. Urbana: University of Illinois Press.

Mannheim, Bruce, and Krista Van Vleet. 1998. "The Dialogics of Southern Quechua Narrative." *American Anthropologist* 100(2): 326–46.

Manrique, Nelson. 2002. *El tiempo del miedo: La violencia política en el Perú, 1980–1996*. Lima: Fondo Editorial del Congreso del Perú.

———1995. "Political Violence, Ethnicity, and Racism in Peru in the Time of War." *Journal of Latin American Cultural Studies* 4(1): 5–18.

Mantilla Falcón, Julissa. 2007. "Violencia sexual contra las mujeres: La experiencia de la Comisión de la Verdad y Reconciliación." In *Fronteras interiors: Identidad, diferencia y protagonismo de las mujeres*, edited by Maruja Barrig, 225–44. Lima: Instituto de Estudios Peruanos.

———. 2005a. "La experiencia de la Comisión de la Verdad y Reconciliación en el Perú: Logros y dificultades de un enfoque de género." In *Memorias de ocupación: Violencia sexual contra mujeres detenidas durante la dictadura*, edited by Ximena Zavala, 67–89. Santiago, Chile: Fundación Instituto de la Mujer; Corporación Humanas.

———. 2005b. "The Peruvian Truth and Reconciliation Commission's Treatment of Sexual Violence Against Women." *Human Rights Brief* 12(2): 1–5.

Martin, Emily. 2013. "The Potentiality of Ethnography and the Limits of Affect Theory." *Current Anthropology* 54(S7): S149–S158.

Martinez HoSang, Daniel, Oneka LaBennett, and Laura Pulido, eds. 2012. *Racial Formation in the Twenty-First Century*. Berkeley: University of California Press.

Massey, Doreen. 1994. *Space, Place, and Gender*. Minneapolis: University of Minnesota Press.

Mattingly, Cheryl. 2014. *Moral Laboratories: Family Peril and the Struggle for a Good Life*. Berkeley: University of California Press.

Mayer, Enrique. 2009. *Ugly Stories of the Peruvian Agrarian Reform*. Durham, NC: Duke University Press.

———. 2002. *The Articulated Peasant: Household Economies in the Andes*. Boulder, CO: Westview Press.

McCall, Leslie. 2005. "The Complexity of Intersectionality." *Signs* 30(3): 1771–800.

McDermott, Raymond P., and Henry Tylbor. 1995. "On the Necessity of Collusion in Conversation." In *The Dialogic Emergence of Culture*, edited by Dennis Tedlock and Bruce Mannheim, 218–36. Urbana: University of Illinois Press.

McElhinny, Bonnie S. 2010. "The Audacity of Affect: Gender, Race, and History in Linguistic Accounts of Legitimacy and Belonging." *Annual Review of Anthropology* 39: 309–28.

———, ed. 2007. *Words, Worlds, Material Girls: Language and Gender in a Global Economy*. New York: Mouton de Gruyter.

———. 2005. "'Kissing a Baby Is Not at All Good for Him': Infant Mortality, Medicine, and Colonial Modernity in the U.S.-Occupied Philippines." *American Anthropologist* 107(2): 183–94.

Meiu, George Paul. 2016. "Belonging in Ethno-Erotic Economies: Adultery, Alterity, and Ritual in Postcolonial Kenya." *American Ethnologist* 43(2): 215–29.

Mendoza-Denton, Norma, and Aomar Boum. 2015. "Breached Initiations: Sociopolitical Resources and Conflicts in Emergent Adulthood." *Annual Review of Anthropology* 44: 295–310.

Mignolo, Walter D. 2011. "Geopolitics of Sensing and Knowing: On (De)Coloniality, Border Thinking and Epistemic Disobedience". *Postcolonial Studies* 14(3): 273–83.

Mignolo, Walter D., and Freya Schiwy. 2003. "Double Translation: Transculturation and the Colonial Difference." In *Translation and Ethnography: The Anthropological Challenge of Intercultural Understanding*, edited by Tullio Maranhao and Bernard Streck, 3–29. Tucson: University of Arizona Press.

Miles, Ann. 2000. "Poor Adolescent Girls and Social Transformations in Cuenca, Ecuador." *Ethos* 28(1): 54–74.

MIMDES (Ministry of Women and Social Development). 2008. *Plan nacional contra la violencia hacia la mujer, 2009–2015*. Lima: MIMDES.

Mitchell, Lisa M. 2006. "Child Centered? Thinking Critically about Children's Drawings as a Visual Research Method." *Visual Anthropology Review* 22(1): 60–73.

Mohanty, Chandra Talpade. 1984. "Under Western Eyes: Feminist Scholarship and Colonial Discourses." *Boundary 2* 12(3): 333–58.

Moraga, Cherríe, and Gloria Anzaldúa. 1981. *This Bridge Called My Back: Writings by Radical Women of Color*. New York: Kitchen Table Press.

Morgan, Lynn M. 2014. "Claiming Rosa Parks: Conservative Catholic Bids for 'Rights' in Contemporary Latin America." *Culture, Health, and Sexuality* 16(10): 1245–59.

———. 1997. "Imagining the Unborn in the Ecuadorian Andes." *Feminist Studies* 23(2): 323–61.

Morgan, Lynn M., and Elizabeth F. S. Roberts. 2012. "Reproductive Governance in Latin America." *Anthropology and Medicine* 19(2): 241–54.

Mujica, Jaris. 2013. "The Microeconomics of Sexual Exploitation of Girls and Young Women in the Peruvian Amazon." *Culture, Health, and Sexuality* 15: S141–SS52.

Muratorio, Blanca. 1998. "Indigenous Women's Identities and the Politics of Cultural Reproduction in the Ecuadorian Amazon." *American Anthropologist* 100(2): 409–20.

Murdock, Donna F. 2003. "Neoliberalism, Gender, and Development: Institutionalizing 'Post-Feminism' in Medellín, Colombia." *Women's Studies Quarterly* 31(3/4): 129–53.

Nencel, Lorraine. 1994. "The Secrets behind Sexual Desire: The Construction of Male Sexuality in Lima, Peru." *Ethnofoor* 7(2): 59–75.

Nouvet, Elysée. 2014. "'Some Carry On, Some Stay in Bed': (In)convenient Affects and Agency in Neoliberal Nicaragua." *Cultural Anthropology* 29(1): 80–102.

Nunura, Juan, and Edgar Flores. 2001. "El empleo en el Perú: 1990–2000." Lima: Ministerio de Trabajo y Promoción del Empleo. http://www.mintra.gob.pe/archivos/file /CNTPE/Diagnostico_Peru_1990_2000.pdf, accessed July 23, 2014.

Oaks, Laury. 2000. "Smoke-Filled Wombs and Fragile Fetuses: The Social Politics of Fetal Representation." *Signs* 26(1): 63–108.

Ochs, Elinor. 2012. "Experiencing Language." *Anthropological Theory* 12(2): 142–60.

———. 1992. "Indexing Gender." In *Rethinking Context: Language as an Interactive Phenomenon*, edited by Alessandro Duranti and Charles Goodwin, 335–58. Cambridge, UK: Cambridge University Press.

Ochs, Elinor, and Lisa Capps. 2001. *Living Narrative: Creating Lives in Everyday Storytelling*. Cambridge, MA: Harvard University Press.

Ochs, Elinor, and Tamar Kremer-Sadlik. 2007. "Introduction: Morality as Family Practice." *Discourse and Society* 18(1): 5–10.

Ødegaard, Cecilie Vindal. 2010. *Mobility, Markets, and Indigenous Socialities: Contemporary Migration in the Peruvian Andes*. Burlington, VT: Ashgate.

Oliart, Patricia. 2010. "Vida universitaria y masculinidades mestizas." In *Políticas educativas y la cultura del sistema escolar en el Perú*, edited by Patricia Oliart, 185–244. Lima: Instituto de Estudios Peruanos.

———. 2007. "Indigenous Women's Organizations and the Political Discourses of Indigenous Rights and Gender Equity in Peru." *Latin American and Caribbean Ethnic Studies* 3(3): 291–308.

———, ed. 2003. *Territorio, cultura e historia: Materiales para la renovación de la enseñanza sobre la sociedad peruana*. Lima: IEP.

Omi, Michael, and Howard Winant. 2015 [1986]. *Racial Formation in the United States*, 3rd ed. New York: Routledge.

Ortner, Sherry B. 2005. "Subjectivity and Cultural Critique." *Anthropological Theory* 5(1): 31–52.

———. 2003. *New Jersey Dreaming: Capital, Culture, and the Class of '58*. Durham, NC: Duke University Press.

———. 1996. "Making Gender: The Politics and Erotics of Gender." Boston, MA: Beacon Press.

Paerregaard, Karsten. 2015. *Return to Sender: The Moral Economy of Peru's Migrant Remittances*. Berkeley: University of California Press.

Pande, Amrita. 2014. *Wombs in Labor: Transnational Commercial Surrogacy in India*. New York: Columbia University Press.

Patosalmi, Mervi. 2009. "Bodily Integrity and Conceptions of Subjectivity." *Hypatia* 24 (2): 125–41.

Paulson, Susan, and Patricia Bailey. 2003. "Culturally Constructed Relationships Shape Sexual and Reproductive Health and Healthcare in Bolivia." *Culture, Health, and Sexuality* 5(5): 483–98.

Pauwels, Luc. 2015. *Reframing Visual Social Science: Towards a More Visual Sociology and Anthropology*. Cambridge, UK: Cambridge University Press.

Pérez Silva, Jorge, Jorge Acurio Palma, and Raúl Bendezú Araujo. 2008. *Contra el prejuicio lingüístico de la motosidad: Un estudio de las vocales del castellano andino desde la fonética acústica*. Lima: PUCP.

Petchesky, Rosalind Pollack. 1987. "Fetal Images: The Power of Visual Culture in the Politics of Reproduction." *Feminist Studies* 13(2): 263–92.

Pilkington, Doris. 1996. *Rabbit Proof Fence*. New York: Hyperion.

Pollock, Della. 2005. *Remembering: Oral History Performance*. New York: Palgrave.

———. 1999. *Telling Bodies, Performing Birth: Everyday Narratives of Childbirth*. New York: Columbia University Press.

Ponce, Ana. 2007. "'Padre y madre para mis hijos': Las familias dirigidas por mujeres." In *Fronteras interiores: Identidad, diferencia y protagonism de las mujeres*, edited by Maruja Barrig, 95–120. Lima: Instituto de Estudios Peruanos.

Poole, Debra. 1997. *Vision, Race, and Modernity: A Visual Economy of the Andean Visual World*. Princeton, NJ: Princeton University Press.

Portocarrero, Gonzalo. 2012. *Profetas del odio: Raíces culturales y líderes de Sendero Luminoso*. Lima: Fondo Editorial PUCP.

Postero, Nancy Grey, and Leon Zamosc, eds. 2004. *The Struggle for Indigenous Rights in Latin American*. Portland, OR: Sussex Academic Press.

Povinelli, Elizabeth. 2010. "The Crisis of Culture and the Arts of Care: Indigenous Politics in Late Liberalism." In *Culture Crisis: Anthropology and Politics on Remote Aboriginal Australia*, edited by Jon Altman and Melida Hinkson, 17–31. Sydney: University of New South Wales.

———. 2006. *The Empire of Love*. Durham, NC: Duke University Press.

Premo, Blanca. 2005. *Children of the Father King: Youth, Authority, and Legal Minority in Colonial Lima*. Chapel Hill: University of North Carolina Press.

Pribilsky, Jason. 2016. "Remaking the *Yanga Kawsay*: Andean Elders, Children, and Domestic Abuse in the Transmigration Logics of Highland Ecuador." In *Transnational Aging: Current Insights and Future Challenges*, edited by Vincent Horn and Cornelia Schweppe, 64–84. New York: Routledge.

Pyyry, Noora. 2015. "'Sensing with' Photography and 'Thinking with' Photographs in Research into Teenage Girls' Hanging Out." *Children's Geographies* 13(2): 149–63.

Quijano, Aníbal. 2000. "Colonialidad del poder y clasificación social." *Journal of World Systems Research* 11(2): 353–80.

Radcliffe, Sarah A., Nina Laurie, and Robert Andolina. 2004. "The Transnationalization of Gender and Reimagining Andean Indigenous Development." *Signs* 29(2): 387–416.

Rae-Espinoza, Heather. 2010. "Consent and Discipline in Ecuador: How to Avoid Raising an Antisocial Child." *Ethos* 38(4): 369–87.

Rafael, Vincente, ed. 2000. *White Love and Other Events in Filipino History*. Durham, NC: Duke University Press.

Ragoné, Helena, and France Winddance Twine, eds. 2000. *Ideologies and Technologies of Motherhood: Race, Class, Sexuality, Nationalism*. New York: Routledge.

Raguz, Maria. 2001. "Adolescent Sexual and Reproductive Rights in Latin America." *Health and Human Rights* 5(2): 30–63.

Rahier, Jean Muteba. 2014. *Blackness in the Andes: Ethnographic Vignettes of Cultural Politics in the Time of Multiculturalism*. New York: Palgrave Macmillan.

Ram, Kalpana, and Christopher Houston. 2015. *Phenomenology in Anthropology: A Sense of Perspective*. Bloomington: Indiana University Press.

Ramos-Zayas, Ana Y. 2011. "Learning Affect, Embodying Race: Youth, Blackness, and Neoliberal Emotions in Latino Newark." *Transforming Anthropology* 19(2): 86–104.

Richard, Analiese, and Daromir Rudnyckyj. 2009. "Economies of Affect." *Journal of the Royal Anthropological Institute* 15 (1): 57–77.

Rifkin, Mark. 2017. *Beyond Settler Time: Temporal Sovereignty and Indigenous Self-Determination*. Durham, NC: Duke University Press.

Ríos-Salas, Vanessa, and Daniel R. Meyer. 2014. "Single Mothers and Child Support Receipt in Peru." *Journal of Family Studies* 20(3): 298–310.

Robbins, Joel. 2007. "Between Reproduction and Freedom: Morality, Value, and Radical Cultural Change." *Ethnos* 72(3): 293–314.

Roberts, Elizabeth F. S. 2012a. *God's Laboratory: Assisted Reproduction in the Andes*. Berkeley: University of California Press.

———. 2012b. "Scars of Nation: Surgical Penetration and the Ecuadorian State." *Journal of Latin American and Caribbean Anthropology* 17(2): 215–37.

Robertson, Jennifer. 2002. "Reflexivity Redux: A Pithy Polemic on 'Positionality.'" *Anthropological Quarterly* 75 (4): 785–92.

Robillard, Chantalle. 2010. "Honourable *Señoras*, Liminal *Campesinas*, and the Shameful Other: Re-Defining Femininities in Bolivia." *Culture, Health, and Sexuality* 12(5): 529–42.

Rose, Nikolas. 1999. *Powers of Freedom: Reframing Political Thought*. Cambridge, UK: Cambridge University Press.

———. 1990. *Governing the Soul: The Shaping of the Private Self*. New York: Rutledge.

Rutherford, Danilyn. 2009. "Sympathy, State Building, and the Experience of Empire." *Cultural Anthropology* 24(1): 1–32.

Safa, Helen. 2005. "The Matrifocal Family and Patriarchal Ideology in Cuba and the Caribbean." *Journal of Latin American Anthropology* 10(2): 314–38.

Sanford, Victoria, Katerina Stefatos, and Cecilia M. Salvi, eds. 2016. *Gender Violence in Peace and War: States of Complicity*. New Brunswick, NJ: Rutgers University Press.

Scheper-Hughes, Nancy. 1992. *Death without Weeping: The Violence of Everyday Life in Brazil*. Berkeley: University of California Press.

Schiffrin, Deborah. 1996. "Language as Self-Portrait: Sociolinguistic Constructions of Identity." *Language in Society* 25(2): 167–203.

Seligmann, Linda. 2009. *Broken Links, Enduring Ties: American Adoption across Race, Class and Nation*. Stanford, CA: Stanford University Press.

———. 1995. *Between Reform and Revolution: Political Struggles in the Peruvian Andes, 1969–1991*. Stanford, CA: Stanford University Press.

———. 1993. "Between Worlds of Exchange: Ethnicity among Peruvian Market Women." *Cultural Anthropology* 8(2): 187–213.

Shepard, Bonnie. 2006. *Running the Obstacle Course to Sexual and Reproductive Health: Lessons from Latin America*. Westport, CT: Praeger Publishers.

Silva Santiesteban, Rocío. 2009. *El factor asco: Basurización simbólica y discursos autoritarios en el Perú contemporáneo*. Lima: Red para el Desarrollo de las Ciencias Sociales en el Perú.

Silverblatt, Irene. 1987. *Moon, Sun, and Witches: Gender Ideologies and Class in Inca and Colonial Peru*. Princeton, NJ: Princeton University Press.

Silverstein, Michael. 1976. "Shifters, Linguistic Categories, and Cultural Description." In *Meaning in Anthropology*, edited by Keith Basso and H. Selby, 11–55. Albuquerque: University of New Mexico Press.

Sinervo, Aviva, and Michael D. Hill. 2011. "The Visual Economy of Andean Childhood Poverty: Interpreting Postcards in Cusco, Peru." *Journal of Latin American and Caribbean Anthropology* 16(1): 114–42.

Smith, Gavin. 1991. *Livelihood and Resistance: Peasants and the Politics of Land in Peru*. Berkeley: University of California Press.

Smith-Oka, Vania. 2013. *Shaping the Motherhood of Indigenous Mexico*. Nashville, TN: Vanderbilt University Press.

Solinger, Rickie. 1992. *Wake Up Little Susie: Single Pregnancy and Race before Roe v. Wade*. New York: Routledge.

Speed, Shannon. 2017. "Structures of Settler Capitalism in Abya Yala." *American Quarterly* 69(4): 783–90.

Spence, Jo, and Patricia Holland, eds. 1991. *Family Snaps: The Meanings of Domestic Photography*. London: Virago.

Steel, Griet. 2008. *Vulnerable Careers: Tourism and Livelihood Dynamics among Street Vendors in Cusco, Peru*. Doctoral dissertation, University of Utrecht. Amsterdam: Rozenberg Publishers.

Stephens, Sharon, ed. 1995. *Children and the Politics of Culture*. Princeton, NJ: Princeton University Press.

Stephenson, Marcia. 1999. *Gender and Modernity in Andean Bolivia*. Austin: University of Texas Press.

Stern, Steve J. 1998. *The Secret History of Gender: Women, Men, and Power in Late Colonial Mexico*. Chapel Hill: University of North Carolina Press.

———. 1982. *Peru's Indian Peoples and the Challenge of Spanish Conquest: Huamanga to 1640*. Madison: University of Wisconsin Press.

Stevenson, Lisa. 2014. *Life beside Itself: Imagining Care in the Canadian Arctic*. Berkeley: University of California Press.

Stewart, Kathleen. 1991. "On the Politics of Cultural Theory: A Case for 'Contaminated' Cultural Critique." *Social Research* 58(2): 395–412.

Stoler, Ann Laura. 2006. "Intimidations of Empire: Predicaments of the Tactile and Unseen." In *Haunted by Empire: Geographies of Intimacy in North American History*, edited by Ann Laura Soler, 1–22. Durham, NC: Duke University Press.

———. 2002. *Carnal Knowledge and Imperial Power: Race and the Intimate in Colonial Rule*. Berkeley: University of California Press.

———. 2001. "Tense and Tender Ties: The Politics of Comparison in North American History and (Post) Colonial Studies." *Journal of American History* 88: 829–65.

———. 1989. "Making Empire Respectable: The Politics of Race and Sexual Morality in 20th Century Colonial Cultures." *American Ethnologist* 16(4): 634–60.

Strong, Pauline Turner. 2005. "What Is an Indian Family? The Indian Child Welfare Act and the Renascence of Tribal Sovereignty." *American Studies* 46 (Special Issue: Indigeneity at the Crossroads of American Studies) (3/4): 205–31.

———. 2001. "To Forget Their Tongue, Their Name, and Their Whole Relation: Captivity, Extra-Tribal Adoption, and the American Indian Child Welfare Act." In *Relative Values: Reconfiguring Kinship Studies*, edited by Sarah Franklin and Susan McKinnon, 468–93. Durham, NC: Duke University Press.

Sue, Cristina A., and Tanya Golash-Boza. 2013. "'It was only a joke': How Racial Humour Fuels Colour-Blind Ideologies in Mexico and Peru." *Ethnic and Racial Studies* 36(10): 1582–98.

Tabbush, Constanza, and María Florencia Gentile. 2013. "Emotions behind Bars: The Regulation of Mothering in Argentine Jails." *Signs* 39(1): 131–49.

Tapias, Maria. 2016. *Embodied Protests: Emotions and Women's Health in Bolivia*. Urbana: University of Illinois Press.

———. 2006. "'Always Ready, Always Clean': Competing Discourses of Breast-feeding, Infant Illness, and the Politics of Mother-Blame in Bolivia." *Body and Society* 12(2): 83–108.

Taylor, Analisa. 2006. "Malinche and Matriarchal Utopia: Gendered Visions of Indigeneity in Mexico." *Signs* 31(3): 815–40.

Taylor, Janelle S. 2004. "Big Ideas: Feminist Ethnographies of Reproduction." *American Ethnologist* 31(1): 123–30.

Tedlock, Dennis. 1983. *The Spoken Word and the Work of Interpretation*. Philadelphia: University of Pennsylvania Press.

Tedlock, Dennis, and Bruce Mannheim, eds. 1995. *The Dialogic Emergence of Culture*. Urbana: University of Illinois Press.

Theidon, Kimberly Susan. 2015. "Hidden in Plain Sight." *Current Anthropology* 56(S12): S191–S200.

———. 2012. *Intimate Enemies: Violence and Reconciliation in Peru*. Philadelphia: University of Pennsylvania Press.

Throop, C. Jason. 2010. *Suffering and Sentiment: Exploring the Vicissitudes of Experience and Pain in Yap*. Berkeley: University of California Press.

———. 2003. "Articulating Experience." *Anthropological Theory* 3(2): 219.

Tickten, Miriam. 2011. *Casualties of Care: Immigration and the Politics of Humanitarianism in France*. Berkeley: University of California Press.

Tomlinson, Matt, and Julian Millie. 2017. *The Monologic Imagination*. New York: Oxford University Press.

Turner, Victor. 1986. "Dewey, Dilthey, and Drama: An Essay in the Anthropology of Experience." In *The Anthropology of Experience*, edited by Victor Turner and Edward Bruner, 33–44. Urbana: University of Illinois Press.

Ulfe, María Eugenia, and Málaga Sabogal Ximena. 2016. "Disputing Visual Memories in the Peruvian Andes: The Case of Huancasancos, Ayacucho." In *Photography in Latin America: Images and Identities across Time and Space*, edited by Gisela Cánepa Koch and Ingrid Kummels, 219–38. Bielefeld, Germany: Verlag.

Underberg, Natalie M., and Elayne Zorn. 2013. "Exploring Peruvian Culture through Multimedia Ethnography." *Visual Anthropology* 26(1): 1–17.

UNICEF. 2007. "Teenage Motherhood in Latin America and the Caribbean: Trends, Problems, Solutions." *Challenges* 4: 1–12. Santiago, Chile: United Nations Publications.

Unnithan, Maya, and Stacy Leigh Pigg. 2014. "Sexual and Reproductive Health Rights and Justice—Tracking the Relationship." *Culture, Health, and Sexuality* 16(10): 1181–87.

Urban, Greg. 1991. *A Discourse-Centered Approach to Culture: Native South American Myths and Rituals*. Austin: University of Texas Press.

Urcioli, Bonnie. 1996. *Exposing Prejudice: Puerto Rican Experiences of Language, Race, and Class*. Boulder, CO: Westview Press.

Van den Berghe, Pierre, and Jorge Flores Ochoa. 2000. "Tourism and Nativistic Ideology in Cuzco, Peru." *Annals of Tourism Research* 27(1): 7–26.

Van Vleet, Krista. 2019. "Between Scene and Situation: Performing Racial and Gendered Alterity in a Cusco Orphanage." *Anthropological Quarterly* 92(1): 111–42.

———. 2017. "Discussion—Diving into the Gap: 'Words,' 'Voices,' and the Ethnographic Implications of Linguistic Disjuncture." In *The Monologic Imagination*, edited by Matt Tomlinson and Julian Millie, 159–70. New York: Oxford University Press.

———. 2009. "'I had already come to love her': Raising Children at the Margins of the Bolivian State." *Journal of Latin American and Caribbean Anthropology* 14(1): 1–23.

———. 2008. *Performing Kinship: Narrative, Gender, and the Intimacies of Power in the Andes*. Austin: University of Texas Press.

———. 2003. "Adolescent Ambiguities and the Negotiation of Belonging in the Andes." *Ethnology* 42(4): 349–63.

———. 2002. "The Intimacies of Power: Rethinking Violence and Kinship in the Andes." *American Ethnologist* 29(3): 567–601.

Van Wolputte, Steven. 2004. "Hang On to Your Self: Of Bodies, Embodiment, and Selves." *Annual Review of Anthropology* 33: 251–69.

Vargas Valente, Rosana. 2010. "Gendered Risks, Poverty, and Vulnerability in Peru:

A Case Study of the *Juntos* Programme." Overseas Development Institute Report, https://www.odi.org/sites/odi.org.uk/files/odi-assets/publications-opinion-files /6246.pdf, accessed July 23, 2014.

Vasquez de Aguila, Ernesto. 2014. *Being a Man in a Transnational World: The Masculinity and Sexuality of Migration.* New York: Routledge.

Vásquez de Velasco, María del Ana. 2009. *Situación general de los hogares INABIF.* Documento de Trabajo. Lima: MIMDES/INABIF.

Vergara, Alberto, and Aaron Watanabe. 2016. "Peru since Fujimori." *Journal of Democracy* 27(3): 148–57.

Villaba, Unai. 2013. *"Buen Vivir* vs. Development: A Paradigm Shift in the Andes?" *Third World Quarterly* 34(8): 1427–42.

Villalobos, Ana. 2014. *Motherload: Making It All Better in Insecure Times.* Berkeley: University of California Press.

Villanueva Flores, Rocío. 2007. "Respuesta del sistema de administración de justicia peruano frente a los casos de violencia sexual contra mujeres ocurridos durante el conflicto armado interno." In *Justicia y reparación para mujeres víctimas de violencia sexual en contexto de conflicto armado interno,* edited by Carlos Martín Berestain, 211–58. Lima: Consejería de Proyectos (PCS).

Vincent, Susan. 2016. "Mobility of the Elderly in Peru: Life Course, Labour, and the Rise of a Pensioner Economy in a Peruvian Peasant Community." *Critique of Anthropology* 36(4): 380–96.

Viola Recasens, Andreu. 2014. "Discursos 'pachamamistas' versus políticas desarrollistas: El debate sobre el *sumak kawsay* en los Andes." *Íconos: Revista de ciencias sociales* 48: 55–72.

Volkman, Toby Alice, ed. 2005. *Cultures of Transnational Adoption.* Durham, NC: Duke University Press.

Vološinov, V. N. 1986. *Marxism and the Philosophy of Language.* Translated by Ladislav Matejka and I. R. Titunik. Cambridge, MA: Harvard University Press.

Wade, Peter. 1997. *Race and Ethnicity in Latin America.* New York: Pluto.

Walmsley, Emily. 2008. "Raised by Another Mother: Informal Fostering and Kinship Ambiguities in Northwest Ecuador." *Journal of Latin American and Caribbean Anthropology* 13(1): 168–95.

Wang, Caroline. 1999. "A Participatory Action Research Strategy Applied to Women's Health." *Journal of Women's Health* 8: 85–192.

Wargo, Jon M. 2017. "'Every Selfie Tells a Story . . .': LGBTQ Youth Lifestreams and New Media Narratives as Connective Identity Texts." *New Media and Society* 19(4): 560–78.

Weber, Katinka. 2013. "Chiquitano and the Multiple Meanings of Being Indigenous in Bolivia." *Bulletin of Latin American Research* 32 (2):194–209.

WEF (World Economic Forum). 2013. *The Peru Travel and Tourism Competitiveness Report.* Geneva: WEF.

Weismantel, Mary J. 2001. *Cholas and Pishtacos: Stories of Race and Sex in the Andes.* Chicago: University of Chicago Press.

———. 1995. "Making Kin: Kinship Theory and Zumbagua Adoptions." *American Ethnologist* 22(4): 685–709.

Weismantel, Mary, and Stephen F. Eisenman. 1998. "Race in the Andes: Global Movements and Popular Ontologies." *Bulletin of Latin American Research* 17(2): 121–42.

Whitten, Norman. 2007. "The Long Durée of Racial Fixity and the Transformative Conjunctures of Racial Blending." *Journal of Latin American and Caribbean Studies* 12(2): 356–83.

———. 2003. *Millennial Ecuador: Critical Essays on Cultural Transformations and Social Dynamics*. Iowa City: University of Iowa Press.

Whitten, Norman, and Dorothea Scott Whitten. 2015. "Clashing Concepts of the 'Good Life': Beauty, Knowledge, and Vision Versus National Wealth in Amazonian Ecuador." In *Images of Public Wealth or the Anatomy of Well-Being in Indigenous Amazonia*, edited by Fernando Santos-Granero, 191–215. Tucson: University of Arizona Press.

Willen, Sarah S. 2014. "Plotting a Moral Trajectory, *Sans Papiers:* Outlaw Motherhood as Inhabitable Space of Welcome." *Ethos* 42(1): 84–100.

Wirtz, Kristina. 2011. "Cuban Performances of Blackness as the Timeless Past Still among Us." *Journal of Linguistic Anthropology* 21(S1): E11–E34.

Wolfe, Patrick. 1999. *Settler Colonialism and the Transformation of Anthropology*. London: Cassell.

Wozniak, Danielle F., and Karen Neuman Allen. 2012. "Ritual and Performance in Domestic Violence Healing: From Survivor to Thriver through Rites of Passage." *Culture, Medicine, and Psychiatry* 36(1): 80–101.

Yanagisako, Sylvia, and Carole Delaney. 1995. *Naturalizing Power: Essays in Feminist Cultural Analysis*. New York: Routledge.

Yon, Ana J. 2014. "Sexuality, Social Inequalities, and Sexual Vulnerability among Low-Income Youth in the City of Ayacucho, Peru." PhD diss., Columbia University.

Ypeij, Annelou, and Annelies Zoomers, eds. 2006. *La ruta andina: Turismo y desarrollo sostenible en Peru y Bolivia*. Quito, Ecuador: Abya-Yala.

Zigon, Jarrett. 2013. "On Love: Remaking Moral Subjectivity in Post-Rehabilitation Russia." *American Ethnologist* 40(1): 201–15.

———. 2007. "Moral Breakdown and the Ethical Demand." *Anthropological Theory* 7(2): 131–50.

Zigon, Jarrett, and C. Jason Throop. 2014. "Moral Experience: Introduction." *Ethos* 42(1): 1–15.

Index

KRISTA E. VAN VLEET is a professor of anthropology and chair of the Department of Anthropology at Bowdoin College. She is the author of *Performing Kinship: Narrative, Gender, and the Intimacies of Power in the Andes.*

Interpretations of Culture in the New Millennium

The University of Illinois Press
is a founding member of the
Association of University Presses.

University of Illinois Press
1325 South Oak Street
Champaign, IL 61820-6903
www.press.uillinois.edu